ACHIEVING

BUZZWORD

COMPLIANCE

DATA ARCHITECTURE
LANGUAGE AND VOCABULARY

By David C. Hay

Foreword by John A. Zachman

Published by:

2 Lindsley Road

Basking Ridge, NJ 07920 USA

https://www.TechnicsPub.com

Cover design by Lorena Molinari

Edited by Lauren McCafferty

First Edition

First Printing 2018

ISBN, print ed.   9781634623704

ISBN, Kindle ed.   9781634623711

ISBN, ePub ed.   9781634623728

ISBN, PDF ed.   9781634623735

Library of Congress Control Number: 2018944766

To Richard Barker and Harry Ellis,

Who invented a profound approach to modeling an enterprise's ontology.

CHRONO-SYNCLASTIC INFUNDIBULA—Just imagine that your Daddy is the smartest man who ever lived on Earth, and he knows everything there is to find out, and he is exactly right about everything, and he can prove he is right about everything. Now imagine another little child on some nice world a million light-years away, and that little child's Daddy is the smartest man who ever lived on that nice world so far away. And he is just as smart and just as right as your Daddy is. Both Daddies are smart, and both Daddies are right.

Only if they ever met each other they would get into a terrible argument, because they wouldn't agree on anything. Now, you can say that your Daddy is right and the other little child's Daddy is wrong, but the universe is an awfully big place. There is room enough for an awful lot of people to be right about things and still not agree.

The reason both Daddies can be right and still get into terrible fights is because there are so many different ways of being right. There are places in the Universe, though, where each Daddy could finally catch on to what the other Daddy was talking about. These places are where all the different kinds of truths fit together as nicely as the parts in your Daddy's solar watch. We call these places chronosynclastic infundibula.

...

Chrono (KROH-no) means time. Synclastic (sin-CLASS-tick) means curved toward the same side in all directions, like the skin of an orange. Infundibulum (in-fun-DIB-u-lum) is what the ancient Romans like Julius Caesar and Nero called a funnel. If you don't know what a funnel is, get Mommy to show you one.

Kurt Vonnegut
Sirens of Titan[1]

TABLE OF CONTENTS

TABLE OF FIGURES

Physical Model

Chapter 6: The Development Process
Reverse Engineering

Create Conceptual Models

Create Logical Models

Chapter 7: Best Practices
Best Practices for Aesthetics

FOREWORD

JohnA. Zachman
© John A. Zachman, Zachman International

I like this book. That should not come as a great shock; I have known David Hay for many years and I have the highest respect for him. Whenever I have any data modeling questions, I call David Hay. I can depend on him for sound, practical, thoughtful advice and clarifications.

We can really appreciate David as he has read about every "data" book known to humankind and has given us a thumbnail sketch of many of them. Clearly, neither he nor anybody else can be an expert in everybody else's work. Life is too short! It is difficult enough to become an expert in one's own work, let alone be an expert in someone else's without devoting sufficient portions of your life, understanding and extending (building on) other's seminal works which then becomes one's own work.

But having some idea about the significant ideas of thought-leaders, practitioners and researchers, and understanding where they fit in the context of an Enterprise is REALLY helpful! Good night! Look at all the references and discussions in "Achieving Buzzword Compliance!" In fact, I would suggest this kind of effort--understanding, summarizing and contextualizing seminal pieces of work--is invaluable to the serious reader. This kind of contribution to the general body of knowledge is what it takes to become a thought leader in one's own right!! Thank you David Hay!

I like the premise of the book too. Clearly, the Information domain is in a kind of pre-puberty stage of development. We do not have an agreed-upon ontological structure or even a lexicon, definitions of the essential concepts of our practices. We think we are communicating with each other but we are simply talking. We do not have a "Periodic Table" equivalent that would form the basis of an articulation of the natural laws that govern our practices. My personal opinion is that we, Information People, are much like the Alchemists of Chemistry before it became Chemistry, that is, before Mendeleev published the early versions of the Periodic Table.

In fact, I do not believe that there is a "discipline," ANY discipline, until the body of serious practitioners have an agreed-upon ontological structure, an identification and formal expression of theoretical constructs, a basis for finding and validating the domain, "laws of nature." Of course, the domain I personally have in mind is the "Enterprise" domain and David Hay takes a significant step in this direction in "Achieving Buzzword Compliance."

By the way, it was Kurt Lewin that said, "there is nothing so practical as a good theory." I would add that if you cannot articulate for me what you are arguing or proposing in the context of "physics" (i.e., laws of nature), I know I am banking on a miracle happening. Magic. Typically, a "silver bullet" ... and there are no "silver bullets."[2]

This is another reason I like "Achieving Buzzword Compliance." David is explaining to us the causes and effects of choices to be made based on his experience and research and the other practical work of acknowledged thought-leaders.

---

[2] Fred Brooks, "No Silver Bullet - Essence & Accidents of Software Engineering" 1986 in Information Processing 86. H.J. Kugler, ed., Elsevier, 1069-1076. (Invited paper, IFIP Congress '86, Dublin) Reprinted in The Mythical Man-Month, 20th Anniversary Edition, Frederick P. Brooks, Jr., Addison-Wesley, 1995.

I wish I could tell you that I was so smart that I knew all of these things from the very beginning. It has taken me 83 years to realize how little I know, have known and will be able to know. There are simply insufficient hours in the day!

In my own domain of interest, I simply happened to observe one day that Data Processing actually was a manufacturing business. We manufacture Enterprises because systems ARE the Enterprise. Unfortunately, the Enterprises were never Engineered! So, actually, we don't manufacture Enterprises, we manufacture PARTS of Enterprises … and the parts don't fit together. They were not *designed* to fit together. We don't do Engineering. Fred Brooks[3] is attributed to saying, "programming is manufacturing, NOT engineering." We only Manufacture … we *build* and run systems. We don't design Enterprises.

I could see patterns in Engineering/Manufacturing that were identical in Architecture/Construction. Then I could identify paradigmatic correlations between the older disciplines of Industrial Product Engineering and Manufacturing and Building Architecture and Construction with my domain of interest, *Enterprise* Engineering and Manufacturing! I used the logic structure of descriptive artifacts of the older disciplines to order the structure of the descriptive representations of the Enterprise. Many years later someone explained to me that I had defined the foundation of an "Ontology." I didn't even know what an Ontology was!!

Here is another reason I like David's book. The *formalisms* (descriptions, models, notations) he postulates and rationalizes from his own extensive PRACTICE, as well as other notable works, map precisely to the structure and *transformations* (I say again "transformations") specified in Column 1 of my ontological classification. Despite our long association and friendship, we came essentially to identical conclusions quite independently. There was zero collaboration. And, there is no discontinuity between my more theoretical work and his very practical work.

Note: We don't completely agree as to some naming choices and categorizations … we are pretty close, but not quite … yet. I think we have a kind-of external schema problem David refers to in his discussion of the ANSI/SPARC Three Schema Approach. We have two different world views of the same Enterprise. David is accounting for every descriptive formalism required to accurately transform the Concepts of Executives and Management into implementations that reflect those Concepts. In contrast, I am trying to devise a classification structure that accommodates every unique thought[4] about the Enterprise that exists upon which the existence of the Enterprise depends.

What is particularly edifying for me is that every formal description that David identifies from his decades of data practice as necessary for transforming the thoughts of Executive Management into operational reality of the Enterprise fit precisely in the structure of my ontological Framework, whether we completely agree as to the classification and naming or not. The practical contents are precisely accommodated by the ontological structure.

Furthermore, the structure of the Column 1 components may well form a pattern that is relevant in other Columns.

---

[3] *Ibid.*

[4] I would have used the word "fact" instead of "thought" but I didn't want to digress into the domain of metaphysics and try to define "truth." I need a single-variable, unique, elementary, ontological (in my terms) "Primitive" name (entity-type) for the all the constituents of every different Cell (category, classification) in my Framework. This would be an ordered classification of all the knowledge upon which the Enterprise is dependent for its existence … an "ontology."

You should have a warm feeling that reality validates Kurt Lewin's observation, "there is nothing more practical than a good theory."

I really like "Achieving Buzzword Compliance" by my friend, David Hay. I am sure we will get the Column 1 classification and names reconciled some day. We are pretty close today. But we are on the right track, transforming the practice of Information Technology (IT) into a discipline in its own right, with an agreed upon lexicon and ontological structure, upon which we can discover and articulate the Enterprise Engineering and Manufacturing "laws of nature."

John A. Zachman

Bakersfield, California 2018

ACKNOWLEDGEMENTS

If I have seen farther, it is by standing on the shoulders of Giants.

-Sir Isaac Newton
Letter to Robert Hooke
1676

One way or another, all the books I've written are thanks to the people who introduced me to data modeling. The first, who unfortunately passed from us last year was Richard Barker, who along with his colleague Harry Ellis, developed the approach to modeling that focused not on the data *per se*, but on the "things of significance" that the data described. They were at the forefront of the efforts to make models accessible to business viewers.

About thirty years ago, I got to be an apprentice to Richard, along with Cliff Longman and Mike Lynott. Their tutelage was instrumental in any success I may have enjoyed since.

Setting out to write a book is seductive. If you have a really good, compelling, idea, you expect that you should be able to turn it out in a few months.

Except, of course, if it is a textbook encompassing a wide subject area, even if you have a lot of experience in a lot of different parts of it, you quickly discover huge holes in what DAMA would call your "body of knowledge".

If you're lucky, though, you have a lot of people you can call on.

For this I thank a group of specialists, who either taught me from scratch or helped me renew my understanding of stuff I already knew.

I first encountered Terry Halpin and Sjirr Nijssen in 1990 by reading their first book on Nijssen's Information Analysis Methodology (NIAM). It was a fascinating book on a very intriguing methodology, but it was troublesome that these people were in The Netherlands and Australia, so I couldn't ask them questions. As it happened, Terry subsequently moved to the United States, renamed the technique to "Object Role Modeling" (ORM) and spent some time with the Business Rules Group, where I met him, and finally got to ask my questions. Over the years, we became well acquainted. I never had the opportunity to work with ORM on a project, but I have great respect for it, and to this day, I am thankful to Terry for helping me make sure I always represent it accurately. I have also had the opportunity to draw upon his colleague Gordon Everest, and I thank him for his patience as well.

I have been studying the Semantic web for some 15 years now, greatly helped by David McComb, and colleagues from his company, Semantic Arts—in particular, Michael Uschold and Dan Cary.

For my knowledge of Data Vault, I have been taught by Kent Graziano, Dan Linstedt, and John Giles. For NoSQL, I have depended on author Dan Sullivan, and specifically for graph modeling, on authors Ian Robinson, Jim Webber, and Emil Eifram.

For my knowledge of OMG's "Business Motivation Model", and their "Semantics of Business Vocabulary and Business Rules" (SBVR), I must express my appreciation to the collection of people that made up the "Business Rules Group". That group was the source of both of these models before they were turned over to the Object Management Group. In addition, my section on

SBVR was thoroughly vetted by the fellow who wrote the book to translate SBVR into English, Graham Witt.

My appreciation must also go to other friends and colleagues who spent an unreasonably long amount of time thoroughly reading, editing, and commenting on this book. This group includes Mike Lynott, Michael Gorman, Irina Webber, Bert Hooyman, Peter Heller, and Cory Casanave.

Other reviewers included Pascal Desmarets and Jim Andrews.

Most of the models in this book were done using SAP/Sybase's great modeling tool PowerDesigner. This is clearly (in my humble opinion, as of 2018) the best tool on the market for the "CASE" modeling I do here. And my personal thanks to Jeff Giles of Sandhill Consulting for, over the last year of so, patiently teaching me the ins and outs of the tool.

Thanks must also go to Steve Hoberman, my friend and publisher, along with his wife Jenn Nichols, for shepherding this book to completion.

And of course, it was my mother who taught me how to write coherently in the first place (back in ancient times). She displayed her talents in later years, by writing a column for the Grand Junction, Colorado *Daily Sentinel*. This is the somewhat conservative small town where I grew up. (Her views have always been more liberal, which made hers the most widely read feature in the paper.) She had to give it up, alas, when she turned 97 years old, because failing eyesight made it hard to use the computer. (But she's still around at 104!)

Of course, I couldn't do this without my dear wife, Jola, putting up with me for all these years, along with my children Pamela and Bob (who have been a continual source of wisdom in my life). My appreciation for them is unbounded.

PREFACE

L et's start with language.

One of the many jobs of data consultants is to help clients understand and manage the disparate ways parts of companies (and/or government agencies) use information. Invariably, this is related to the different ways they use language. There are various words for the same (approximately the same?) thing. Conversely, the same word can mean very different things in different contexts. Indeed, very often, there is one word that expresses the core of an enterprise's business—yet the underlying meaning of that word is completely different for different players.

But what about us? Are we data modeling/architecture/governance/quality people any more effective in describing what *we* do? What, for example, do we mean by the term "logical data model"?

How many definitions exist for this seemingly straightforward term? Surely each of you has met someone who defines it differently from the way you do.

Vendors have particular definitions, but these aren't necessarily consistent with others in the industry (or, for that matter, with other models *they* support).

And there is "conceptual data model": Is it a Zachman row one thing (à la Steve Hoberman[5])?. Or is it a Zachman row two thing (à la John Zachman[6])? Perhaps instead it's a Zachman row three thing (à la Graeme Simsion[7] and me[8])?♦

How about "physical data model"? Just how physical is it? For that matter, what do we mean by "data modeling" itself? Does it present a prospective database design? Or a description of the underlying business?

Can't we, the data experts, at least come up with consistent definitions for the words we use in our own field. His book is about a *particular set of definitions* for these and other terms.

About the title of this book. According to the Cambridge Business English Dictionary[9], a *buzzword*♠ is "a word or expression from a particular subject area that has become fashionable because it has been used a lot" ♣.

---

[5]   Steve Hoberman. 2015. Data Model Scorecard: Applying the Industry Standard on Data Model Quality. (Technics Publications). Pp. 68, 167.

[6]   John Zachman. 1987. "A Framework for Information Systems Architecture," *IBM Systems Journal*, 26:3 (IBM Publication G321-5298).

[7]   Graeme Simsion and Graham Witt. 2005. *Data Modeling Essentials, Third Edition*. (Morgan Kaufmann). pp. 273-5.

[8]   David C. Hay. 2006. *Data Model Patterns: A Metadata Map*. (Morgan Kaufmann). P. 10.

♦   Spoiler alert: It's all of those.

[9]   Cambridge Business English Dictionary (Cambridge University Press). Retrieved March 5, 2018 from https://dictionary.cambridge.org/us/dictionary/english/buzzword?q=Buzzword.

♠   In this book, all words and phrases with a specialized definition are in *boldface italics*, and also appear in the glossary (Appendix A).

♣   In the hope for this book to be translated into other languages, your author recognizes that this word does not

The data architecture field is rife with terms that have become "fashionable". Some of the terms begin with very specialized meanings, but as they spread, they lose the precision of their technical definitions and become, well, "buzzwords". To be sure, there are a lot of words described in this book that have not yet achieved buzzword status. Perhaps we can head those off.

This book, then, is about cutting through the hype to arrive at **buzzword compliance**, the state where you fully understand the concrete meanings of the terms used in the data architecture industry. Where there are disagreements, this is discussed and attempted to be resolved.

That is, this book is an attempt to rationalize the various definitions of these terms. Terms are introduced and explained in the body of the work, and defined more concisely in the Glossary.

The book will attempt to explain both *conceptual* models and those on a current list (as of 2018) of the *technologies* that exist for managing data.

Of necessity, the book must provide at least basic descriptions of each technique presented. In each case, the definitions are meant to be detailed enough to understand the language and terminology of each technique—while recognizing that a full understanding will require additional reading in the books where they are more completely described. Thus, both the Glossary and the Bibliography are important parts of this book.

In the *conceptual* world, this book will address the vocabulary that includes entity/relationship modeling, of course, but also the Semantics of Business Vocabulary and Rules (SBVR), Object Role Modeling, and The Semantic Web. And of course, we'll discuss my favorite: essential data modeling.♦

In the *technological* world, we have to deal with terms describing relational database design, object-oriented design, "dimensional" modeling, data vaults, and NoSQL. In this context, NoSQL is a catch-all term for various attempts to go beyond relational database design, including document databases, key-value databases, column databases, and graph databases. Note that this book is being published in 2018. Next year the technology realm could be completely different.♥

While you may initially disagree with some of the definitions presented here, I ask for your patience. That is, I ask you to read this book thoroughly before you draw any firm conclusions. Please *do* write to me♠ with any (positive or negative) reactions you have to anything you read here.

I hope at least to provide you with some insights into the problem of naming, even if you don't fully accept each solution I propose.

. . .

Some 30 years ago, I discovered that as an amateur philosopher, I was really at heart something called a "data modeler" at heart—and it turned out I could make that into a paying profession! In

---

translate well into Polish, Japanese, or pretty much any other. Even so, the idea of technical words whose meanings are not universally understood should not be completely unknown in any culture.

♦ About capitalization: historic model terms like "logical data model" and "conceptual data model" are shown without initial capitalization. Those created by someone with a specific meaning already defined (and typically their own acronym, like "ORM") have initial capital letters.

♥ The conceptual modeling realm, however, should change less. There will be much better tools, but the requirement to capture the nature of the business does not go away.

♠ Please send any comments to ACommonVocabulary@essentialstrategies.com.

the decades since then, the field has grown from only a handful of us to thousands who claim that title.

The problem, however, is that not all "data modelers" are doing the same things.

When you *hire* a data modeler, what do you get? A modeler of the business? A database designer? A data warehouse developer? Some combination of these?

On the other hand, if you are *looking for a job* as a data modeler, what skills exactly are you offering?

If the prospective employer is looking for one thing but you are offering something quite different, you both will be disappointed.

This book is an attempt to clarify that conversation.

At the very least, for those of you who are new to this field, the book should help you become more fully *buzzword compliant.*

Consider this to be my version of a **chrono-synclastic infundibula**.

David C. Hay
ESSENTIAL STRATEGIES
INTERNATIONAL
Houston, Texas USA

CHAPTER 1: INTRODUCTION

A **datum**♥ is something given or admitted as a basis for reasoning or inference.[10] A collection of these, of course, are **data**♠. To model data is to provide a (usually graphical) representation of a set of data in a domain.♣ A **data model** may either represent a domain in the world (such as a business, government agency, industry, or branch of science), or it may represent a specific collection of data using a particular database technology.

Data modeling is a critical component aspect of data management. The modeling process enables enterprises to discover and document how data from different parts of the enterprise fit together. Since the data modeling industry is about the process of definition, it is important to understand the vocabulary that supports that process.

A model of a domain in the world is very different from a model of a particular database that manages the data that constitutes that domain. It is common to confuse one with the other. To accurately represent data modelling in this book will require addressing both domain-oriented models and the technologically-based database designs that support them.

Data modeling ultimately comes in two flavors: "domain-oriented" (also called "conceptual") and "technologically-oriented". A **domain-oriented** or **conceptual** data model is a picture of the underlying structure of an enterprise's information. This model addresses the **universe of discourse**.[11] It describes various things of significance to the enterprise, and makes assertions about how they are related to each other. It is not in any way concerned with the *technology* that might be used to manage information. It captures the language of the business and elaborates upon it. There are three sub-categories of this model. **overview model**, **semantic model**, and **essential model**.

A **technologically-oriented data model**, on the other hand, creates a picture of the way data will be managed and stored, using one or more particular kinds of technology. This kind of model addresses the designs of databases and the software that will manage them. In this book, we will be concerned with two kinds of technologically-oriented models: **logical data model** (described using terms such as "hierarchical", "relational", "object-oriented", etc.), and **physical model**, which describes characteristics of a physical database. Examples of physical model characteristics include **tablespaces** (physical data groupings) and **partitions** (separate physical files).

♥ Throughout this book, the convention is that specialized terms are represented in **bold face** Entity type names are represented by **Bold Face (calibri font)** and have initial capital letters. In your glossary, you have a standard for fonts.

[10] Various editors. *Merriam-Webster On-line Dictionary*. "datum". Retrieved February 6, 2017 from http://merriam-webster.com.datum.

♠ Note that this means that the word "data" is, properly speaking, plural. Since the purpose of this book is to clarify our use of language, this is a good place to start.

♣ "Domain - a sphere of knowledge, influence, or activity" - *Webster's Online Dictionary*. "Domain". Retrieved 9/12/2017.

[11] Simsion, Graeme. 2007. *Data Modeling Theory and Practice*. (Technics Publications).

Ideally, a technologically-based data model represents the structures that are present in an enterprise's domain-oriented models. Often, though, the database designer must adjust these structures to accommodate physical constraints imposed by technology.

It is, however, the conceptual model that provides the definitions of terms and the interconnections among them that describe constraints on the enterprise itself. Designers then use these definitions—along with knowledge of relevant physical constraints—in order to define new databases and applications that use available technology. The effective combination of the domain-oriented and technologically-oriented models then creates a foundation for creating broad-scoped systems.

As this book will demonstrate, proper conceptual data modeling leads to less complex systems, thereby reducing support costs and increasing the reusability opportunities for future initiatives. Technology-oriented models, on the other hand, are then used by designers to address the trade-offs that must be made in order to implement the conceptual models. The introduction of technology can increase the complexity of the model.

Why is it so critical to make sure everyone is "on the same page" about data modeling? There are three key benefits that arise when we confirm and document understanding of different perspectives.

> **Formalization**
> A conceptual, domain-oriented data model documents a concise definition of business structures and relationships among them. Formal definition imposes a discipline on the structure of data. This formality reduces the possibility of data anomalies occurring when actually gaining access to and storing data. A clearly-defined technologically-oriented model—which should be based on the conceptual model—provides a sound architecture for a database as well as the applications it supports.

> **Scope Definition**
> Whether enterprise-wide or for a particular subject area, a conceptual data model can help articulate the boundaries for a system effort. Subject areas can be defined clearly in terms of the data they use and produce. Dependencies are made clear by data models, allowing implementation sequences to be identified.

> **Knowledge Retention and Documentation**
> A conceptual data model can preserve corporate memory regarding a system or project, simply by capturing knowledge in an explicit form.

> This captured knowledge serves as documentation for future projects. The process of design is itself an exercise in making trade-offs. The elegant conceptual model of the business has to be squeezed into a technology that at any point in time has very real, specific constraints. The designer adapts the model to fit those constraints. Over time, the result may become complex enough that a subsequent analyst may have difficulty identifying just *why* a particular design decision was made.

> Having the conceptual model of the business, however, provides a reference point. In the future, when those constraints are no longer around thanks to new technology, a new design can be developed based on the original model.

> The conceptual data model, then, becomes a reusable map to help business professionals, project managers, analysts, and developers understand data structure within the environment. In much the same way that cartographers learned and documented geographic landscapes so that others can better navigate, the modeler enables others to

understand an information landscape.[12] [13] The technological model then provides a similar map, this time to help people understand the systems themselves.

NOTE:

This book contains descriptions of a wide variety of approaches to modeling, organized into five major categories. In each case, the objective is not to replace the detailed documentation available for an approach. For these, the reader should consult the sources referenced in the Bibliography. Rather, the idea here is to define each approach, describing its important aspects well enough for the reader to understand what it is, and to clarify how it differs from the others.

---

[12]   Steve Hoberman. 2009. Data Modeling Made Simple: A Practical Guide for Business and IT Professionals, Second Edition. (Technics Publications). Pages 27-29.

[13]   David C. Hay. 2011. *Enterprise Model Patterns: Describing the World*. (Technics Publications). Pages xvii-xxvi.

CHAPTER 2:
OVERVIEW OF TYPES

This section will begin with a history of data modeling. From there it describes three approaches to a suggested cataloguing of data modeling types. In other words, this begins the definitions of the *vocabulary* of the data modeling industry *itself*.

A Bit of History

For a comprehensive history of both data and object modeling, consult *UML and Data Modeling: A Reconciliation*[14]. To describe the history of *data* modeling requires reference to its creators, which is where we will begin.

> ### *Charles Bachman (1969)*[15]
> In the summer of 1969, Charles Bachman published his **Data Structure Diagram**", that was the precursor to the modern entity/relationship diagram. For these diagrams, he defined an ***entity*** as "a particular object being considered".[16] A particular personal computer and Jerry Seinfeld are examples of entities. For purposes of his drawings, however, he showed not entities but **entity classes**, where **entity class** is defined as "an entire group of entities which are sufficiently similar, in terms of attributes that describe them, to be considered collectively". That is, descriptions of *entities* are *instances* of an *entity class*. In our example "a particular instance of personal computer" is probably an instance of **Personal Computer**, while "Jerry Seinfeld" is an instance of **Person**.
>
> An **entity set**, is "a different kind of entity grouping—one that associates a group of entities of one entity class with one entity of a differnet entity class in a subordinate relationship."[17] That is, in Mr. Bachman's view, an entity set is a *model* of two or more entity classes with a relationship between them. This should not be confused with the word "set" in the mathematical sense, which, like "entity class" can also refer to a group of entity instances.
>
> His models, graphically, consist of one or more named rectangles (entity classes), and named arrows between pairs of them. If it is optional from the source, the arrow line is dashed. The arrows always represent one-to-many relationships, with the arrow on the many end. In his original article, cited here, he shows some standard configurations of models, including hierarchies and networks. The models do not display attributes.

---

[14]   David C. Hay. 2011. *UML and Data Modeling: A Reconciliation.* Appendix B. (Technics Publications). p. 150.

[15]   Charles W. Bachman, "Data Structure Diagrams," *ACM Data Base* (1:2) 1969 Summer, pages 4 - 10.

[16]   Ibid.

[17]   Ibid.

➤ *Peter Chen (1976)*[18]

In the mid-1970s Dr. Peter Chen published a graphical notation to describe **entity-relationship modeling**. As did Mr. Bachman, he started by defining an **entity** as something real or imaginary that is of interest. Unlike Mr. Bachman, however, he called "entity classes"—categories of entities—**entity types**.[♠] Dr. Chen's approach differs from both Mr. Bachman's and most of his successors in its representation of **relationships** and **attributes**. relationships are shown with a separate diamond-shaped symbol on the relationship line, and attributes are shown in separate—attached—circles, instead of as annotations on the entity types, as was done in subsequent approaches.

➤ *Clive Finkelstein and James Martin (Martin: 1985[19]; Finkelstein: 1989[20])*

Clive Finkelstein and James Martin created an overall approach to developing systems called **Information Engineering (IE)**. Among other things, this is the source of the **waterfall approach** to the systems design process: Begin with **Strategy**, follow with **Requirements Analysis**, then **Design**, **Construction**, and finally, **Implementation**. Included in this approach was a data modeling technique that was less complex than Dr. Chen's. Among other things, they included neither representation of attributes nor of identifiers. These concepts, however, were later added by LogicWorks in their tool called **ERwin**. The Erwin version eventually prevailed in the marketplace, and became "Information Engineering" as generally understood. This expanded version is definitely oriented towards relational database design.[21]

➤ *US Air Force, Robert G. Brown (1981-93)*

Integration DEFinition for Information Modeling (IDEF1X) is a notation that is specifically directed to designing relational databases. It is based on two independent efforts. **IDEF1** was developed for the United States Air Force in 1981, as part of its **Integrated Computer Aided Manufacturing (ICAM)** program. The **Logical Database Design Technique (LDDT)** had been developed in 1982 by Robert G. Brown of The Database Design Group entirely outside the IDEF program and with no knowledge of IDEF1. In 1993, however, IDEF1X was officially published, combining features from both IDEF1 and LDDT.[22]

---

[18] Peter Chen "The Entity-Relationship Model: Towards a Unified View of Data", *ACM Transactions on Database Systems*, Vol. 1, No 1, (March 1976), pages 9-36.

[♠] Over the years, data modelers have become careless, referring to the boxes in their models as being about "entities" instead of "entity types". This might not matter, except that about 1990, the "object-oriented analysts" came along and asserted their intellectual superiority because they understood the difference between an "object" and an "object class". In the interest of reclaiming our intellectual position, this author is going to stick to referring to "entity types" (that is, "entity classes") as the contents of a data model.

[19] James Martin and J. Leben. 1989. *Strategic Information Planning Methodologies*. (Prentice Hall).

[20] Clive Finkelstein. 1989. *An Introduction to Information Engineering: From Strategic Planning to Information Systems*. (Addison-Wesley).

[21] Donna Burbank and Steve Hoberman. 2011. *Data Modeling Made Simple with CA ERwin Data Modeler R8*. (Technics Publications).

[22] Wikipedia, IDEF1X, citing *FIPS Publication 184* released of IDEF1X by the Computer Systems Laboratory of the National Institute of Standards and Technology (NIST). 21 December 1993.

IDEF1X is analogous to the IE notation, but it focuses on whether a relationship is identifying or not to a great degree. It is strongly oriented towards relational database design.

IDEF1X is still used extensively by the United States Department of Defense. LogicWorks included some of its conventions in ERwin's version of Information Engineering.

Thomas Bruce published what became the definitive textbook on IDEF1X in 1992[23].

> ### ➢ *Richard Barker and Harry Ellis* **(1990)**[24]
> Richard Barker and Harry Ellis developed an approach to modeling data that was specifically oriented toward presenting the model to non-technical business people. The graphical approach is schematically simpler, but the method includes strict rules for naming relationships as business assertions. The **Barker/Ellis Notation** ensures that a non-data modeler can clearly understand (and dispute, if necessary) each drawing.♥

> ### ➢ *G.M. Nijssen and Terry Halpin (1989)*[25]
> **Object Role Modeling (ORM)** is an approach quite different from the other data modeling techniques described here. "Rather than representing entity types as analogues of relational tables, it shows relationships (that contain one or more "roles" in ORM parlance) to be such analogues. Like the Barker/Ellis notation, it makes extensive use of language in making the models accessible to the public, but unlike other modeling techniques, it has much greater capacity to describe business rules and constraints."[26]

> ### ➢ *Object Management Group (OMG) (V1.3 - 2000: v2.0 – 2005)*[27]
> **The Unified Modeling Language (UML)** brought together the works of various players to address modeling not only data ("class" modeling), but also process flows, events and responses, as well as software components. The notation is clearly oriented toward object oriented design. Only "class models" concern us here.

> ### ➢ *World Wide Web Consortium (W3C) (2000-2004)*[28]
> Building on the World Wide Web's ability to share globally pictures and documents, the **Semantic Web** consists of a standard for registering all definitions (with the owner of each) on the web. Each term is assigned a specific kind of **Uniform Resource Locator (URL)** called a **Universal Resource Identifier (URI)**. Included in this global vocabulary are some "reserved words" used in three languages for manipulating these definitions: **Resource Definition Framework (RDF)** (defining the language of the world), **RDF Schema (RDFS)** (recognizing classes and relationships), and the **Web Ontology Language (OWL)** (drawing inferences).

---

[23] Thomas Bruce. 1992. Designing Quality Databases with IDEF1X Information Models. (Dorset House)

[24] Richard Barker. 1990. CASE*Method: Entity Relationship Modeling. (Addison Wesley)

♥ Full disclosure requires your author to acknowledge that the Barker/Ellis technique was his introduction to this field and remains his favorite.

[25] Gerardus Maria Nijssen and T Halpin. 1989. Conceptual Schema and Relational Database Design. (Prentice-Hall).

[26] David C. Hay. 2011. UML … op. cit. p. 150.

[27] Object Management Group. 2015. *Unified Modeling Language™ (UML®)* Version 2.5. Can be downloaded from *http://www.omg.org/spec/UML/2.5/PDF/*.

[28] World Wide Web Consortium. 2004. The Semantic Web. Described on https://www.w3.org/standards/semanticweb/.

> ➤ **Business Rules Group / Object Management Group (2008)**[29]
>
> In the early 2000s, the Business Rules Group sought a way to capture and define *business rules* in a coherent, natural language way. From this came the **Semantics of Business Vocabulary and Rules**™ (SBVR), adopted by the Object Management Group as a standard for describing business rules. While its objective is to describe the constraints that apply to an enterprise's operations, it includes some very good guides to capturing rigorously an enterprise's semantics.

For a more thorough comparison of data modeling techniques, see "Appendix C – Types of Notation", below.

Summary of Data Model Types

Over the years, people have attempted to organize data in several diverse ways. The most popular of these approaches to organization are described here.

The Ontology Version (323 BCE)

One could characterize each of the models described in this document as an **ontology** of the enterprise. That is, each is a model of *what exists*. The word "ontology" ("οντολογία") is, after all, the world's first 2400-year-old hot new buzzword.

Originally (323 BCE), this was "that department of metaphysics that relates to the being *or essence* of things, or to being in the abstract."[30]

Now (in 2018 CE), an *ontology* is a catalog of terms describing the types of things that are *assumed to exist*...

...in a domain of interest

...with rules governing how those terms can be combined to make valid statements

...along with "sanctioned inferences" that can be made.[31]

For those who prefer a more arcane definition, an **ontology** is "an explicit *specification* of a *conceptualization*".[32]

That is, a "body of formally represented knowledge that is based on a *conceptualization*: the objects, concepts, and other entities that are assumed to exist in some area of interest and the relationships that hold among them. A conceptualization is an abstract, simplified view of the world that we wish to represent for some purpose. Every knowledge base, knowledge-based system, or knowledge-level agent is committed to some conceptualization, explicitly or implicitly." [33] An ontology describes one of those.

---

[29] Object Management Group. 2017. Semantics of Business Vocabulary and Rules™. Available at: http://www.omg.org/spec/SBVR/1.4.

[30] Various Editors. 1971. The Compact Edition of the Oxford English Dictionary. (Oxford University Press).

[31] Knowledge Based Systems, Inc. 1994. "Information Integration for Concurrent Engineering". Prepared for Armstrong Laboratory AL/HRGA.

[32] Tom Gruber. 1993. "A translation approach to portable ontology specification". Knowledge Acquisition 5(2):199-220. P. 199. Quoted in: Asuncion Gomex-Perez, Mariano Fernandez-Lopez and Oscar Corcho. 2005. Ontological Engineering. (Springer). Page 6.

[33] Tom Gruber. 1992. "What is an Ontology?" Retrieved 2/27/2018 from *http://www-ksl.stanford.edu/kst/what-is-an-*

Examples of ontologies are conceptual glossaries, data models, and collections of statements using the semantic web.

The ANSI / SPARC Version (1975 CE)

In 1975, the American National Standards Institute's Standards Planning and Requirements Committee (ANSI/SPARC) published their "three-schema approach" to database management. The three schemas[♦] were:

➤ *External Schema:*

"The various users of the database management system operate on sub-sets of the total enterprise model which are relevant to their particular needs." These subsets are represented as "external schemas".

➤ *Internal Schema:*

"The 'machine view' of the data is described by the internal schema. This schema describes the stored representation of the enterprise's information."

➤ *Conceptual Schema:*

This "embodies the 'real world' view of the enterprise being modeled in the database. It represents the current 'best model' or 'way of doing business' for the enterprise." It encompasses as many of the external schemas as possible, and is the foundation for defining appropriate internal schemas.

The ANSI committee viewed the problem from the point of view of a database management system.[34] Over time, however, it became clear that the three schemas could be viewed from the point of view of data management itself. Figure 1 shows the schemas laid out.[35]

While the ANSI committee saw the **external schema** as the domain of application programs, it is true that the external schemas also represent the different views of various *people* in the enterprise, with numerous ways of examining the same body of data. Every one of us, over the course of our lifetimes, assembles a vision of the world, with a particular set of assumptions and inferences. When we come together, we use language as best we can to communicate. But each world view remains our own.

The ANSI/SPARC description of the **internal schema** in fact glossed over the fact that there were actually two things going on: First is the organizational approach used by any particular data management technology (e.g. relational ("Relnl" in the figure), XML, hierarchy, network, flat files, etc.). This is called by some the **logical schema**. The second part of the internal schema then contains the description of *how* the data are stored, (i.e., record implementation techniques, field implementation techniques, syntax of data values, etc. This may be called the **physical schema**.)

---

ontology.html.

[♦] Purists would recognize the Greek roots of "schema" and call the plural "schemata", but that far, even your author isn't willing to go…

[34] Donald A. Jardine, Editor. 1977. *The ANSI/SPARC DBMS Model.* (The North-Holland Publishing Company).

[35] Hay. 2011. *UML… op. cit.* Pages 136-137.

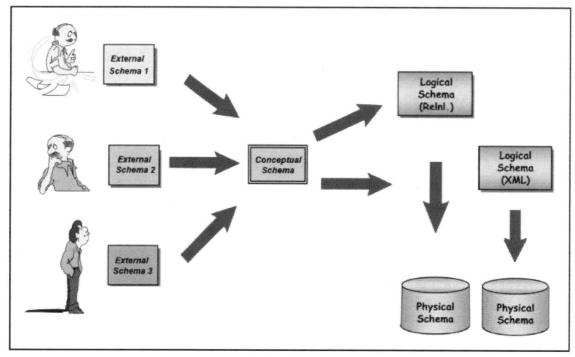

Figure 1: The Three (well four, actually) Schema Architecture

It is the **conceptual schema** that brings all of these views together in a single representation that embodies the concepts of the domain of interest as a whole. Each of the *concepts* of all relevant external schemas must be represented in some way in a conceptual model, in a way that does not conflict with other views of the same data. Similarly, new *technology* can be added to the logical and internal views, without affecting any of the conceptual or external views.

It is the *independence* of the three kinds of schemas that can make systems more robust. Different external views can be added without affecting the logical or physical views. Similarly, technologies may change internal schemas, but do not affect the external views.

The John Zachman Version (1987, 1992, 2008 CE)

John Zachman published a "Framework for Information Architecture" in 1987[36] and, along with John Sowa, extended it in 1992.[37] This framework is a two-dimensional matrix that originally described all aspects of system development. In 2008, he updated the framework to make it a "Framework for *Enterprise* Architecture".[38]

Figure 2 shows the matrix that comprises the latest version of the **Zachman Framework.**

---

[36]   John Zachman. 1987. "A framework for information systems architecture", *IBM Systems Journal*, Vol. 26, No. 3. (IBM Publication G321-5298).

[37]   John Sowa and J. A. Zachman. 1992. "Extending and Formalizing the Framework for Information Systems Architecture", *IBM Systems Journal*, Vol 31, No 3. IBM Publication G321-5488.

[38]   Zachman, John and Stan Lock. The Zachman Framework™. (Retrieved 2011 from *http://zachmaninternational.com/index.php/home-article/13#maincol.*)

	What (Inventory)	How (Process)	Where (Distribution)	Who (Responsibility)	When (Timing)	Why (Motivation)
Executives	Inventory Identification	Process Identification	Distribution Identification	Responsibility Identification	Timing Identification	Motivation Identification
Business Managers	Inventory Definitions	Process Definitions	Distribution Definitions	Responsibility Definitions	Timing Definitions	Motivation Definitions
Architects	Inventory Representation	Process Representation	Distribution Representation	Responsibility Representation	Timing Representation	Motivation Representation
Engineers	Inventory Specifications	Process Specifications	Distribution Specifications	Responsibility Specifications	Timing Specifications	Motivation Specifications
Technicians	Inventory Configuration	Process Configuration	Distribution Configuration	Responsibility Configuration	Timing Configuration	Motivation Configuration
Enterprise	Inventory Instantiation	Process Instantiation	Distribution Instantiation	Responsibility Instantiation	Timing Instantiation	Motivation Instantiation

Figure 2: The Zachman Framework

The Columns

The *columns* represent the dimensions of any effort:

➢ **What?** (the *inventory* column):
Structures used to build the architecture.

➢ **How**? (the *process* column):
Activities performed in an enterprise or in an automated system.

➢ **Where?** (the *distribution* column):
Business locations and/or technology locations.

➢ **Who?** (the *responsibility* column):
People, organizations, and roles.

➢ **When?** (the *timing* column):
Intervals, events, cycles, and schedules.

➢ **Why?** (the *motivation* column):
Goals, strategies, and means, plus policies and rules.

Rudyard Kipling put it well in his *Just So Stories* (1902) [39]:
I keep six honest serving-men
(They taught me all I knew);
Their names are What and Why and When
And How and Where and Who.

---

[39] Rudyard Kipling. 1902. *Just So Stories*. "The Elephant's Child". (Digireads.com Publishing).

While there are many interconnections among the columns, this book is primarily concerned with column *one*: the "resources" of interest (comprising the domain of interest in an enterprise) that are described by *data*.

The Rows

The *rows* represent the various perspectives bring to the enterprise table by different players . The row names were defined in 2008 as follows.

> **The first three are not about technology, but about the business itself.**

✓ **Executive perspective**
Identification of basic concepts, used for defining the overall scope of efforts.

✓ **Business Managers' perspectives**
Definition of terms, as seen by the executive leaders and other "owners" of the data in the enterprise.

✓ **Architect's perspective**
Relatively abstract representation of the essence of the enterprise by the architects. This is called a "system" by Mr. Zachman, reflecting the works of cybernetisist Stafford Beer, where the word means "a group of elements dynamically related in time according to some coherent pattern…with a PURPOSE".[40]

Actually, it's much more complicated than that: hence Mr. Beer's book. But this definition will suffice for Mr. Zachman's purposes.

> **The next two are more specifically about a technology:**

✓ **Engineers' perspectives**
Specification of technology—both database and program design.

✓ **Technicians' perspectives**
Configuration of target systems in detail.

> **And finally:**

✓ **Enterprise's perspective**
Instantiation as seen by the enterprise workers to whom the system is finally delivered.

Each cell of the matrix, then, represents a particular perspective's view of a particular kind of thing. For example, an *architect's* view of *resources (data)* typically consists of entity/relationship diagrams. The *executive's* view of *functions* typically involves process models. And so forth.

Object Management Group (OMG): Model-driven Architecture (MDA) (2001-2014 CE)

In the late 1990s, the Object Management Group (OMG) created the suite of modeling techniques called the **Unified Modeling Language (UML).**[41] As part of UML's implementation, in 2001, the OMG articulated (and trademarked) what they called **Model Driven Architecture®(MDA®)**. Initially, this was an approach meant to unite UML and other OMG standards "necessary to

---

[40]   Stafford Beer. 1979. *The Heart of Enterprise.* (John Wiley & Sons), page 7.

[41]   Object Management Group. 1997. UML Specification Version 1.1. (Retrievable at http://www.omg.org/members/cgi-bin/doc?ad/97-08-11.zip.) (OMG Members only).

support interoperability with specifications that address integration through the entire systems life cycle: from business modeling to system design, to component construction, to assembly, integration, deployment, management, and evolution, to future integration standards."[42]

It MDA distinguished between "platform-independent models" (or PIM) and "platform-specific models"(or PSM). It only peripherally acknowledged, however, that there might also exist "computationally-independent model" (or CIM), which is sometimes referred to as a "domain model". While the CIM need not be explicitly present in a particular usage of the MDA scheme, MDA accommodates it consistently in the same overall architecture."[43]

The **Platform-Independent Model (PIM)** describes the business without regard to any technology that might be involved in implementing the model. Alternatively, the **Platform-Specific Model (PSM)** is derived by performing some transformation on the PIM. The platform-independent model still contains some characteristics of a technology even if the PIM does not contain anything specific to a particular vendor's version of the technology..

Another account of MDA® is told by Donald Chapin[44] and summarized by Danette McGilvray in her book *Executing Data Quality Projects*[45]:

➤ **Environment model –** A sketch that includes primary entities.

➤ **Class of platform (technology) independent model (CPIM) –** A model of the semantics of a business.

➤ **Class of Platform (technology) specific model (CPSM) or Vendor Platform Independent Model (VPIM) –** An arrangement of data to be used by a particular data management technology to accommodate technical constraints and expected usage.

➤ **Vendor platform specific model (VPSM) –** A model that organizes data on one or more physical media.

In 2014, the OMG published a better-developed description of the MDA®. First, it expressed the mission of MDA® more clearly: "The MDA® approach represents and supports everything from requirements to business modeling to technology implementations. By using MDA® models, we are able to better deal with the complexity of large systems and the interaction and collaboration between enterprises, people, hardware, software." [46] The MDA® then described the following architectural "layers" of models:

➤ **"Business or Domain Models.** These are models of the actual people, places, things, and laws of a domain. The "instances" of these models are "real things", rather than representations of those things in an information system. In MDA®, domain models have historically been called **Computation Independent Models (CIM).**

[42]   Object Management Group (OMG). 2001. Model Driven Architecture (MDA) - ormsc/2001-07-01. (Retrieved, 7/2017, from: http://www.omg.org/cgi-bin/doc?ormsc/2001-07-01).

[43]   Ibid.

Object Management Group. 2008. Working Paper: "MDA Foundational Model Applied to Both the Organization and Business Application Software".

[45]   Danette McGilvray. 2008. Executing Data Quality Projects: Ten Steps to Quality Data and Trusted Information. (Morgan Kaufmann).

[46]   Object Management Group. 2014. Model Driven Architecture® (MDA®) MDA Guide rev. 2.0. Page 1. (Retrieved 7/2017 from http://www.omg.org/cgi-bin/doc?ormsc/14-06-01).

> ➤ **"Logical System Models.** These model the way the components of a system interact with each other, with people, and with enterprises, to assist an enterprise or community in achieving its goals." [47] They are independent of particular vendors' approaches to data management, although each is specific to a particular approach. We often call these "PIM" or "Platform Independent Models".

> ➤ **"Implementation models.** These models show the way in which a particular system or subsystem is implemented to carry out its functions. Implementation models are typically tied to a particular implementation technology or platform. These are referred to as "PSM", or "Platform-specific Models".

This Book's Clarification Data Model Categories (2018 CE)

The rows of John Zachman's Framework give us perfect reference points for describing (in the "data" column) what kinds of *data* models are of interest to the data management community. The "schemas" in the ANSI/SPARC vision and the "perspectives" in the Zachman version both provide raw materials that allow data modelers to define a set of model terms.

This chapter briefly describes each of the kinds of models. For more detailed explanations, refer to Chapter 4 and Chapter 5. To model the first three perspectives is to model the *enterprise* (either a commercial business or a government agency).

Conceptual Data Model

The term **conceptual data model** can be used to describe all of the first three of John Zachman's perspectives. Specifically, it refers to a model that describes elements of the business without respect to any particular data management or other technology.

More specific terms can be used to describe each of the kinds of models in the first three rows:

Overview Model

The **overview model** is a model (or perhaps only a sketch) of the primary concepts that concern an area of interest for an enterprise. Its purpose is to establish a context for the remaining modeling efforts.

Note that **scope** is defined here. This model may be used to define a single subject area (part of the business), or it could be the start of an Enterprise Model to address the enterprise as a whole. In either case, it would be just a selection showing the most important entity types within that scope, but it could also identify the subject areas (in terms of those entity types) to be addressed in more detail in the models to follow. [48]

The Overview Model corresponds to Object Management Group's **Environment Model.**

Semantic Model

There are at least five ways to display the information about the enterprise's language – the **Semantic Model**. The first two are graphical methods, which can be more intuitive to understand *if* the pictoral representations are chosen with care. Recognize though, that since it

---

[47] Ibid.

[48] Hoberman. 2009 Data Modeling … Op. cit.

will cover many terms the diagram can quickly become very complicated. It is therefore essential that the overall scope of any diagramming effort be divided into managable subject areas. The latter three methods are text-based, which means that they can grow more comfortably, but again, organizing even these models into subject areas is necessary to keep them manageable.

➢ **Entity/relationship diagram**

This kind of diagram is a model of the language used in the enterprise. Its purpose is to capture the language of the enterprise—the set of terms (with their definitions) that are used to carry out its daily business. The models in this category come from extensive interviews with the shop foremen, middle managers, , accountants, etc who are responsible for the daily conduct of business.

➢ **Fact-based model**

This is a version that explicitly represents "facts"—assertions of what is true about the enterprise. Most common are **Object Role Modeling (ORM)** and **Fully Communication-Oriented Information Modeling (FCO-IM)**. Among other things, they include the abilirty to represent constrants that cannot be shown in an entity/relationship diagram. These also can very quickly expand into very large models. As with entity / relationship modeling, it is essential that the overall scope of any diagramming effort be divided into manageable subject areas.

➢ **Glossary of terms**

A **Glossary** is a collection of terms in a natural language, such as English. Each term is clearly defined **intrinsically**. (This is called the **Aristotlean** approach to definitions.) That is, the definition of a term begins with specifying the general category of which the term is a member of ("genus" to Aristotle), and adds characteristics that distinguish it from others in that same category ("differentiae" to Aristotle). [49] This is as opposed to an **extrinsic** definition, which simply lists examples of the term. Extrinsic is a much weaker form.

The problem with either of these, though, is that a glossary still doesn't do enough to represent relationships between terms.

➢ **Semantics of Business Vocabulary and Rules**

Semantics of Business Vocabulary and Rules (SBVR*)* specification from the Object Management Group (OMG) "provides an unambiguous, meaning-centric, multilingual, and semantically rich capability for defining *meanings of the language used by people* in an industry, profession, discipline, field of study, or enterprise. This specification is conceptualized optimally for business people rather than automated processing. It is designed to be used for business purposes, independent of information systems designs to serve these business purposes." [50] Again, this is not a graphical representation, but it does provide a disciplined approach to describing terms in a natural language.

➢ **Semantic Web**

The **Semantic Web** encompasses a worldwide collection of terms, each with a clear definition and record of ownership. It also includes an approach to creating the sentences in which they are used. First, each term is defined on the World Wide Web identified with a

---

[49] Robert Arp, Barry Smith, and Andrew D. Spear. 2015. *Building Ontologies with Basic Formal Ontology*. (MIT Press). P. 69.

[50] Object Management Group. 2015. "Semantics of Business Vocabulary and Business Rules" (SBVR). (Version 1.3 found on *http://www.omg.org/spec/SBVR/1.3/PDF*).

specialized "Uniform Resource Locator" (URL), called its **Universal Resource Identifier (URI)**.[*] The Semantic Web encompasses three intersecting languages based on the "Extensible Markup Language" (XML): **Resource Definition Framework (RDF), RDF Schema (RDFS)**, and the **Web Ontology Language (OWL)**. Each of these languages is expressed via a set of "reserved words" which are themselves defined as URIs.

In a typical enterprise, many people will be consulted to acquire these definitions; this means that the vocabulary captured will be extensive, with some conflicting terminology between departments. For this reason, the semantic model is called a **divergent model.**

Essential Data Model [*] –

The **essential data model** is a model of those *things of significance* to the enterprise that define its *essential* or *fundamental* nature. Its purpose is to capture the *fundamental, underlying* nature of the enterprise.

The term "essential data model" is derived from your author's experience with **essential data flow diagrams,** described initially by Steven McMenamin and John Palmer in their 1984 book, *Essential Systems Analysis.*[51]

That is, they were questioning how to move from the "*current* physical system" (representing activities as seen by participants) to a "*new* physical system", (to be created by development efforts). Both sets of authors in this field identified the "logical" model of a prospective system, but they were hard pressed to describe it in detail. They were unclear as to what such a "logical" model would consist of

The pioneers in **"structured systems analysis"**, Tom DeMarco (in 1978[52]), and Chris Gane, and Trish Sarsen (in 1979[53]), developed an approach to diagramming the nature of data flows through an organization. These **data flow diagrams** describe **processes** which transform data from one form to another, **external entities** (such as "customers" and "vendors") which are the ultimate source and destination for data, **data stores**(such as "pending orders") where data await processing, and of course the lines with represent the **data flows** (flow of data) from one external entity, process, or data store to another. The notations in the two books are different, but the underlying concepts are the same.

In both cases, data flow diagram are developed in two steps:

First the analyst describes a **current physical data flow diagram** describing **data flows, processes** and **data stores** in terms of the current mechanisms—paper forms and reports, computer system outputs, and the like. This is then converted to a **logical data flow diagram** that instead describes the underlying nature of those flows. The idea is that the logical data flow diagram would become the basis for designing new systems.

---

[*] NOTE: "Locators" are "uniform". "Identifiers are "universal". Retrieved 5/1/2018 from *https://www.w3.org/Addressing/URL/uri-spec.html.*

[*] The use of "essential model" to describe John Zachman's "Architects' View" was introduced by David C. Hay in his 2011 book, UML ... op. cit.

[51] Steven McMenamin and John Palmer. 1984. *Essential Systems Analysis.* (Yourdon Press).

[52] Thomas DeMarco. 1978. Structured Analysis and System Specification. (Prentice-Hall).

[53] Chris Gane C. and Trish Sarson. 1979. *Structured Systems Analysis: Tools and Techniques.* (Prentice Hall).

The only problem was, how is that transformation from "physical" to "logical" data flows and stores supposed to be done? Of course clever analysts can use their intuition, but it a more disciplined and rigorous approach is called for.

So, Messrs. McMenamin and Palmer took on the task of defining the "true requirements" of a system. "To find these requirements—called the system's *essence*—you need a framework to organize your understanding of them. We begin this framework by defining *essence* as all characteristics of a planned response system that would exist if the system were implemnted with perfect technogy."[54]

✓ ***Remove physical references.*** For each data flow or data store that describes a physical thing (like "Sales Order"), a computerized or manual report should simply describe the contents (e.g., sales, production completions).

✓ ***Sub-divide processes to the most "atomic" level, consisting of process "fragments".*** Examine each process and divide it into component processes. Then do the same with each of those. You know you've reached the "atomic" level when a fragment is small enough that, once it starts, it cannot be terminated until it has completed its function.

✓ ***Identify all "external events" that affect this part of the enterprise.*** These include anything that occurs in the world, having an impact on the enterprise, but is out of the enterprise's control. Examples include when a sales order is received, when a machine in the factory breaks, or when a hurricane passes over or near an enterprise facility.

✓ ***Define essential processes.*** For each external event, gather the process fragments that are invoked—from the first fragment to occur after the event happens, to the one where the enterprise's response is complete, and all in between. All of the affected fragments together may be considered a set—one level up—that constitutes an *"essential process"*.

Thus, an **essential data flow process** is defined as "the complete response by an enterprise to a particular external event." The result of this process is recognition that these activities (e.g. processes or functions) are essential to the enterprise's operation. On the Zachman Framework, this is the *Architect's View* of *Activities*.

This yields a "planned response system that would exist if the system were implemented with perfect technology.

Looking now at **essential data *model*** diagrams, as opposed to **essential data *flow*** Diagrams, we are still on row three. However, the data model in column 1 concerns data *structure*, while the data flow diagram in column 2 is about data *processing*. But again we are talking about data structures that would exist if they were managed with perfect technology.

Reviewing the detailed definitions from the semantic model allows us to identify patterns of data structure; this, in turn, will produce a more abstract (and more generally applicable) essential data model. These will likely include different terms that mean the same thing, or recognition that different concepts may in fact be sub-types of a single, more general concept.

The overall structure of the essential model should have many fewer pieces than the corresponding semantic model. This is called an "integrated" or **convergent model.** The Object Management Group, however, refers to it as a **Computationally Independent Model.**

---

[54] McMenemin and Palmer. *Op. cit. p. 16.*

Technology-specific Models

Technology-specific models should certainly reflect the conceptual descriptions previously described, but here they also reflect the data management technology used to manage those concepts. To varying degrees, the data models must be tinkered with to allow particular kinds of data management systems to be able to manipulate them on a timely basis. Here trade-offs are required to balance, for example the space required for data and the response time required for particular kinds of queries.

All of this is to say that there is more variety in the technological models than in the conceptual ones. The representations of the later have stabilized as the elements of understanding a business have matured. No matter how technology may change, the issues of capturing what is a business' essence will not change significantly.

In the world of technologies, however, an appropriate trade-off this year may be quite inappropriate when the technology changes. In this book, while the conceptual modeling techniques have developed over the last four decades, the technologies represented were developed over the last 20 years—some of them in the last five. What is represented this year may not be appropriate next year. Stay tuned!

Logical Data Model

The logical data model represents the domain being modeled, in terms of a specific data management technology.

NOTE: This is not just one kind of modeling notation. When ANSI came up with its "Three Schema Architecture" in 1975 (see page 10), the only varieties of logical model were "hierarchical" and "network". Relational Databases came along three years later and changed everything, Things have gotten more confusing since then. Among those being used in 2018 are:

➢ **Hierarchical**
  This model recognizes that some things can be linked in hierachies, with multiple "branches" for each "root". This makes retrieval of high level elements very fast, but retrieval of categories of lower level elements very slow.

➢ **Relational**
  Relational theory was defined by Dr. Edward Codd in 1970. (See page 97, below) It took until 1978 before relational technology became available. In relational databases, entity types are represented as two-dimensional tables. Each set of columns whose values identify instances of a table (that is, a row) constitutes a **primary key**. A relationship between this table and another table is represented by a copy of the other table's *primary keys*; this copy is called a **foreign key.**

➢ **Dimensional**
  Dimensional modeling represents entity types as **facts** and **dimensions**, organized for retrieval.

➢ **Object-oriented**
  Object-oriented models represent entity types as **object classes** and relationships as **associations**.

➢ **XML Schema**
  An XML script that defines the meaning of XML tags for other XML scripts. XML Schema tags include various kinds of *components:*

✓ Declarations – components that can appear in XML instances covered by this schema, such as `element, attribute,` and `notation.`

✓ Definitions – components that are internal to the schema, such as `data type, model group,` *attribute group* and `identity constraint.`[55]

> ## NoSQL♦

The NoSQL models describe data in terms of documents, where a "document" refers to a piece of code in a lightweight data-interchange format (such as JavaScript Object Notation or eXtensible Markup Language). There are currently frsions of this:[56]

✓ Key-value – Every item in the database is stored as an attribute name or key, together with its value. The value, however, is totally opaque to the system; data can only be queried by the key.

✓ Column-oriented – Of all the NoSQL variations, this structure is closest to relational. It uses a sparse, distributed, multi-dimensional, sorted map to store data. Each record can vary in the number of columns that are stored. Columns can be grouped together for access in column families, or columns can be spread across multiple column families. Data [are] retrieved by primary key per column family.

Key value stores and column-oriented stores are useful for a narrow set of applications that only query data by a single key value. These approaches appeal because of their performance and scalability, which can be highly optimized due to the simplicity of the data access patterns and opacity of the data itself.

✓ Graph – Graph databases use graph structures with nodes, edges and properties to represent data. In essence, data are modeled as a network of relationships between specific elements. Its main appeal is that it makes it easier to model and navigate relationships between entities in an application.

✓ Document – Instead of taking a business subject and breaking it up into multiple relational structures, document databases frequently store the business subject in one structure called a **document**. For example, instead of storing **Student**, **Course**, and **Registration** information in three distinct relational structures, properties from all three will exist in a single document called **Registration**. Document-oriented modes are generally focused on application, whereas table-oriented models are more focused on data.

In the Object Management Group's Model Driven Architecture®, this is called a **Platform Independent Model (PIM).**

Physical Data Model

A **physical data model** may or may not be graphical in form, but it represents—in whatever way seems reasonable—the technology for *storing data* on a **storage medium.** Its purpose is to represent data as they are stored on one particular medium. This may be described in terms of tablespaces, partitions, or whatever other terminology is appropriate.

---

[55] Priscilla Walmsley. 2002. *Definitive XML Schema.* (Prentice Hall).

♦ …meaning "not just SQL", not "no SQL".

[56] MongoDB, Inc. 2017. "Top 5 Considerations When Evaluating NoSQL Databases". (Retrieved 9/9/2017 from *https://www.mongodb.com/collateral/top-5-considerations-when-evaluating-nosql-databases.*

In the Object Management Group's Model Driven Architecture®, this is called a **platform specific model (PSM).**

About Metadata[57]

The last kind of model to be addressed is that which describes *metadata.*

During the 1990's the concept of *data warehouse* swept the information technology industry. After many years of trying, it appears finally to be possible for a company to store all of its data in one place where they can be reported and analyzed.

One of the problems that arose from this effort was the realization that if a senior executive is going to ask a giant database a question, it is necessary to know just what is in the database and what kinds of questions to ask. In addition to the data themselves, therefore, it is necessary to keep data *about* the data. The term coined for "data about data" during the 1990s was *metadata.*

As with all buzzwords, once invented, the term "metadata" has taken on a life of its own. It is variously described as

- *Any data about the organization's data resource.*[58]

- *All physical data and knowledge from inside and outside an organization, including information about the physical data, technical and business processes, rules and constraints of the data, and structures of the data used by a corporation.*[59]

- *The detailed description of instance data; the format and characteristics of populated instance data: instances and values, dependent on the role of the metadata recipient.*[60]

Several significant points come out of these definitions:

First of all, as Mr. Marco pointed out, there is a difference between **business metadata** and **technical metadata**. The business user of metadata is interested in definitions and structures of the language as terms for the kinds of information to be retrieved. The technician is concerned with the physical technologies used to store and manage data. Both of these points of view are important, and both must be addressed.

Second, the subject is concerned with more than just data. It is, as Mr. Brackett said, "*any* data about an organization's data resource". Once you have started looking at the structure of an organization's data, you have to also account for its activities, people and organizations, locations, timing and events, and motivation.

Third, as Ms. Tannenbaum pointed out, the "meta" aspect of the question is a matter of point of view. There is metadata relative to the data collected by the business. There is also "meta-meta-data" which is used to understand and manage the metadata[*]

---

[57]   This section is extracted from David C. Hay. 2006. *Data Model Patterns: A Metadata Map.* (Morgan Kaufmann).

[58]   Michael H. Bracket, 2000. *Data Resource Quality.* (Addison-Wesley). p. 149.

[59]   David Marco. 2000. *Building and Managing the Meta Data Repository.* (John Wiley & Sons). p. 5.

[60]   Adrienne Tannenbaum. 2002. *Metadata Solutions.* Addison-Wesley. p. 93.

[*]   While delivering a lecture on cosmology one day, Sir Arthur Eddington gave a brief overview of the early theories of the universe. Among others, he mentioned the Indian belief that the world rested on the back of a giant turtle,

This last point is illustrated in Figure 3 Here, the bottom row shows examples of things in the world that are often described in information systems. Julia Roberts is a real human being. The Wall Street Branch of a bank is a physical place were business is performed. Checking account 09743569 is a particular account held in that bank by a particular customer (say, Julia Roberts, for example). The customer of that account may then perform an actual ATM withdrawal at a specific time.

Metadata Literature	**Elements of metadata (metadata model)**	Objects: "Entity Class", "Attribute"	Objects: "Entity Class" "Attribute" "Role"	Objects: "Table" "Column"	Object: "Program module", "Language"
Data Management (Metadata)	**Data about a database (a data model)**	Entity class: "Customer" Attributes: "Name" "Birthdate"	Entity classes: "Branch", "Employee" Attributes: "Employee.Address" "Employee.Name" Role: "Each Branch must be managed by exactly one Employee"	Table: "CHECKING_ACCOUNT" Columns: "Account_number" "Monthly_charge"	Program module: ATM Controller Language: Java
IT Operations (Instance Data)	**Data about real world things (a database)**	Customer Name: "Julia Roberts"; Customer Birthdate: "10/28/67"	Branch Address: "111 Wall Street" Branch Manager: "Sam Sneed"	CHECKING_ACCOUNT. Account_number: = "09743569" CHECKING_ACCOUNT. Monthly_charge: "$4.50"	Transaction Date: 5/20/2018 Time: 19:36 Amount: $400.00
	Real world things	Julia Roberts	Wall Street branch	Checking account #09743569	ATM Withdrawal

Figure 3: Data and Metadata

The next row up shows, in the first three columns, the data that might describe those three things: Julia Roberts has the customer name "Julia Roberts", and a birth date. The Wall Street Branch has an address and a branch manager. The checking account has an account number and a monthly charge. In the fourth column the first row from the bottom shows a transaction that carries out the ATM withdrawal. Data include "Date", 5/20/2018, "Time", 19:36, and "Amount", $400.00. These are the things that would concern the person managing data for the banking business.

Note that each of the terms was described as to what it was: "customer name", "branch manager", "account number", and so forth.

The third row from the bottom collects those descriptors and labels them in turn. This is to create what in the data administration world is called the **metadata**. There are two components to these labels: first are the names of the things of significance being described by the business data, such as "Customer" and "Branch"; second, each of these is in turn described by attributes, such as

---

adding that it was not a particularly useful model as it failed to explain what the turtle itself was resting on.

Following the lecture Eddington was approached by an elderly lady. "You are very clever, young man, very clever," she forcefully declared, "but there is something you do not understand about Indian cosmology: it's turtles all the way down!"

"Name", "Address", and "Birthdate". We also discover, in the case of the bank branch that there are really two things of significance ("Branch" and "Manager") and that they are related to each other. ("Each Branch must be managed by exactly one Manager.")

In the checking account column, we see that "Checking Account" is actually the subject of a table in a database. The table is called CHECKING_ACCOUNT and has columns "Account_number" and "Monthly_charge".

The ATM program described in the second row simply as "Java code" actually is a program module with the name, "ATM Controller", written in the language "Java".

As we can see, the metadata row itself encompasses several different kinds of objects ("Entity Class", "Attribute", "Table", "Program Module", etc.) The assignment of this book, represented by the top row, is to show how these objects all relate to each other.

Metadata don't just describe data. They describe how the organization understands, not only its data, but also its activities, people and organizations, geography, timing, and motivation.

Yes, metadata describe the entities and attributes of an entity-relationship model, and the tables and columns by which these are implemented in a computer system. But they also provide structure for describing the activities of the organization and the computerized processes that implement these activities. They describe who has access to data and why. They describe the kinds of events and responses that are the nature of an organization's activities. They describe where the data and processes are. And they describe the motivation and business rules that drive the whole thing.

The top row then describes the elements of the metadata language itself: Entity Class, Table, Program Module, etc.

So, from all this, we'll settle on the following definition of metadata:

> **Metadata** are the data that describe the structure and workings of an organization's use of *information, and which describe the systems it uses to manage that information.*

One anomaly has revealed itself in the line between business data and metadata. The information about what constitutes a legal value for a "Product Category" or an "Account Type" in the business model is often captured in separate "reference tables". To reflect these validation structures, a typical data model often has many **...type** entity classes (**Account Type**, **Status**, **Day of the Week**, etc.) describing legal values for attributes. These are part of the business database.

But because they are in fact constraints on the values of other attributes in the same database, they are also included in the category of *metadata*. Where a table designer would be required to specify the domain of a column, the data modeler who is instructing the designer, must now provide the values that constitute that domain.

Here you have business data acting as metadata.

Be aware, of course, that even this line between business data and metadata is not as clear-cut as it seems. **Product Type**, for example, is about reference data that constrains many attributes in a business model. Even so, specification of the list of product types is very much the domain of the business, not the data administrator. This plays both the roles of business data and metadata. Probably more in the metadata manager's domain would be Product Category. There should be relatively fewer of these, and the list should be relatively stable.

Chapter Summary

Table 1 summarizes the four general approaches to classifying models.

Table 1: Different Views

The ANSI/SPARC Approach	The Zachman version (Perspectives)	OMG's Model Driven Architecture®[♦]	Models from this book
External	2. Business Manager	(Business domain model)	Semantic model
	6. Enterprise	...	\<delivered system\>
Conceptual	1. Executive	Environment model	Overview
	3. Architect	Class of platform independent model	Essential model
Internal	4. Engineer	Class of platform specific / vendor platform independent model (logical system model)	Logical model
	5. Technician	Vendor platform specific model (implementation model)	Physical model

Figure 4 summarizes the key points of this chapter.

> ➤ The **Overview** model provides a synopsis of the most important concepts for the enterprise. This is typically prepared in cooperation with the company *executives*.

> ➤ The **Semantic** data model captures the enterprise's *semantics*–the terms, concepts, and definitions that constitute the language of the enterprise. This is typically described as *divergent*, since it captures the views of a broad collection of players. This is prepared in cooperation with the enterprises *business management.*

> ➤ The **Essential** data model integrates the elements of the semantic model, providing a more concise view of the fundamental things of significance to the enterprise. This typically models entities, attributes, and relationships, making use of patterns to provide a more abstract view. This is prepared in cooperation with data and enterprise *architects*.

Note that the three of these constitute ***Conceptual Models,*** representations of the enterprise that have no technological components.

[♦] Donald Chapin, 2008. "MDA Foundational Model Applied to Both the Organization and Business Application Software. Object Management Group (OMG) working paper" (March, 2008).

Quoted in Danette McGilvray. 2008. Executing Data Quality Projects: Ten Steps to Quality Data and Trusted Information.tm. (Morgan Kaufmann). Pp 48-49.

➢ The **Logical** data model reflects the structures of the *Essential* model, but adds elements that reflect the technology being adopted. For example, this could include relational columns and keys, object-oriented classes and associations, and XML tags. These are developed in cooperation with database and system *designers*.

➢ And then **Metadata** describe all of these models.

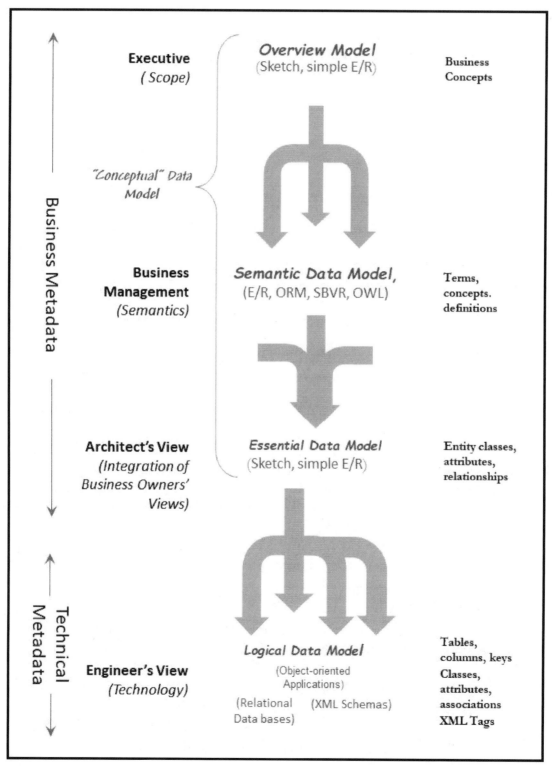

Figure 4: Kinds of Data Models - Schematic

CHAPTER 3:
ABOUT NOTATIONS

I n addition to the problem with defining *terms* for the data modeling world is that of agreeing on *notations*. Just as different people use different terminology for the same things and use the same terms to describe different things, different people use different graphic conventions to describe the same and different things.

Experiences

One problem with notation is that each modeler begins by learning one particular convention. It is difficult not just to master the syntax of a notation, but also to make up for the shortcomings of using it to represent a particular situation. Each notation is inherently better at describing some things than others. If the assignment calls for things that are difficult to describe in one's preferred notation, that notation is stretched and tweaked to make it work. The modeler's way of solving problems is influenced by the modeling notation's fit for addressing each one.

This means that if someone else comes along with a different notation—even one that might make some of the difficult problems easier to solve—the modeler often resists it. The modeler has already described the world in his native notation.

Notation Objectives

The assignment of this book is to bring some peace and coherence to the data modeling community. This section will briefly describe the most popular notations used today, along with guidance as to where each is most appropriate. Understand, however, that each of the following notations *can* be used for any of the kinds of modeling being described here. Subtle differences make (in your author's opinion) each more suited for some tasks than for others.

There are actually three levels of conventions that must be defined in the data-modeling arena. The first is **syntactic** convention, which deals with the symbols used. These conventions are the primary focus of this chapter. The second convention defines the organization of model diagrams. These **positional** conventions dictate how to lay out entity types. Messrs. Ellis and Barker have defined a very effective set of positional conventions to enhance the aesthetic power of each diagram;[61] they are described in the section of this book on Best Practices for Aesthetics in Chapter 6 (page 157). Finally, there are conventions about how the *meaning* of a model may be conveyed. Such **semantic** conventions describe standard ways for representing common business or technical situations. These are the data model "patterns", first described by your author in *Data Model Patterns: Conventions of Thought*,[62] and subsequently by Martin Fowler,[63] Len Silverston,[64] and

---

[61] Barker. 1990. *Op. cit.*

[62] David C. Hay. 1996. Data Model Patterns: Conventions of Thought (Dorset House).

[63] Martin Fowler. 1997. Analysis Patterns; Reusable Object Models (Addison Wesley).

[64] Len Silverston, W. H. Inmon, Kent Graziano. 1997. *The Data Model Resource Book*. (John Wiley).

others. These are what provide the power of *essential* modeling, described later in the section by that name.

Regardless of the symbols used, conceptual data (or object) modeling is intended to describe the things about which an enterprise wishes to collect data, along with the relationships among them. For this reason, these three sets of conventions are, in principle, completely independent of each other. Given any of the syntactic conventions described here, you can follow any of the available positional or semantic conventions.♦ In practice, however, promoters of each syntactic convention typically also promote at least some positional conventions. Moreover, as we will see below, different syntactic conventions are more appropriate for the specific kinds of data models this book is describing.♥

For a set of tables comparing the Barker Ellis, Information Engineering, IDEF1x, and Unified Modeling Language notations, see Appendix C.

Evaluating Notations

When evaluating syntactic conventions, it is important to remember that data modeling has two audiences. The first is the business community, which uses the models and descriptions to verify that the business analysts understand the environment of the enterprise and its requirements. The second audience is the set of systems designers, who use the structures in the models (and the business rules the structures impose) as the basis for computer database and system designs.

Different techniques are better for one audience than another. Models used by business analysts must be clear and easy to read by the non-technical public. This often means that these models may describe less than the full extent of detail available. First and foremost, they must be accessible by a viewer not originally interested in data modeling. Models for designers, on the other hand, must be as complete and rigorous as possible, expressing as much detail as possible.

This evaluation, then, is based both on the technical completeness of each technique and on its readability. *Technical completeness* is defined in terms of the representation of:

- ➢ **Entity types and attributes**
- ➢ **Relationships**
- ➢ **Unique identifiers**
- ➢ **Sub-types and super-types**
- ➢ **Constraints between relationships**
- ➢ **"Enumerated" types**
- ➢ **User-defined types (both entity types and data types)**

A technique's *readability* is characterized by its graphic treatment of relationship lines and entity-type boxes, as well as its adherence to general principles of good graphic design. Among the most important of these principles are that each symbol should have exactly one meaning, and that each concept should be represented by exactly one symbol. Moreover, a diagram should not be cluttered

---

♦ Note that there are some fundamental differences between the way object-oriented designers look at the world and the way data-oriented designers do. The two can communicate with each other, but it must be understood that the world is treated very differently. For more on this, see David C. Hay. 2011. *UML and Data Modeling...* op. cit.

♥ Be aware, however, that some of the techniques for addressing semantics (particularly The Semantic Web and Semantics for Vocabulary and Business Rules (SBVR)) are basically not graphic at all. Here its linguistic skill called for, not aesthetics.

with more symbols than are absolutely necessary, and the graphics in a diagram should intuitively express the concepts involved. Your author has written several articles on this subject.[65]

Each technique has strengths and weaknesses in the way it addresses each audience. As it happens, most are oriented more toward designers than they are toward the user community. These produce models that are very intricate; they focus on ensuring that all possible constraints are described. Alas, this completeness often comes at the expense of readability. The following notations dominate the field as of 2018:

> **Data Structure Diagram** – Charles Bachman invented what was to become entity/relationship modeling. It featured boxes and directed lines.

> **Entity-Relationship Model** – Peter Chen created this version, noteworthy because relationships are represented by the rhombus symbol linked to entity types with simple lines..

> **Information Engineering**—Clive Finkelstein and James Martin combined data modeling with an approach to systems development. This was merged with the IDEF1X notation by LogicWorks, Inc. to produce the ERwin tool.

> **Entity/Relationship Diagram** – Harry Ellis and Richard Barker created the notation used in Europe's SSADM methodology and originally by the Oracle Corporation.

> **Integration DEFinition for Information Modeling** (IDEF1X)—This technique is supported and extensively used by the United States Department of Defense. It is a complex representation with multiple kinds of symbols to link relationship lines to entity class boxes.

> **Fact-based Modeling** (including **Object Role Modeling (ORM)** and **Fully Communication-oriented Modeling (FCO-IM)**)—These techniques differ from entity/relationship versions in their approach to modeling factual assertions.

> **The Unified Modeling Language (UML)**—This supports the object-oriented world.

> **The Extended Markup Language Schema (XML Schema)**—This is not strictly a data-modeling language, but it demonstrates some interesting data-structure ideas.

Table 2 presents the eight notation schemes with indications of what kind of modeling each is most appropriate for. The table shows how suitable each notation is for each of the kinds of models we are discussing here.

A few notes about the evaluations. As will be described in Chapter 4, attempts to represent the semantic model graphically suffer from the fact that, since they are attempting to capture a diverse set of views of the language of the company, they all will have difficulties capturing a "divergent" population of entity types. At the very least, rigorous definitions of and organization into subject areas will be required.

Also, for the essential model, aesthetics will be important, since this must be approved by managers not conversant with data-modeling techniques.

Note that UML is billed as an "object modeling" technique, rather than as a "data (entity/relationship) modeling" technique; in fact, there are some very specific ways in which UML represents the world quite differently. See "UML and Entity/Relationship Modeling in Chapter 5,

---

[65] For example, David C. Hay. 1998. "Making Data Models Readable". *Information Systems Management* 15(1) Winter, 1998, pp 21-33. This can also be found at *http://www.essentialstrategies.com/publications/modeling/makingrd.htm.*

below (page 113). The notation, however, can be adapted to represent the same things represented in an essential entity/relationship diagram.[*] The comparison shown in Table 2 is in terms of each technique's symbols for describing entity types (or "object classes", for the UML), attributes, relationships (or object-oriented "associations"), unique identifiers, sub-types, and constraints between relationships.

Note that only UML can display any or all of the following:

> **Enumeration**
> **Relationship constraints**
> **Derived data types**
> **Derived attributes**

As will be seen in Chapter 4, the task of capturing the semantics of an enterprise may be better done with text than with diagrams. This begins with a glossary of the terms discovered (see page 173), and carried out either via either the business rule approach (OMG's "Semantics of Business Vocabulary and Rules", shown on page 53), or the World Wide Web Consortium's "Semantic Web" (See page 57).

For a more comprehensive comparison of data modeling techniques, see Appendix C.

Table 2: Notations and Kinds of Data Models

	Overview	Semantic Model	Essential Model	Logical Model	Physical Model
Bachman	Strong	Divergent	Good aesthetics	Conceptual only	Can convert to DDL
Chen	Poor aesthetics	Divergent	Poor aesthetics		
Information Engineering	Not suitable	Divergent	Aesthetics can be Addressed	Strong (Relational)	Can convert to DDL
Barker / Ellis	Strong	Divergent	Strong	Not as detailed as required.	Can convert to DDL, XML Schema, and Java
Object Role Modeling	Not suitable	Strong, but divergent			Can convert to DDL
IDEF1X	Poor aesthetics	Poor aesthetics	Poor aesthetics	Strong (Relational)	Can convert to DDL
UML	Poor aesthetics	With adjustments to approach[66]	Conceptually different. Aesthetics can be addressed	Strong (Object-Oriented)	Can Convert to DDL, Java
XML Schema	Not suitable	Not suitable	Not suitable	Strong (XML-Canonical Model)	Not suitable

---

[*] Indeed, your author demonstrated this in his second book on data model patterns (*Enterprise Model Patterns: Describing the World*), where all of the models were presented using UML notation, while keeping the discipline borrowed from the Barker / Ellis approach.

66 Hay. 2011. UML and Data Modeling … op. cit.

CHAPTER 4:
DETAILS – CONCEPTUAL

The conceptual models are not concerned in any way with the technology that might be involved in capturing and managing data. Rather, they are concerned with describing things of significance to enterprises and relationships among them. There are three kinds:

> ➤ **Overview Model** – an executive summary.
> ➤ **Semantic Model** – in the language used by the enterprise.
> ➤ **Essential Model** – the distillation of the Semantic Model into fundamental concepts.

Specifically:

An **Overview Model** usually comprises a relatively small number of entity types, highlighting the most important concepts. The purpose is to make possible a conversation between analysts and top management.

A **Semantic Model** describes the enterprise's language as it exists—jargon, technical terms, inconsistencies, and all. It may or may not be a *graphical* representation, even though in all cases there are strong rules about how we construct definitions. A set of **entity/relationship diagrams** could be developed in the specific terms used by each department. Since most enterprises could have hundreds (or thousands) of terms to gather, creating an entity/relationship diagram may be excessive—difficult to create systematically, and difficult to display.

An alternative *graphic* approach is fact-based **Object Role Modeling**, but again, the number of terms involved can quickly make it become very large. This is made worse by the fact that classes and attributes are depicted as separate symbols.

In the case of both entity/relationship and fact-based models, it is important to organize the models by subject area, and to present them to the public in relatively small pieces. (See Chapter 7, "Best Practices for Aesthetics", for more on this subject.)

Text compilation alternatives include

> ➤ **Glossary**

> ➤ **"Semantics of Business Vocabulary and Rules" (SBVR)** ◆

> ➤ The **Semantic Web**
>   ✓ Universal Resource Identifiers (URIs)
>   ✓ Resource Definition Framework (RDF)
>   ✓ RDF Schema (RDFS)
>   ✓ Web Ontology Language (OWL).

Whichever approach is used—graphic or textual—because it will capture terms as used, with variations, throughout the enterprise, it is called a **divergent models.**

An **essential data model** is a diagram that comprises abstractions of the terms captured in the semantic model. That is, where one department (in, for example, an equipment manufacturing company) is concerned only with **Compressors** and another is concerned with **Pumps**, it is more

---

◆ From the standards organization, the Object Management Group (OMG).

manageable to describe the more general category **Product**. Note that this can be shown by classifying **Pump**, **Compressor**, and **Other Product** as sub-types of **Product**. ("Sub-types" will be discussed below.)

A Note About Model Scope

Presumably, an *overview* model represents an enterprise as a whole (or a major division of it, at least). A *semantic* model, on the other hand, will begin by collecting terms from a specific area, but ideally will eventually cover a large part of an enterprise. The semantic model can thus become an *enterprise data model*, or it can be developed simply to address a particular *subject area*— one project or part of the enterprise.

In the ontology world, a model that covers the language of the world as a whole is called an *upper ontology*, while a model that only addresses a particular subject area (that is, a "domain") is called a *domain ontology*[67].

A recent example is the **Basic Functional Ontology**, created by the Institute for Formal Ontology and Medical Information Science (IFOMIS). It sees the world as divided between "**substantial entities** or **continuants**, and **process entities** or **occurrents**."[68]

> **Continuants**
> Entities that *continue* or *persist* through time, including: (1) independent objects (for example, people like Julia Roberts and organizations like Microsoft), and inanimate things (such as a computer or smart phone); (2) dependent continuants, including qualities (such as a person's temperature and height), and functions (such as the ability of a switch to turn on a light); together with (3) the spatial regions these entities occupy at any given time (like Cleveland, Ohio).

> **Occurrents**
> Entities that *occur* or *happen*, variously referred to as "events" or "processes" or "happenings", which we take to comprise not only (1) the processes that unfold in successive phases (for example, business processes) but also (2) the boundaries or thresholds at the beginnings or ends of such processes (e.g., "Process xy-23 start time"), as well as (3) the temporal and spatiotemporal regions in which these processes occur (such as, for financial accounting, "Third Quarter, 2017").

All of these upper ontologies attempt to model the basic language of the world, without regard to the particular pieces of it one may be interested in.

A model that only addresses a particular area of interest, however, is called a *Domain Ontology*. For example, one a domain ontology could address only one project, department, or specialty.

One ontology of note, at least in the world of enterprises (both commercial and governmental), is the first part of your author's book *Enterprise Model Patterns: Describing the World.*[69] It purports to be

---

[67] Alan Rector, Robert Stevens, Jeremy Rogers and the CO-ODE and BioHealth Informatics Teams, School of Computer Science, University of Manchester. "Simple Bio Upper Ontology". (Retrieved, 2/18/2017, from *http://www.cs.man.ac.uk/~rector/ontologies/simple-top-bio/*).

[68] Andrew D. Spear. 2006. "Ontology for the Twenty First Century: An Introduction with Recommendations". *Institute for Formal Ontology and Medical Information Science (IFOMIS).* (For more information, see *http://ncorwiki.buffalo.edu/index.php/Basic_Formal_Ontology_2.0* .)

[69] David C. Hay. 2011. *Enterprise Model Patterns: Describing the World.* (Technics Publications).

an Upper Ontology, using the graphical representation of entity/relationship models. It describes the world in terms of *continuants* (people and enterprises, geographic locations, and physical assets) and *occurrents* (activities and times). Rather than representing a true upper ontology, however, perhaps it is a domain model whose domain is the world of enterprises.

The Overview Model

The **overview data model** is just that: a synopsis of the enterprise's information structure. An analyst/modeler will typically sketch out this model on a whiteboard, during the strategic planning phases of a project, in response to discussions of objectives and other information concerns.. Before the meeting, however, the analyst/modeler must do some research:

> **Basic Elements** – What are the *basic elements* of the enterprise's organization? (employees, customers, divisions, departments, locations, etc.?)

> **Product and Service Types** – What are the *categories* of *products* and/or *services* the enterprise offers?

> **Motivation** – What issues in the business *sparked* the initiation of this effort?

In 2005 The Object Management Group published a general-purpose business model it calls the **Business Motivation Model (BMM)** . Specification of this model "The Business Motivation Model specification provides a scheme or structure for developing, communicating, and managing business plans in an organized manner. Specifically, the Business Motivation Model does all of the following:

> ➢ "It identifies factors that motivate the establishing of business plans.

> ➢ "It identifies and defines the elements of business plans.

> ➢ "It indicates how all these factors and elements inter-relate. Among these elements are those that provide governance for and guidance to the business Policies and Business Rules." [70]

Figure 5 shows an overview of the model. An initial version of the model was presented by your author in his 2003 book, *Requirements Analysis: From Business Views to Architecture.*[71] A more complete version of Mr. Zachman's **motivation (why)** column constitutes Chapter 7, "Motivation", of your author's 2006 book *Data Model Patterns: A Metadata Map.*[72]

In 2010, the Business Motivation Model was made an official standard by the Object Management Group, and has been updated in minor ways since then.[73]♥ This can be used as an organizing tool for the *overview* segment of any strategic planning session. The Business Motivation Model consists of the following entity types:

> ➢ **End** – Something that the enterprise sets out to accomplish.

---

[70] Object Management Group. 2015. "Business Motivation Model, Verrsion 1.3". (Available as of 4/17/2018 at *http://www.omg.org/cgi-bin/BMM/1.3.)*

[71] Hay. 2003. Requirements … Op. cit.

[72] Hay. 2006. Metadata..*op. cit.* pp. 273-342.

[73] Object Management Group. 2015. "Business Motivation …" *Op. cit.*

♥ The definitions that follow are all from Business Motivation … *Op. cit.*

✓ **Vision** - An End that is a desired future state of the enterprise, without regard to how the enterprise achieves it.

✓ **Desired Result** – An End that is a target or state that the enterprise intends to maintain.

  – **Goal** – A **Desired Result** that is a specific statement about a condition of the enterprise to be brought about or sustained through appropriate **Means** (BMM). A **Goal** is an *amplifier* of a **Vision**. Whereas a **Vision** describes a future state of the enterprise in general, a **Goal** is one of the steps to be taken to accomplish that **Vision**. By definition, a **goal** is narrower than a **Vision**.

  – **Objective** – An attainable, time-limited, measurable **Desired Result** that will help the enterprise achieve its **goals.**

➢ **Means** – Any capability that may be called on, activated, or enforced to achieve an enterprise's objectives.

  ✓ **Mission** – An overall method for the ongoing operation of the enterprise. (That is, what the business is or will be doing on a day-to-day basis.)

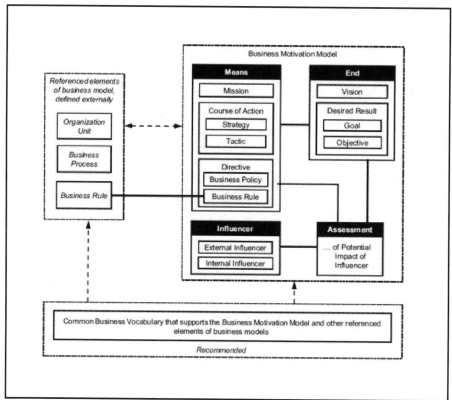

Figure 5: Business Motivation Model - Overview[74]

✓ **Course of Action** – An approach or plan for configuring some aspect of the enterprise. This involves *the use of* things, processes, locations, people, timing, or motivation.

  – **Strategy** – The essential Course of Action attempted to achieve an enterprise's End—particularly its Goals. Moreover, a Strategy must be *to carry out* exactly one Mission.

  – **Tactic** – A **Course of Action** (BMM) that represents one or more details of a **Strategy**. A **Strategy** may be *implemented via* one or more **Tactics**.

---

[74] Object Management Group. 2015. "Business Motivation ..." *Op. cit.*

In general, **Strategies** address **Goals**, while **Tactics** address **Objectives**.

- **Directive** – A specification that constrains **Courses of Action**. There are two kinds of **Directives**:
  - **Business Rule** – A Directive that is "the set of conditions that govern a business event so that it [the event] occurs in a way that is acceptable to the business".[75] For example (for an airline or travel agency) "Each flight booking request for a return journey must specify the return date."
  - **Business Policy** – A non-actionable Directive that guides the activities of the business or governs them in a general way. Note that it "governs"; it does not control or shape Courses of Action. For example, to say that "We will not permit on-site visits" constrains the **Tactics** available for meeting the Strategy to "increase market share". It does not specify what those Tactics should be.

Both external and internal factors constitute **Influencers** of the business, and the extent of that influence is determined by one or more **Assessments**.

The first data strategy meeting, after introductions, should begin with the modeler's confirmation of the enterprise's vision (What do they want to be?) and mission (How do they want to accomplish it?). What strategies and tactics have they laid out so far? From that, extract some key nouns that represent good candidates for *entity types*. This can result in an initial sketch of an entity/relationship model, either privately on paper, or with a group on a whiteboard.

The meeting should also articulate the *goals* and *objectives* of this effort. These are laid out in the context of strategies and tactics for the business, along with any issues that interfere with meeting the enterprise's goals and objectives.

The meeting, then, should result in formalization of the **vision, goals** and **objectives**, along with this entity/relationship model sketch, complete with definitions of all terms that came up. Once these results are published, a possible follow-up meeting can confirm these results.

The Overview Data Model should be limited to a dozen or so entity types—each with a proper definition. Where possible, include "many-to-many" relationships between each pair, with two role names for each relationship.

The Semantic Data Model

Semantics is "the branch of linguistics and logic concerned with meaning."[76] The objective of the semantic model is to capture the language actually used by the enterprise to describe the meaning of things of significance to it. Ideally, the semantic model should be constructed from interviews of many people throughout the enterprise. Unfortunately, this means that semantic "irregularities" will certainly show up As we've discussed, different people may call the same thing (or at least what appears to be the same thing) by different terms,. Different people also use the same term to describe different things. Ideally, this means that the various people involved should at some point get together in a room to attempt to harmonize the language.

---

[75] Barbara von Halle. 2002. *Business Rules Applied*. (John Wiley and Sons). p. 28.

[76] Various editors. Oxford Living Dictionaries. "semantics". (Retrieved 7/6/2017 from https://en.oxforddictionaries.com/definition/semantics).

For example, many companies have one term (word or expression) which is at the center of their operations. Unfortunately, in nearly every case, there are at least two or three (or more) definitions of that word, depending on who you talk to. For example, in a highway department, the enterprise's business is "road". But what does "road" mean? To a planner (or the person trying to get to a hotel from the airport), it's a network of *lines*; to a land manager, it is the *area* that constitutes a right-of-way; to an engineer, it is a solid, consisting of a *volume* of asphalt or cement.

What that means is that "road" should not appear on the model. "Route segment", "right-of-way", and "material component" would be better terms to use.

The enterprise can represent its semantics in numerous ways. Graphic models are sometimes easier to understand, but usually not well suited for a very large model. Easier to manage are the several forms that are text-based. Before diving into detail, here we'll summarize the approaches to semantic modeling:

> **Graphical Representations**
>   ✓ **Entity/relationship model**
>   A graphic representation of the things of significance to an enterprise, plus relationships among them.
>
>   ✓ **Fact-based modeling**
>   A family of conceptual modeling languages, based in the analysis of natural verbalization (also referred to as "plausible sentences") that might occur in the business domain. Two are presented here:
>   – **Object Role Modeling**
>   …which was formalized as a first-order logic by Terry Halpin in 1995[77]
>   – **Fully-Communication-Oriented Information Modeling (FCO-IM),**
>   … published by Guido Bakema, Jan Pieter Zwart, and Harm van der Lek in 2002[78], with updated documentation in *Fact Oriented Modeling with FCO-IM* in 2015.[79]
>
> **Text Representations**
>   ✓ **The Glossary**
>   A simple list, with definitions.
>
>   ✓ **Semantics of Business Vocabulary and Rules** (SBVR)[80]
>   Object Management Group's approach to describing an enterprise's business rules.[81]

---

[77] Terry Halpin. 1995. Conceptual Schema Conceptual Schema & Relational Database Design, Second Edition. (Prentice Hall).

[78] Guido Bakema, J.P. Zwart, H. van der Lek. 2002 Fully Communication Oriented Information Modeling (FCO-IM). Privately published. (Available at http://fco-im.nl/index.php?option=com_content&view=article&id=47:fully-communication-oriented-information-modeling-&catid=35:books&Itemid=55).

[79] Jan Pieter Zwart, Marco Engelbart, Stijn Hoppenbrouwers. 2015. *Fact Oriented Modeling with FCO-IM*. (Technics Publications).

[80] A more English-language description of SBVR can be found in: Graham Witt. 2012. *Writing Effective Business Rules: A Practical Method*. (Morgan Kaufmann).

[81] Object Management Group. 2017. "Semantics of Business Vocabulary and Business Rules: Version 1.4." (Available at *http://www.omg.org/spec/SBVR/1.4/PDF./*).

✓ **The Semantic Web**[82]
Based on the World Wide Web, the Semantic Web combines the capture of terms on the World Wide Web, plus languages for describing the meaning and implications of those terms.

More detailed descriptions of each of these follow.

Graphic Representations

One possibility for capturing *graphically* the semantics of an enterprise is to create a full entity/relationship model, with one entity type box for each term. This will also require capturing the relationships for all entity type pairs. Since there will be a lot of them, this may involve creating a *very large diagram*. This is a **divergent model.** The essential model, an alternative described below (page 72), is an example of a **convergent model.** A plotter, if available, can create wall-sized pictures and provide a place to mark them up and make changes. But even with helpful markup, it can still be difficult to comprehend such a vast picture.

Since it may be used in both semantic and essential models, it is necessary here to begin with a brief description of the entity/relationship diagram.

Entity/relationship Diagram

As Richard Barker wrote, "In its simplest form, entity relationship modelling involves identifying the things of importance in an enterprise (known as **entity types**), the properties of those things (known as **attributes**), and how they are related to one another (known as **relationships**)."[83]

Syntax is "the way in which linguistic elements (as words) are put together to form constituents as phrases or clauses."[84] This is as opposed to **semantics**, the study of meaning[85]. In the case of conceptual modeling, the linguistic elements are both words and symbols.

The syntax of entity/relationship diagramming will apply to all three kinds of conceptual models. For this book, your author is partial to the syntax and modeling discipline laid out by Richard Barker and Harry Ellis.[86] As described in the previous chapter, other systems of notation may also be used. (See Appendix C for a list of such systems.) The Barker/Ellis approach, however, is preferable for creating models that will be presented to non-technical business people. Specifically, it has the following advantages:

➢ **Graphic Simplicity** – Relationships are solid or dashed, and there is one symbol that may annotate one end. Identifying relationships are marked with an unobtrusive symbol only.

➢ **Linguistic Rigor** – Each relationship name lends itself to creating a strong—easily disagreed with—statement about the enterprise.

---

[82] Created by the World Wide Web Consortium (W3C), original documentation may be found at *https://www.w3.org/standards/semanticweb/*. There are, however numerous books on the subject. (See Appendix B: Bibliography).

[83] Barker. 1989. *Op. cit.*

[84] Various editors. Merriam Webster On-line Dictionary. "Syntax". (Merriam Webster). Retrieved 2/12/2017 from https://www.merriam-webster.com/dictionary/syntax.

[85] Various editors. *Merriam Webster On-line Dictionary.* "Semantics". (Merriam Webster On-line Dictionary). (Retrieved 2/12/2017 from *https://www.merriam-webster.com/dictionary/semantics*).

[86] Barker. 1989. *Op. cit.*

Here follows a detailed description of the Barker/Ellis syntax and discipline.

Entity Type

An **entity type** is the definition of a set of **entities**—things of significance to the enterprise, about which it wishes to collect information. Dr. Chen originally used his modeling effort to address "entities", or things of interest. His drawings, however, only concerned "classes" of entities—"entity types". That is, the drawing doesn't represent "Charlie Brown", or a particular piano. Rather, it represents the classes "Person", and "Musical Instrument". ♠

Figure 6 shows the entity types from a example entity/relationship model.

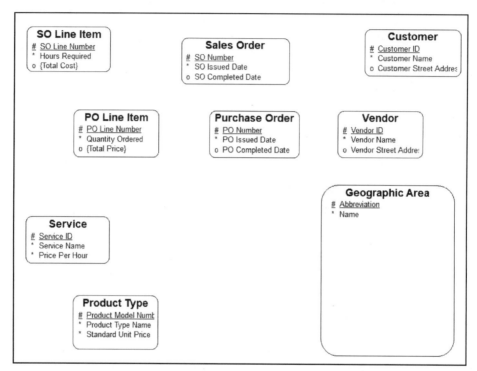

Figure 6: Sample Entity Types

Specifically:

➤ **Customer**

An enterprise or person who has purchased a **Service**♣ from us or who is likely to do so.

➤ **Sales Order**

A contract between our company and a **Customer** who wishes to receive a specified service from us, in exchange for financial compensation.

➤ **SO Line Item**

An entry on a **Sales Order** that describes a **Service** a customer has requested.

♠ Unfortunately, over the years, data modelers became lazy, using the term "entity" to describe each box. That was acceptable, until the object-oriented community asserted their intellectual superiority when they pointed out that they knew the difference between "object" and "class".

Data specialists who are professional always understood that distinction as well. They knew the difference between "entity" and "entity type". It is time for all to acquire this discipline.

♣ Henceforth, entity type names will be shown bold-faced in the sans serif "Calibri" font.

> ➢ **Service**
> The definition of a kind of activity that we are willing to perform for compensation.

> ➢ **Vendor**
> An enterprise or person who is able to sell us a **Product Type** of interest.

> ➢ **Purchase Order**
> A contract between our company and a **Vendor** who is prepared to deliver one or more specified **Product Types** to us, in exchange for compensation.

> ➢ **Purchase Order Line Item**
> The fact that a particular **Product Type** is being ordered on a particular **Purchase Order**.

> ➢ **Product Type**
> The definition of a kind of product that is available for purchase.

> ➢ **City**
> "1. a large, important town.
>
> 2. In the United States, an incorporated municipality, whose boundaries and powers of self-government are defined by a charter from the State in which it is located.
> 3. In Canda, a municipality of the highest rank.
>
> 4. In Great Britain, a borough or town with a royal charter."[87]

> ➢ **State**
> "One of the territorial and political units constituting a federal government, as in the United States."[88]

> ➢ **Country**
> "A land; whole territory of a nation or state."[89]

About Sub-types

Note that in Figure 7, above, **City, State,** and **Country** are shown as boxes inside the box for **Geographic Area**. This means that they are *sub-types* of **Geographic Area**. That is, every instance of **City** is, by definition, also an instance of **Geographic Area**. Similarly, every instance of **State** and **Country** is also an instancs of **Geographic Area**. On the other hand, each instance of **Geographic Area** must in fact also be an instance of either **City, State,** or **Country**.

This means, among other things, that each sub-type *inherits* both the *relationships* and *attributes* of the super-type.

Thus, the sub-types of **Geographic Area** actually have the following attributes:

> ✓ **City**
> – (Abbreviation)
> – (Name)

> ✓ **State**
> – (Abbreviation)
> – (Name)

---

[87] Various editors. *Webster's New World Dictionary.* 1964. "City". (World Publishing Company), p. 267.

[88] *Ibid.* "State", p. 1424.

[89] *Ibid.* "Country". p. 338.

✓ **Country**
  – Country Telephone Code
  – (Abbreviation)
  – (Name)

If the relationship lines from **Purchase Order** and **Sales Order** had gone to the outside entity type (**Geographic Area**), then each of the sub-type entity types would also inherit those relationships. Since they only are related to **City**, then only that one is *the site of* **Purchase Order** and **Sales Order**.

In the Barker/Ellis notation, sub-types are shown as boxes *inside* the super-type boxes. This makes the model more compact. This approach also makes it graphically clear that an instance of a sub-type *is* also an instance of the super-type.

NOTE:

By convention, all sub-types under the Barker/Ellis approach are both *complete* (each instance of the super-type must be an instance of one of the sub-types) and *mutually exclusive* (an instance of the supertype can only be an instance of one sub-type.) Other approaches don't follow this constraint, but Messrs. Barker and Ellis have found it to improve the overall discipline of the modeling process.

Attribute

If an entity type is a class of "things of significance about which one desires to hold information", the *attribute* defines an element of that thing – "a characteristic evaluated for or describing instances of an entity [type]."[90] That is, each *attribute* will hold one and only one value for each instance of the *entity type*.♥

In the Barker/Ellis notation, attributes are shown as descriptors on the entity box. For example, on Figure 6, note the attributes for each of the entity types shown:

✓ **Customer**
  – Customer ID
  – Customer Name
  – Customer Street Address

✓ **Vendor**
  – Vendor ID
  – Vendor Name
  – Vendor Street Address

✓ **Sales Order (SO)**
  – SO Number
  – SO Issued Date
  – SO Completed Date

---

[90]   Hay, *UML... op. cit*. Page 194.

♥   Note that this is a constraint, inherited from relational theory, that provides rigor to the semantic and essential models. It is relaxed in some kinds of logical models.

✓ **Purchase Order (PO)**
- – PO Number
- – PO Submitted Date
- – PO Last Received Date

✓ **SO Line Item**
- – SO Line Number
- – Total Hours
- – Total Cost

✓ **PO Line Item**
- – PO Line Number
- – Quantity
- – Total Cost

✓ **Service**
- – Service ID
- – Service Name
- – Price per Hour

✓ **Product Type**
- – Product Model Number
- – Product Type Name
- – Standard Unit Price

✓ **Geographic Area**
- – Abbreviation
- – Name

✓ **Country**
- – Telephone Country Code

Relationships

In entity / relationship modeling, ***relationship*** is a pair of directed assertions about one entity type's association with another entity type.

The Barker/Ellis approach to data modeling places special emphasis on rigorously naming relationships.

If this is supposed to be an ***Ontology***, representing *what exists* in a domain, simply listing things (or classes of things) is not sufficient. Note that this means the "verb phrase" in each relationship will always be "to be" (in the form of "must be" or "may be").

What is also needed are *assertions* about how these things are related to each other. For example, in Figure 7, the diagram makes a series of assertions that are important if the viewer is to understand the diagram's meaning:

- Each **Sales Order** <u>must be</u> *to sell to* one and only one **Customer**. That **Customer**, on the other hand <u>may be</u> *buyer in* one or more **Sales Orders**.

- Each **Sales Order** <u>may be</u> *composed of* one or more **SO Line Items**, <u>each of which</u> <u>must be</u> *to sell* one and only one **Service**.

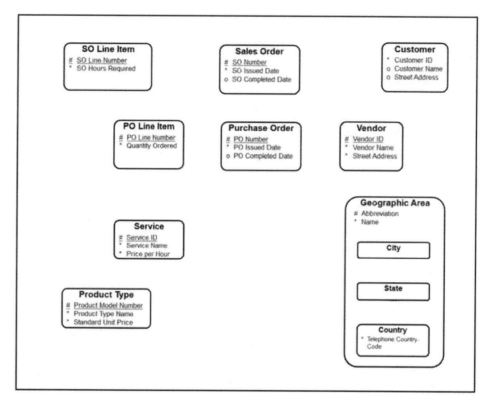

Figure 7: Sample Entity/Relationship Diagram (with Relationships)

The syntax for relationships

Notice that the above discussion about how to construct relationships made use of straight-forward English sentences to describe them. As a reader, you may notice the similarity in their structures, but thinking about that does not interfere with your being able to understand them. There's a reason for that. This is the contribution of Messrs. Ellis and Barker to the body of knowledge.

First, the notation is relatively simple and intuitive.

➢ **Optionality:**

If a half-line is *solid* next to the *subject* of a relationship, that relationship is *mandatory*. That is, for each instance of the subject entity type, at least one instance of the object entity type <u>must be</u> present. If it is *dashed*, the relationship is *optional*. That is, there may or may not be any instances of the object entity type for an instance of the subject. It <u>may be</u> present.

➢ **Cardinality:**

If the relationship next to the *object* of the relationship *is* decorated by a chevron (*"crow's foot"*), there may be <u>one or more</u> instances of this entity type for each instance of the subject entity type.♦ If there is *no crow's foot*, then there can only be <u>exactly one</u> instance of the object entity type for each instance of the subject entity type.

♦ In Figure 7, the vertical lines on relationship lines next to **SO Line Item** and **PO Line Item** denote that these are identifying relationships. These will be discussed further below.

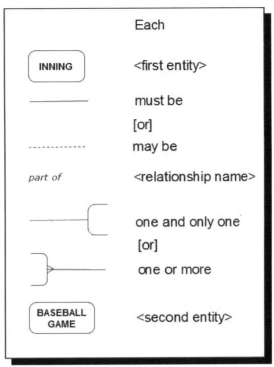

Figure 8: How to Read a Relationship

Second, relationship names are constructed to result in strong assertions abou the nature of the relationship.

Figure 8 shows how to construct a simple English sentence from the names assigned to each relationship end.

The reading starts from one end and collects the relationship name and the optionality of the line from that end, and then picks up the cardinality from the other end. For example, "Each **Inning** <u>must be</u> *part of* <u>one and only one</u> **Baseball Game**." "Each **Baseball Game** <u>may be</u> *composed of* <u>one or more</u> **Innings**."

Two of the relationships shown on Figure 7, then are:

- Each **Sales Order** <u>must be</u> *to sell to* <u>one and only one</u> **Customer.**
  (Each **Customer** <u>may be</u> *responsible for* <u>one or more</u> **Sales Orders**.)

- Each **Purchase Order** <u>must be</u> *to buy from* <u>one and only one</u> Vendor.
  (Each **Vendor** <u>may be</u> *responsible for* <u>one or more</u> **Purchase Orders.**)

Now we can combine and read the other relationships:

- Each **Sales Order** <u>may be</u> *composed of* <u>one or more</u> **Sales Line Items** (where each **Sales Line Item** <u>must be</u> *to sell* <u>one and only one</u> **Service**).

- Each **Service** <u>may be</u> *sold via* <u>one or more</u> **Sales Order Line Items** (where each **Sales Order Line Item** <u>must be</u> *part of* <u>one and only one</u> **Sales Order**).

We can discuss the meaning of these assertions without actually examining the details of the model at all. This is because the relationship names have been carefully selected so that they may to be assembled into strong assertions that the subject matter expert must agree with or not.

The best way to "proofread" the relationship names is to read them aloud. There are three things to test for:

1) Are they grammatically correct?

2) Do they make sense?

3) Do they sound true?

Of course the reason you willl present this to reviewers is to determine if they are *actually* true.

Traditionally, the language around relationship names are called ***verb phrases***. With the Barker/Ellis approach, however, the "verb" in the verb phrase is always "to be"; the *meaning* of the relationship itself is conveyed by a prepositional phrase (or, occasionally, an infinitive). (Think of Grover's "over and under" words, in the American kids' television show, "Sesame Street".)

This is also consistent with the view that we are dealing with ***ontologies***—descriptions of *what exists.*

Domains

In conceptul data modeling, a ***domain*** is "a set of validation rules, format constraints and other properties that apply to one or more attributes."[91] ♣

A domain provides a means of standardizing the characteristics of the attributes.

Figure 9 shows a "meta" model describing ***Attributes***, ***Domains***, and some related concepts.

In any of the *conceptual models* (*overview, semantic,* or *essential*), an **Attribute** may have one or more *discrete* values (a **Discrete Attribute**), like "Status". Alternatively, it may have a *range* of values (a **Continuous Attribute**), like "Temperature". **Other Attributes**, like dates, are neither continuous nor discrete.

Domains can be defined in different ways:

➢ **Value Set**

Note that the set of values (a **Value Set**) described here is not the same as the list of codes (a **Code Set**) that will be addressed when the logical and physical models are taken up. For example, here you can recognize that the attribute "Canadian Province" will have a **Value Set** with one entry per province. When the model is populated, however, there will be one or more **Code Sets**, first in various languages and second in various forms (e.g., codes, abbreviations, names, etc.). Each **Code Set** may be *composed of* one or more **Valid Codes**.

Note that while each **Value Set** may be represented by one or more **Code Sets**, it is sometimes useful to identify a single **Code Set** as the standard representation of the **Value Set**. For example, in conventional usage, the set of US States is primarily described by the **Code Set** called "US State Names in English".♠

---

[91] Barker. 1990. *Entity… op. cit.* p. G1-3.

♣ Note that this is in the context of modeling data attributes. This should not be confused with "domain" which describes a subject area.

♠ Unfortunately, the Canadians must have <u>two</u> standard representations of the **Value Set** "Canadian Provinces": "Canadian Province Names in English" and "Canadian Province Names in French".

➢ **Value Expression**

These domains are defined by **value expressions**— the rules that values must comply with in order to be valid. For example, Line Item "extended price" is defined as Line Item "unit price" * Line Item "Quantity".

➢ **Range**

These domains allow a **range** of values of the same data type that are between one (or more) minimum and maximum values. Some ranges can be open-ended. For example, Delivery Date for an order must be no earlier than the Order Date.

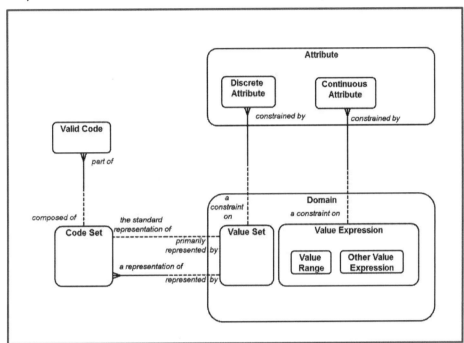

Figure 9: Metamodel of Domains

➢ **Other Domains**

✓ **Data Type**

Attributes may be constrained simply by their **data type**. For example, Integer, Character(30), and Date are all data type domains.

✓ **Data Format**

Data format domains use patterns. Patterns may define valid values via templates and masks, such as those found in "postal code" and "telephone number". They may also be character limitations (e.g. alphanumeric only, or alphanumeric with certain special characters allowed).

Derived Attributes

The principles of relational theory—as translated into entity/relationship modeling—dictate that every attribute must describe a single, atomic value for an entity class. It is often useful, however, to make interim calculations.[92] By convention (at least in the Barker/Ellis notation),

---

♠ This technique and syntax was originally developed for a product called MITROL in the 1970's by a group of software visionaries from the Massachusetts Institute of Technology. Your author first used the approach in the

computed attributes are surrounded by curly braces ({ }). In some cases, these are simple calculations within an entity type.

For example, as shown in Figure 10:

SO Line Item ({Total Cost}) = **SO Line Item** (Hours Required) * **SO Line Item** ({Price Per Hour})

In other cases, a value for a derived attribute may be *inferred* from an attribute in a parent entity. For example:

SO Line Item ({Price Per Hour}) = INFER-THRU (*to sell*, **Service**, Price Per Hour)

Morover, going the other direction, it is possible to *summarize* across values for an attribute in a child entity type, to populate a derived attribute in a parent entity type. For example:

Sales Order ({SO Value}) = SUM-THRU (*composed of*, **SO Line Item**, {Total Cost})

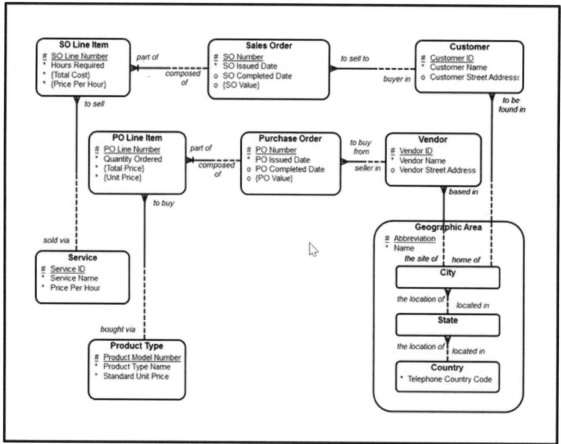

Figure 10: Derived Attributes

Note that these expressions represents theoretical calculations in a conceptual view of things. It may be possible—when this is implemented –to evaluate the derived attributes when they are queried. This means that the result makes use of the most current components. It also adds to the processing time for the query. An alternative is to store the results of the calculations when

early 1980s. Learn more from: Teamco, Inc. 1980. Mitrol. Retrieved 9/11/2017 from http://www.mitrol.com/html/history.html#top.

[92] Also presented in Hay. 2011. *Enterprise Model Patterns… op. cit.* pp. 305-306.

the source data are captured. This, however makes it necessary to recalculate the value any time one of its components are changed. That is, it is a design decision whether to do the calculations when the data are captured or when they are retrieved. The model simply represents the fact that derived values exist.

Note that the conceptual model is simply defining the nature of defined attributes. It is the designer who must evaluate expected use patterns and determine—for purposes of creating a particular physical model which approach is is the better use of processing resources.

Fact-based Modeling

An alternative *graphical* approach to capturing semantics is **fact-based modeling,** a family of conceptual modeling languages that originated in the late 1970s as the "Natural-language Information Analysis Method" (NIAM). This method was originally formulated by Sjir Nijssen from the Netherlands, based on work by Eckhard Falkenberg from Germany. Later they both moved to the University of Queensland (Australia), where they met Terry Halpin, who worked with them to enhance the method further. Mr. Halpin provided the first full formalization of the method[93]. Subsequently, along with Dr, Njissen, Mr. Halpin co-authored the first book on the topic.[94] In the early 1990s, Halpin developed an extended version of NIAM called "Object Role Modeling (ORM)". These languages are based in the analysis of natural verbalization (plausible sentences) that might occur in the business domain. Fact-based languages view the world in terms of objects, the facts that relate or characterize those objects, and the role that each object plays in each fact.[95]

Fact-based modeling includes an extensive and powerful constraint system that relies on fluent automatic verbalization and (more than with entity/relationship modeling) automatic checking against the concrete examples. Fact-based models do not use attributes. This reduces the need for intuitive or expert judgment by expressing the exact relationships between objects (both entities and values). The most widely used of the FBM variants is **Object Role Modeling (ORM),** which was formalized in first-order logic by Terry Halpin in 1989, and described in detail in several books.[96]

Fully-Communication-Oriented Information Mo*deling* (FCO-IM), was published online by Guido Bakema, Jan Pieter Zwart, and Harm van der Lek in 2002,[97] with more accessible documentation contained in the 2015 book, *Fact Oriented Modeling with FCO-IM.*[98]

---

[93] Terry Halpin. 1989. "A Logical Analysis of Information Systems: Static Aspects of the Data-Oriented Perspective". PhD thesis. University of Queensland.

[94] Gerardus Maria Nijssen and T Halpin. 1989. *Conceptual Schema and Relational Database Design.* (Prentice Hall).

[95] Nijssen and T Halpin. 1989. *Op. cit.*

[96] Among them is the one from which is derived the history above: Terry Halpin and T. Morgan. 2008. *Information Modeling and Relational Databases.* (Morgan Kaufmann). pp. 106-107.

[97] Guido Bakema, J.P. Zwart, H. van der Lek. 200 "Fully Communication Oriented Information Modeling (FCO-IM)", pp. 24-37. Privately published. (Available at *http://www.casetalk.com/downloads/book/FCO-IMbook.pdf*).

[98] Jan Pieter Zwart, Marco Engelbart, Stijn Hoppenbrouwers. 2015. *Fact Oriented Modeling with FCO-IM.* (Technics Publications).

Object Role Modeling (ORM)

Object-Role Modeling (ORM) is a model-driven engineering approach with typical examples of required information or queries, which may be presented in any external formulation familiar to users. The model then verbalizes these examples at the conceptual level, in terms of simple facts expressed in a *controlled natural language*. This controlled natural language is a restricted version of natural language that is unambiguous, so the semantics are readily grasped by humans; itis also formal, so it can be used to automatically map the structures to lower levels for implementation.[99]

ORM is about **facts** and **fact types**. A **fact** is "an atomic or conjunctive proposition taken to be true by the relevant business community. An **atomic fact** can't be split into two or more facts involving the same object types without information loss, and is either an **elementary fact** or an **existential fact**. An elementary fact applies a logical predicate to one or more objects. An existential fact simply asserts the existence of a single object."[100]

As with the distinction between **entities** and **entity types** described previously, a **fact** is a single assertion about one or more objects in the world. A **fact type** is a collection of facts of a given kind.

Figure 11[101] illustrates an ORM model. Here are two versions of a model of fact types derived from the fact sentence: "the moon (that is, Earth's moon) orbits the Earth". Similar fact sentences could be:

- ✓ "Europa orbits Jupiter"
- ✓ "Ganymede orbits Jupiter"
- ✓ "Phobos orbits Mars"

Together these examples allow us to infer the following *atomic fact type*:

- **Moon** orbits **Planet**

…and suggests the following *constraint pattern*:

- Each **Moon** *orbits* <u>one and only one</u> **Planet**♥,

A *role* (a part in a relationship) is depicted by a *role box*, connected to the object type that hosts the role. The solid dot attached to a role means "must". (In other words, the role is mandatory for instances of its object type.)

- Every **moon** <u>must</u> orbit a **planet**.

The horizontal line above "orbits" depicts a uniqueness constraint: each **moon** can orbit <u>only one</u> **planet**.

From the other direction . . .

- Each **planet** is *orbited by* <u>one or more</u> **moons**.

---

[99] This chapter is derived from Terry Halpin. 2015. *Object-Role Modeling Fundamentals*. (Technics Publications). Page 3.

[100] *Ibid*. Page 5.

[101] *Ibid*. pp. 9-13.

♥ In Halpin's book, text in the sentences, (Each", at most one", etc.) is in bold case. Entity type names are not emphasized (although they do have initial capital letters). In order to stay consistent with the rest of this book, however, the typography here is reversed. Only entity type names are in bold face. Relationship names are in italics.

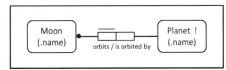

Figure 11: The Compact ORM Model

No solid circle is attached to a role, which means that that role is optional. That is, a **Planet** may exist without any **Moons**. The absence of any adjacent line in this fact type means that the Planet may be orbited by many moons. The exclamation point by the name "Planet" means that it may exist even if it plays no elementary fact roles.

Atomic facts inform us about *roles* played by objects. In this case, a Moon plays the role of orbiting around a Planet, and the Planet plays the role of being orbited. The two drawings also show two additional facts: a moon or planet is each identified by its relationship to a single value (in each case, its name). These simple reference schemes are shown in two different ways:

➢ **Compact Form – Figure 11 shows them in a compact form using** *reference modes*: **each Moon is** *referenced by* **(identified by) its name (".name"), and each Planet is referenced by its name (".name").**

➢ **Extended Form – Figure 12, on the other hand, shows the reference schemes of Moon and Planet more explicitly as** *injective* **(mandatory 1:1) relationships.**

The solid dot next to **Moon** means that it is **mandatory**:

✓ Each instance of **Moon** <u>must have</u> "MoonName".

The solid line over "has" means that

✓ Each instance of **Moon** has <u>only one instance</u> of "MoonName".

From the other direction, the two solid lines over the *is of* role means that

✓ Each **Moon Name** is of <u>at most one</u> **Moon**, *and* this name provides the preferred (primary) reference for **Moon**.
✓ Since the text that is **Moon Name** may exist without having a **Moon** to refer to, there is no circle on the role next to **Moon Name**.

The explicit reference scheme for Planet is handled in exactly the same way.

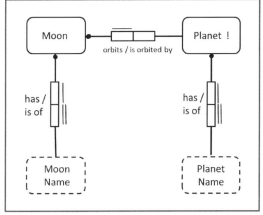

Figure 12: The Expanded ORM Model[102]

---

102   *Ibid.* Page 11. (Drawing Copyright © 2015, by Terry Halpin).

Modeling Constraints

One of the advantages of ORM is its ability to describe constraints. In the interest of maintaining discipline and coherence in the model, Barker/Ellis entity/relationship models are subject to several unspoken constraints. These are either not followed in other approaches, or (in the case of ORM) they are made explicit.

> **Multiple Inheritance**
> Entity/relationship models are typically about networks. Hierarchies only appear when sub-type or super-type structures occur. From Aristotle, each "thing" will have two kinds of characterisitcs: **essential characteristics** and **accidental characteristics**. "an *essential property of an object* is a property that it must have, while an *accidental property of an object* is one that it happens to have but that it could lack"[103] .For example, an automobile, a pick-up truck, and a sport utility vehicle are all examples of "Vehicle". Each are based on transport by wheels and they carry something. The "vehicle-ness" of them is an *essential characteristic*, so they cannot be described as being in another fundamental group. Of course, each may have a particular color, horsepower, or body style; these are "accidental" characteristics. While the data about these accidental characteristics should be collecteded and modeled, they are not part of the vehicle's essential nature.

The constraint of multiple inheritance is given in Barker/Ellis entity/relationship models. In ORM, however, the constraint does not exist. A class can have two parents (see Figure 13 for an example). In this case, **Party** is an invented term for collecting together **Person** and **Organization.** It may be argued that "partyness" is not quite the Aristotlean "essential' property of each, but since it was defined as such, it is certainly a good candidate. Even so, it could be argued as well that a **Person** is fundamentally a **Lifeform**, and an **Organization** is fundamentally a **Social Construction**. Whether these are true assertions in a deep philosophical sense or not, ORM can at least describe them as the entity/relationship diagram cannot.

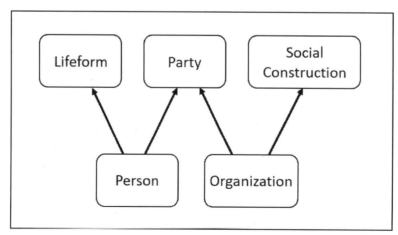

Figure 13: ORM Multiple Inheritance

103   Teresa Robertson, Philip Atkins. 2016. "Essential vs. Accidental Properties". Stanford Encyclopaedia of Philosopby. Stanford University. (Retrieved 4/17/2018 from https://plato.stanford.edu/entries/essential-accidental/.

➤ **Not only binary relationships**

In creating semantic relationships, it is common to have ternary, quaternary, or other degrees of relationships. In each case, the relationship can be reorganized to a set of **binary relationships.** The Barker/Ellis entity/relationship notation only permits binary relationships. To keep the model "tidy", your author highly recommends this restriction.

Even so, many assertions may well involve more than two classes. The ORM permits this, as in the fact type shown in Figure 14: "A Person played a Sport for a Country".

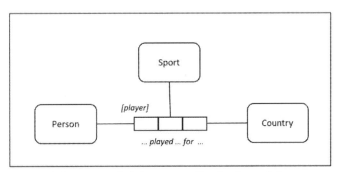

Figure 14: Ternary Relationships

➤ **All entity sub-types in a super-types are** *complete* **and** *disjoint*

If each instance of a super-type with multiple sub-types may be an instance of *only one* sub-type, the sub-types are ***disjoint***. That is, an instance of the super-type *cannot* also be an instance of *more than one* sub-type. This is the assumed constraint on all super-types in the Barker/Ellis notation.

In addition, all *other* entities that do not have inheritance relationships must also be disjoint. An airline flight may not be an instance of an airport.

Another Barker/Ellis rule states that there is no instance of a super-type that is *not* an instance of *one and only one* sub-type. That is, the population of the set of sub-types ***completely*** encompasses the population of the super-type.

This can be finessed by including an **other...** sub-type (e.g., **other project type, other company type**, etc.). After you've come up with all the sub-types you can think of, "Other..." neatly covers the ones you didn't think of.

ORM, on the other hand provides for explicitly noting whether a set of sub-types is ***disjoint, complete***, or both. Figure 15 shows an ORM diagram with sub-types related to super-types with solid arrows. Here you see examples of both constraints, plus the combination representing the entity/relationship diagram constraints. In each case, the constraint is represented by a line (between the sub-type arrows) with a circle and one or more symbols inside it.

As with the Barker/Ellis constraint, a **Person** is shown as being either a **Male Person** or a **Female Person**, but not both. This is signified by the "X" (for "eXclusion") in the middle of the circle. In addition, this model asserts that there are no alternatives to these two.[*] This is represented by the solid circle.

---

[*] That is, this is what the model is asserting. The purpose of any model is to provide the basis of discussion as to what is actually true.

In Figure 15, each instance of **Animal** *may* be *either* a **Cat** or a **Dog** (asserted by the "X"), but not both. The list of sub-types is **disjoint**. There is nothing here, however, to prevent the animal from being an Iguana. As such, the set of sub-types is not *complete.*

Finally, the Figure shows that each Team Member must be *either* a Player or a Coach. In the domain of this model, the member cannot be anything else. The list of sub-types is *complete*. There is nothing here, however, to prevent a coach from also being a player. This is not *disjoint.*

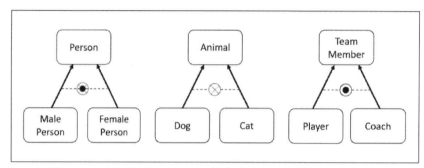

Figure 15: Sub-types: Disjoint and Exclusive

These are but two of the many constraints that can be expressed in ORM. For a listing of all the possible constraints that can be expressed in ORM, see "Appendix D–ORM Constraints".

➢ **Ring Constraints**
One important category of constraints is **ring constraints**. To understand ring constraints, it is necessary first to show that this category of constaints does not apply to Barker/Ellis entity/relationship diagrams. In Figure 16, you see an entity/relationship diagram of a set of **Countries** surrounded by one or more **Boundaries**, which separate them from other **Countries**. Specifically, each **Boundary** may be a *border on* one **Country** and a *border with* another **Country**. That is, a **Boundary** may be defined between Belgium and the Netherlands and another between Germany and Belgium. Note that there is nothng in the model that prevents a **Boundary** being defined between Belgium and itself. It also does not say whether or not, if Belgium is on the boarder with the Netherlands the Netherlands should, in principle, also be on the border with Belgium.

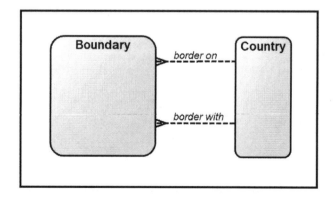

Figure 16: E/R Ring Constraints

ORM permits us to make exactly those assertions. In Figure 17, a "fact type" is that one **Country** borders another **Country**. (The exclamation point means that instances of the class Country can exist without this fact. The bar below the fact type means each fact encompasses both halves.) Attached to the fact type are two "ring constraint types", nested inside each other.

In Figure 17, "the ring constraint shape is compound, combining two ring constraints. The first ring constraint ensures that no country borders itself...For example, Belgium cannot border Belgium. In this case, the borders relationship is said to be ***irreflexive***. [This is represented by the smaller circle with a line through the right part.]

"The second ring constraint ensures that if the fact that a given country borders another given country is recorded, then so is the inverse fact that the second country borders the first country. For example, if Belgium borders France, then France must border Belgium. In this case, the borders relationship is said to be ***symmetric***. [This is rrepresented by the larger oval with two black circles.] Hence, in this example, the borders fact type is both irreflexive and symmetric."[104]

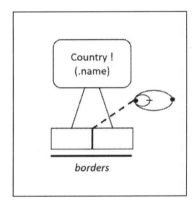

Figure 17: ORM Ring Constraints

Fully Communication Oriented Information Modeling (FCO-IM)

Fully Communication-Oriented Information Modeling (FCO-IM), also derived from NIAM, is similar in notation and approach to ORM. It differs from ORM in that instead of having different symbols for fact type and object type, it uses the fact type symbol to represent both concepts.

Figure 18 shows an example of what in FCO-IM is called an **Information Grammar Diagram**. Specifically, it is diagramming the **fact type** "Mentorship".

Fact Modeling (either ORM or FCO-IM) is a very powerful approach for capturing subtleties of relationships. Like entity/relationship modeling, however, (especially since attributes are themselves graphic objects) it can become very large.

An example of a *FCO-IM* model is shown in Figure 18. This is based on the following facts:

1. "There is a student whose first name is 'Peter'...

---

[104] Terry Halpin. 2005. "Irreflexive and Ring Constraints", derived from "Verbalizing Business Rules, Part 12", *Business rules Journal*. Vol 6. Issue 10.

2.   ... and whose surname is 'Johnson'."

This fact on the diagram is shown by two circles with "first name" and "surname" attached to two fact boxes, "1" and "2".

3.   "There is a teacher whose teacher code is BLC."

This fact on the diagram is shown by the circle with "teacher code" attached to fact box "3".

4.   "The mentor of Peter Johnson is BLC."

On the diagram, this fact is shown by fact box 4 linked to the complete fact "There is a student whose first name is Peter and whose surname is 'Johnson'." (Link 01), and attached to fact box 5 linked to the fact "There is a teacher whose teacher code is BLC." (Link 02)

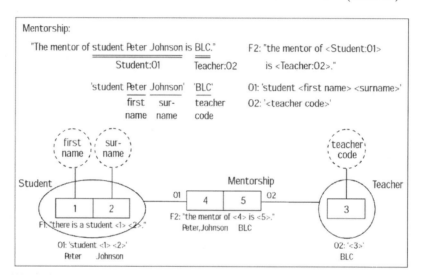

Figure 18: FCO-IM Information Grammar Diagram Model[105]

Text Representations

Since graphic techniques tend to produce large and difficult-to-manage diagrams, it's better to address semantics using language itself. Three approaches are most common in 2018:

- ✓ **Glossary** – a list of terms and definitions.
- ✓ **Semantics of Business Vocabulary and Rules (SBVR)** – an approach to building ontologies based on the search for business rules.
- ✓ **The Semantic Web** – an approach to building ontologies derived from and based on the World-wide Web.

These are each described in more detail in the following sections.

The Glossary

The most straightforward way to capture definitions is via a *Glossary*. The glossary captures each term and groups them by topic as appropriate, along with a *well-formed* definition.

---

[105] Jan Pieter Zwart, etc. al. 2015. *Op. cit.*

This book contains its own glossary of terms as Appendix A. In addition to each term's definition, this glossary includes the chapter and page number of its first appearance. The definitions are "well-formed"— following the best practices referred to in Chapter 7. (See page 162.)

The problem with a glossary, however, is that, while a definition can refer to *other terms*, there is no *systematic* way to do so. The relationships among terms are a very important part of the semantics of an enterprise. The data model described above is one way to address that, but the other lexical approaches described here are more effective for a large body of terms.

Semantics of Business Vocabulary and Rules (SBVR)

Most of the modeling described so far is about creating **ontologies** – descriptions of *what exists*— that is, John Zachman's "what" (*resource / data)* column. This does not address the circumstances under which something *must* or *may* exist, or *must not* or *may not* exist. Mr. Zachman's "why" (*motivation*) column addresses this more thoroughly.

The motivation column is in fact itself addressed by a model in its own right, published originally by an enterprise of linguists and modelers known as The Business Rules Group. Development eventually moved to the Object Management Group, who published the model in 2005, calling it the "Business Motivation Model". It is described more fully in the *Overview Model* discussed earlier (page 31). For our purposes here, the model is reproduced as Figure 19.

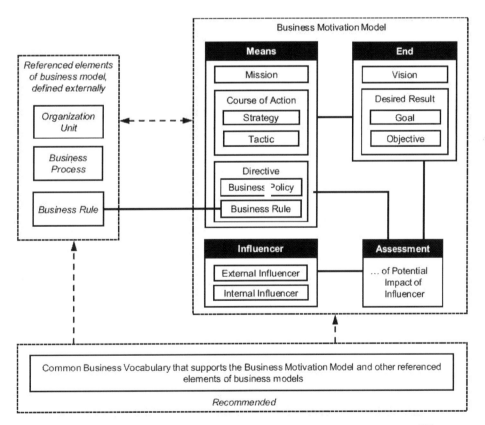

Figure 19: Business Motivation Model - Overview[106]

---

[106]   Object Management Group. 2015. "Business Motivation…" *Op. cit.*

Notice that in that model **Business Rule** shows up as a kind of **Directive**—that is, a kind of **Means**.

The Term **Business Rule** has been given different definitions by different authors,[107] but a reasonable definition is by Barbara von Halle, as "the set of conditions that govern a business event so that it happens in a way that is acceptable to the business."[108] In the OMG Motivation Model, this is in support of a more general Directive—the **Business Policy.**

Note that the model is based on a "Common Business Vocabulary that supports the Business Motivation Model and supports other referenced elements of business models."

That is, even to describe business rules, we have to get the language sorted out. To be sure, the capture and documentation of business rules is every bit as important to the success of an automated system as is the documentation of the ontology that describes things that are addressed by that system. Here, however, we will focus on the latter—the ontology.

For both the business rules and the ontology, the heart of the assignment is *semantics*—as defined previously, "the branch of linguistics and logic concerned with *meaning*."[109] Semantics is about the language the business uses, both to describe what the business *is about* and *how it works*. For this reason, the Business Rules Group published another work that was also subsequently adopted by the Object Management Group as a standard. Specifically, it was published in January 2008 as **The Semantics of Business Vocabulary and Business Rules (SBVR)**.[110] The document was truly comprehensive, but (being the product of a committee) its style made it rather tough reading for the average citizen.

For this reason, Graham Witt has since published what could be called an "English translation of SBVR". It is officially called *Writing Effective Rules: A Practical Method.*[111] As he puts it, SBVR "represents a comprehensive analysis of the linguistic and logical concepts underlying natural language discourse about an enterprise and its activities, in particular the rules that govern that enterprise."[112] Mr. Witt then sets out to make that analysis accessible to all.

The assignment in both documents is to describe rules in natural language. Among other things, this means recognizing the two basic kinds of rules:

> **Operative Rules** – These describe "what must or must not happen in particular circumstances, as in the following examples:
> ✓ Each <u>flight booking request</u> *for* a <u>return journey</u> must *specify* the <u>return date</u>.
>
> ✓ A <u>flight booking request</u> *for* a <u>one-way journey</u> must *not specify* a <u>return date</u>."[113]

> **Definitional Rules** – These rules "constrain how we define various constructs created by the enterprise (or the industry within which it operates). The definitions in this category can

---

[107] Graham Witt. 2012. *Writing Effective Business Rules.* (Morgan Kaufmann). pp. 1-2.

[108] von Halle. 2002. *Op. cit.* P. 28.

[109] Various editors. Oxford Living Dictionaries. "semantics". (Retrieved 7/6/2017 from https://en.oxforddictionaries.com/definition/semantics).

[110] Object Management Group. 2015. "Semantics of Business Vocabulary and Rules (SBVR)". (Available at *http://www.omg.org/spec/SBVR/*).

[111] Witt. *Op. cit.*

[112] *Ibid.* P.56

[113] *Ibid.* p. 13.

be captured for an *ontology* or a *glossary.* The following are constructs that can be defined using definitional rules:

✓ An <u>infant passenger</u> *is* by definition a <u>passenger</u> whose <u>age</u> is less than <u>2 years</u> *at* the <u>time of travel</u>.

✓ A <u>flight</u> *is* by definition either a domestic flight or an international flight.

✓ A <u>flight</u> *has* by definition exactly one <u>origin port</u>.

✓ <u>Close of business</u> *is* by definition <u>5 pm</u> (local time)."[114]

Since all definitions in the world are expressed as collections of business terms, it is the relationships among these terms that constitute *facts* (or, more correctly, *fact types*) that are important here. Mr. Witt is careful to distinguish **facts** (assertions about particular entities in the world ("Employee #1234 was assigned to Project #567") from **fact types** (assertions about entity types ("An <u>employee</u> may be assigned to a <u>project</u>").

Understand that the objective of SBVR (and of Mr. Witt's book) is to address *business rules,* The relevant fact types include not just existential assertions describing an *ontology* (what exists), but also prescriptive or restrictive assertions describing what *must or may (or must not or may not) be done with the things that exist.*

Thus, it is the *operative rules* that are business rules about constraints on how an enterprise must conduct business. The *definition rules,* however, are about the "things of significance" that are also the domain of ontologies and data models. These include:

➤ **Formal term definition** – which defines business terms in a formal manner.
  This must be one of the following:

  ✓ Formal intentional definition
    An **intentional definition** of a term consists of the **hypernym** of the term, plus characteristics that distinguish it from other members of the same set.♥ From the field of linguistics, a "hypernym" is "a word with a broad meaning constituting a category into which words with more specific meanings fall; a superordinate. For example, colour is a hypernym of red".[115]
    – An <u>employer</u> *of* <u>a person</u>
      is by definition
      an <u>enterprise</u> that *employs* that <u>person.</u>

  ✓ Formal extensional definition
    An **extensional definition** of a term consists of a complete disjoint list of the terms that are the *hyponyms* of that term. From the field of linguistics, "hyponym" is "a word of more specific meaning than a general or superordinate term applicable to it. For example, spoon is a hyponym of cutlery."[116]

---

[114] *Ibid.* p. 14.

♥ This is also known as the "Aristotelian" definition. See: Robert. Arp, Barry Smith, Andrew D. Spear. 2015. Building Ontologies with Basic Formal Ontology. (Cambridge, MA: MIT Press).

[115] Various editors. English Oxford Living Dictionaries. "hypernym". (Retrieved 7/6/2017 from https://en.oxforddictionaries.com/definition/hypernym).

[116] Various editors. English Oxford Living Dictionaries. "hyponym". (Retrieved 7/6/2017 from https://en.oxforddictionaries.com/definition/hyponym).

- An <u>immediate family member</u> *of* a <u>person</u>
  is by definition
  a <u>parent</u>, <u>sibling</u>, <u>spouse</u>, or <u>child</u> of that <u>person</u>.

➢ **Categorization scheme enumeration** – which defines members of a *categorization scheme* that are *mutually exclusive* (no individual object can be a member of more than one category in the scheme) and *jointly exhaustive* (each member of the class with which the scheme is associated must belong to a category in the scheme):
  - A <u>person</u>
    is by definition
    either an <u>adult</u> or a <u>minor</u>.

➢ **Category transition constraint** – specifies allowed or disallowed transitions between categories or statuses.
  - A transition *of* the <u>status</u> *of* a <u>customer</u> from <u>current</u> to <u>prospect</u>
    is by definition
    impossible.

➢ **Complex concept structure rules:**
These include:

✓ Cardinality – the number (or minimum or maximum number) of components for a particular concept:
  - A <u>flight</u>
    has by definition
    exactly one <u>destination port</u>.

✓ Equivalence – a pair of components within a particular concept that are the same.
  - The <u>destination city</u> *of* the last or only <u>return flight</u> *of* a <u>return journey</u>
    is by definition
    the same as the <u>origin city</u> *of* the first or only <u>outgoing flight</u> *of* that <u>return journey</u>.

✓ Set constraint – specifies that two sets within a concept must be identical.
  - The set of <u>passengers</u>
    booked on each <u>flight</u>
    specified in a flight <u>booking confirmation</u>
    is by definition
    the same as the set of <u>passengers</u>
    booked on each other <u>flight</u>
    specified in that <u>booking confirmation</u>.

➢ **Valid value definition** – a set of valid values (or a range) for a particular concept.
  - <u>Water temperature</u>
    is by definition
    at least <u>0°C</u> and *at most* <u>100°C</u>.

➢ **Data calculation algorithm** – for computed (or otherwise derived) attributes.
  - The <u>year-to-date sales total</u> *for* a <u>product</u> *on* a <u>date</u>
    is by definition *calculated as:*
    the sum of the <u>extension</u> *for* each <u>order line</u> *for* that <u>product</u> that
    - *has* an <u>order date</u> within the same <u>calendar year</u> *as* that <u>date</u>, and
    - *was* not *cancelled within* the same <u>calendar year</u> *as* that <u>date</u>.

> **Conversion factor definition –** defines a value that can be used to convert from one unit of measure to another.
> - 1 foot
>   *is* by definition
>   12 inches.

> **Standard format definition –** provides a pattern or format constraint for values of a term."[117]
> - A valid <u>flight number</u>
>   *is* by definition *composed of*
>   a valid <u>airline code</u> followed by up to <u>4</u> <u>digits</u>

Since Mr. Witt's book is on *natural language* expressions of rules, he makes a point to include a chapter on grammar—the rules that govern the components of those natural expressions. Unlike some college grammar texts, Mr. Witt's is clearly designed to cover the particular collections of nouns, verbs, and adverbs used in this context.

Both the documentation of SBVR and Mr. Witt's book describe these issues in much more detail than we have room for here.♥ The reader is encouraged to consult either or both for more information.

The Semantic Web

The third linguistic (i.e. non-graphical) approach to capturing semantics is ***The Semantic Web***. In 1990, Tim Berners-Lee invented the World Wide Web. It manipulated *documents* and *pictures* for people to share world-wide. While the international success of it pleased (and overwhelmed) him, he was still not satisfied: He and his colleagues wanted the ability to manipulate *ideas*. The assignment:

> **Define *every term* in the world,**
> …with each definition (with provenance) located uniquely on the World Wide Web.

> **Be able to manipulate all terms**
> …via natural language sentences.

> **Be able to deal with**
> …classes and sub-classes.

> **Be able to**
> …infer assertions from other assertions.

Over the period from 2004 until 2012, he and the World Wide Web Consortium (W3C) created *the Semantic Web* – which satisfied all four of these requirements. Thus, this mechanism for storing semantics on a world-wide platform had four components:

> **Universal Resource Identifier (URI)**
> Every term, (plus the special terms for each language) has an identified location on the *World Wide Web*.

---

[117]   Graham Witt. Ibid. p. 85-88.

♥ …although, in your author's opinion, Mr. Witt's book is much easier to read.

> **Resource Definition Framework (RDF)**
> RDF is a framework for representing information in the Web...RDF graphs are sets of subject-predicate-object triples, where the elements may be IRIs, blank nodes, or datatyped literals.[118] All sentences are formed with the structure:
>
> > <subject> <predicate> <object>.
>
> As created, RDF makes use of XML for its syntax, which is a highly structured form of English. Since its introduction, however, a more compact (and more intuitive) syntax called "Turtle" has been developed. This syntax is used to present the Semantic Web as it is described in more detail below.

> **Resource Definition Framework Schema** (Sem Web) **(RDFS)**
> This is an extension of RDF that allows for specification of classes and relationships.

> **Web Ontology Language (OWL)**
> This is a further extension of RDF, allowing for specification of inferences that are assertions derived from other assertions.

Note that, in addition to documentation available from the W3C[119, 120, 121], there are also numerous text books on the semantic web. Two of particular interest are:

> **Semantic Web for the Working Ontologist, Second Edition**[122]
> This is a very good introduction, well written and easy to follow. It uses the Turtle format for describing assertions. The various languages of the Semantic Web are constructed of XML, but that makes them difficult to follow. Turtle is a much more compact and intuitive way to describe the assertions. Except where noted, Turtle is used in this book as well.

> **A Developer's Guide to the Semantic Web**[123]
> This is the definitive textbook on the topic. It is well written and thorough, with a set of case studies that support every section. It includes not only a comprehensive description of the Semantic Web itself, but also applications, such as Dbpedia.org and Schema.org, as well as guidance for creating semantic web applications. It does use the underlying XML to describe each assertion, however, which means it is only for serious students.

There are some new tools available on the market that purport to be able to provide graphic versions of the Semantic Web models, but they were not available to your author as of this writing.

The book you are holding cannot begin to cover the material described in those other works, but what follows is a brief synopsis.

---

[118] World Wide Web Consortium. 2014. *RDF 1.1 XML Syntax: W3C Recommendation 25 February 2014.* (Retrieved 6/2017 from https://www.w3.org/TR/2014/REC-rdf-syntax-grammar-20140225/).

[119] World Wide Web Consortium. 2014. *RDF 1.1: Terse Triple Language.* (Retrieved 6/2017 from *https://www.w3.org/TR/turtle*).

[120] World Wide Web Consortium. 2014. *RDF Schema 1.1: W3C Recommendation 25 February 2014.* (Retrieved 6/2017 from https://www.w3.org/TR/rdf-schema/).

[121] World Wide Web Consortium 2012. *OWL 2 Web Ontology Language Primer* (Second Edition). (Retrieved 6/2017 from https://www.w3.org/TR/owl2-primer/).

[122] Dean Allemang, Jim Hendler. 2011. *Semantic Web for the Working Ontologist: Effective Modeling in RDFS and OWL.* (Morgan Kaufman).

[123] Liyang Yu. 2014. *A Developer's Guide to the Semantic Web*, Second Edition. (Springer).

Universal Resource Identifier (URI)

Each term in a domain is located on the World Wide Web via a **Universal Resource Identifier (URI)**. These are specialized versions of *uniform resource locators* (URLs).♣ For example:

> ➤ `esi: http://essentialstrategies.com/#customer`
> … holds Essential Strategies International's (esi's) definition of "customer".

The **term** being addressed follows the **octothorpe** (#)♥ at the end of the string (in this example "#customer").

Adjacent to the term is a uniform resource locator (URL) where this definition may be found. Moreover, that URL (e.g., "http://essentialstrategies.com/") plays the role of being a **namespace**. The term "namespace" is borrowed from object-oriented programming to describe "a declarative region that provides a scope to the identifiers (the names of types, functions, variables, etc) inside it. Namespaces are used to organize code into logical groups and to prevent name collisions that can occur especially when your code base includes multiple libraries."[124]

In this case, the URL is serving as a namespace to catalogue the "owner" or the "cataloguer" of the identified term.

To the left of this namespace URL is an abbreviation (called a **qname**), which, in the Turtle presentations, can henceforth can be used instead of spelling out the entire URL (e.g., "esi:").

Thus, the example above ("`esi:http://essentialstrategies.com/#customer`"), can be shortened to "`esi:customer`". Thus, if John Zachman (JAZ) has a URI `jaz: http://johnazachman.com#customer`, it would be a simple matter to compare `esi:customer` with `jaz:customer`.

(For example, John Zachman's definition ("`jaz:Customer`") might be limited to parties that have paid for their products, while ESI's definition might include everyone who's placed an order.)♣

Every term, then, is defined in the context of a host site.

Every Semantic Web script begins with lines to define each of the q-names, starting with those that constitute the laguages themselves:

```
@prefix owl: <http://www.w3.org/2002/07/owl#> .
```

♣ **Buzzword Compliance Alert:** "URL" stands for *uniform* resource locator. "URI" stands for *universal* resource identifier. (And for the record, "UML" stands for *unified* modeling language.)

♥ Yes, it is true that in 2018, the current year's name of the # symbol is "hashtag". This is a new terminology, however. Previously, in the US, it was called a "pound sign". In the UK, it was called a "number sign". Both names go back many centuries to the symbol's linguistic roots. In the 1960s, however, when Bell Labs developed the high-tech new Touch-Tone® telephone, and they decided to add a key with that symbol—they settled on "octothorpe". (It has eight points.) In one stroke, they had dealt with a major(?) trans-Atlantic conflict.

It didn't catch on, however. It took the fire lit by Twitter and other social media to coin a word that stuck (at least until 2018).

124 Microsoft. C# Language Reference. (Retrieved, 4/10/2017 from https://docs.microsoft.com/en-us/dotnet/csharp/language-reference/keywords/namespace).

♣ This example is, of course, fictitious.

```
@prefix rdf: <http://www.w3.org/1999/02/22-rdf-syntax-ns#> .
@prefix xml: <http://www.w3.org/XML/1998/namespace> .
@prefix xsd: <http://www.w3.org/2001/XMLSchema#> .
@prefix rdfs: <http://www.w3.org/2000/01/rdf-schema#> .
```

One line defines the ontology being presented.

```
@prefix esi: <http://essentialstrategies.com/OWL#> .
```

This is followed by specification of the default ontology (used if none is specified).

```
@base <http://essentialstrategies.com/OWL> .
```

The next line, then, identifies the script as a type of ontology:

```
<http://essentialstrategies.com/OWL> rdf:type owl:Ontology ;
rdfs:comment "Achieving Buzzword Compliance in Data Modeling" .
```

Resource Definition Framework (RDF)

RDF is a *language* that provides an English (or other natural) language way of manipulating all terms. Its structure is simplicity itself:

<subject><predicate><object>.

…or it would be if it weren't represented using XML. For our purposes, that is unnecessary, so here you'll just see the more intuitive Turtle version of the examples that follow.

For example, using the Turtle representation, we could assert that:

➢ `stb:Starbucks mw:serves cga:Coffee`
The subject is "stb:Starbucks". The predicate is "mw:serves". The object is "cga:Coffee".

The owners of the (imaginary here) *namespaces*, then, would be:

✓ stb: Starbucks Corporation
✓ mw: The Merriam-Webster Dictionary
✓ cga: The Coffee Growers' Association

Thus, any domain of interest can be represented by sets of <subject><predicate><object> **triples.** That is, a collection of triples can comprise a script that describes something in the world.

Any vocabulary can be used for constructing triples. RDF, however, does include some **reserved words** that contribute semantically to the sentences. A complete list of these are shown in Appendix B.

Of these, the most important place to start is with "`rdf:type`". "Rdf:type" means that the subject is an example of the category **(type)** that is the object. For example:

➢ `stb:StarbucksEchoLaneSite rdf:type mw:CoffeeShop.`

That is, "`stb:StarbucksEchoLaneSite`" is a member of a category (in this case "`mw:CoffeeShop`".) ♠

♠ Note the convention, derived from RDF's XML roots, to eliminate the spaces between words using "camelCase". That is, the initial letter of the second and all following words are capitalized, but spaces are removed.

Note that, whenever you see "rdf:type", you can substitute "is an instance of" ♥. Indeed, in the Turtle notation, this is abbreviated simply "a" (for "is a"). That is:

➢ `stb:StarbucksEchoLaneSite` **a** `mw:coffeShop.`

RDF Schema (RDFS)

RDF Schema adds language for describing membership of instances in classes. The word in RDFS for a semantic group is **class.** In any modeling exercise, each term that describes a class has to be designated an instance of the RDFS term **class.** For example:

➢ `mw:coffeeShop a rdfs:class`

That is, "mw:coffeeShop" is an instance of an "rdfs:class". Moreovoer, we can now assert that The Echo Lane site for Starbucks is itself a member of that class:

➢ `stb:StarbucksEchoLane a mw:coffeeShop`

The complete list of RDFS reserved words will be found in Appendix B.

The Semantic Web is considerably more versatile than is even the most business-oriented data model, but it is useful to see where they match. Figure 20 shows our sample entity/relationship model again.

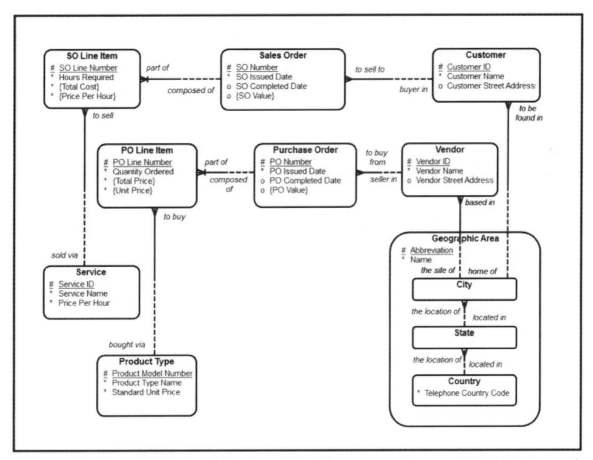

Figure 20: Sample Entity/relationship Diagram as Semantic Web Example

---

♥ It is unfortunate that neither Messrs. Barker or Ellis, nor your author were part of the W3C meetings that came up with these names. At the very least "rdfs:type" should have been "rdfs:aTypeOf".

Each of the entity types is known in the Semantic Web world as a *class.* This is initially defined as an rdfs:class, which is a sub-type of the universal class called rdfs:resource.

Script 1 shows each of them in RDFS format. For example, **"esi:Customer"** is an "`rdf:class`", defined as "An enterprise or person who has purchased(or is in the process of purchasing) a service from us." The sample structure applies to all the owl:classes listed in Script 1♦.

Script 1: Semantic Web Classes

```
esi:City rdf:type owl:Class ;
     rdfs:subClassOf esi:GeographicArea ,
     [ rdf:type owl:Restriction ;
        owl:onProperty esi:theLocationOf ;
        owl:qualifiedCardinality "1"^^xsd:nonNegativeInteger ;
        owl:onClass esi:State
   ] ;
     rdfs:comment """" """"
        1. A large, important town.
        2. In the United States, an incorporated municipality, whose
        boundaries and powers of self-government are defined by a charter
        from the State in which it is located.
           3. In Canada, a municipality of the highest rank.
        4. In Great Britain, a borough or town with a royal charter.

        [ Webster's New World Dictionary. 1964. \"City\". (New York:
        World Publishing Company). p. 267.
        ]"""" .

esi:Country rdf:type owl:Class ;
     rdfs:subClassOf esi:GeographicArea ;
     rdfs:comment """"
        "A land; whole territory of a nation."

        [ Webster's New World Dictionary. 1964. \"Country\". (New York:
        World Publishing Company). p. 338.]"""" .

esi:Customer rdf:type owl:Class ;
   rdfs:comment
        "An enterprise or person who has purchased(or is in the process
        of purchasing) a service from us." .

esi:Geographic Area rdf:type owl:Class ;
     rdfs:comment
        "A bounded, spherically two-dimensional place on the Earth." .

esi:ProductType rdf:type owl:Class ;
     rdfs:comment
        "The definition of a kind of Product (typically identified by a
        \"model number\") that is available for sale." .

esi:POLineItem rdf:type owl:Class ;
     rdfs:subClassOf
     [ rdf:type owl:Restriction ;
        owl:onProperty esi:partof ;
```

♦ The web ontology language (OWL) will be discussed below. In fact, owl:class is exactly equivalent to rdfs:class.

```
          owl:qualifiedCardinality "1"^^xsd:nonNegativeInteger ;
          owl:onClass esi:PurchaseOrder
      ] ;
      rdfs:comment
      "The fact that a particular ProductType is being ordered on a
      particular PurchaseOrder." .
```

esi:**PurchaseOrder** rdf:type owl:Class ;
    rdfs:comment
    "A contract between our company and a Vendor who is prepared to
    deliver one or more specified ProductTypes for financial
    compensation." .

esi:**SOLineItem** rdf:type owl:Class ;
    rdfs:subClassOf
    [rdf:type *owl:Restriction* ;
      owl:onProperty esi:**partOf** ;
      owl:qualifiedCardinality "1"^^xsd:nonNegativeInteger ;
      owl:onClass esi:**SalesOrder**] ;
    rdfs:comment
    "An entry on a SalesOrder that describes a Service for us to
    provide." .

esi:**SalesOrder** rdf:type owl:Class ;
    rdfs:comment
    "A contract between us and a Customer who wishes to receive one
    or more specified services from us, in exchange for financial
    compensation." .

esi:**Service** rdf:type owl:Class ;
    rdfs:comment
    "The definition of a kind of activity that we are willing to
    perform for financial compensation." .

esi:**State** rdf:type owl:Class ;
    rdfs:subClassOf esi:**GeographicArea** ,
    [rdf:type *owl:Restriction* ;
      owl:onProperty esi:**theLocationOf** ;
      owl:qualifiedCardinality "1"^^xsd:nonNegativeInteger ;
      owl:onClass esi:**Country**
    ] ;
    rdfs:comment
    """One of the territorial and political units constituting a
    federal government, as in the United States.

    [Webster's New World Dictionary. 1964. \"State\". (New York:
    World Publishing Company). p. 1424.]""" .

esi:**Vendor** rdf:type owl:Class ;
    rdfs:comment
    "An enterprise or person that offers product types for sale." .

Web Ontology Language (OWL)

Definition

The **Web Ontology Language (OWL)** is an extention of RDF Schema that incorporates
the ability to define properties of classes. These include ***datatype properties*** (known to the

relational world as "attributes") and *object properties* (known to the relational world as "relationships"). In addition, software can be applied to OWL statements to make logical inferences from other statements.

Changed Assumptions

The Semantic Web is different from the data modeling/database world, because its goal is not to construct a **database repository**. Rather, its goal is to construct an **ontology**—a description of what exists. This reflects a different orientation from that usually taken by data modelers and database designers.

Data people have traditionally worked from this viewpoint:

✓ **Closed World Assumption**: If it doesn't *follow the specified rules,* then it <u>must be false</u>. (Or, at least, it is *not acceptable* in our database.)

People in the Semantic Web world, on the other hand, are considering the assertions with a different assumption:

✓ **Open World Assumption**: If the rules don't completely *rule it out*, the assertion *may be true.*

For example, a relational database has the rule:

- Each **City** must be *located in* one and only one **State**.
- A **City** named "Portland" is specified without a value for a **State**.

Closed world: **Rejected**! (It violates the *must be one State* rule.)

Open world: **Accepted provisionally** (…but take note for future research.)

- A **City** named "Portland" is specified as being *located in* the **State** named "Maine".

Closed world: **Accepted**!

Open world: **Accepted**!

- A second **City** named "Portland" is specified as being *located in* the **State** named "Oregon".

Closed world: **Rejected**! (It violates the *must be one State* rule.)

Open world: **Accepted provisionally** – This raises a question:

- Are the **State** named "Maine" and the **State** named "Oregon" the same State? *or*
- Is the **City** that is located in "Maine" a different **City** from the **City** that is located in "Oregon"?

The complete list of OWL reserved words may be found in Appendix B. Here are the most important ones:

Datatype Properties

All of the elements that describe each entity type in an entity/relationship model are called "properties" in the semantic web. Specifically, each *attribute* is called a *datatype property*, and each *relationship* (from the point of view of each subject class) is called an *object property*.

From the entity/relationship diagram in Figure 20, above, Script 2 shows each **attribute** as an `owl:DatatypeProperty`. Here we hark back to RDF Schema for the terms of this property. That is, in each case, the `rdfs:domain` is the class (entity type) that it is a property of, while the `rdfs:range` is one from a set of standard XML ("xsd:") data types that define it.

Thus, in the Script 2 example, "esi:`Contract_Number`" is an `owl:Datatype`Property that is "`A user-entered text that uniquely identifies instances of Contract`". It is a property of (that is, `rdfs:domain`) the class "**esi:Contract.**" The range of values it can take (that is, "`rdfs:range`") are defined by the XML data type "integer".

Script 2 Semantic Web Datatype Properties

```
esi:Abbreviation rdf:type owl:DatatypeProperty ;
     rdfs:domain esi:GeographicArea ;
     rdfs:range xsd:string ;
     rdfs:comment
     "A very short text that identifies each instance of the class,
     GeographicArea." .

esi:ContractNumber rdf:type owl:DatatypeProperty ;
     rdfs:domain esi:contract ;
     rdfs:range xsd:string ;
     rdfs:comment
     "A user-entered text that uniquely identifies instances of
     Contract" .

esi:CountryTelephoneCode rdf:type owl:DatatypeProperty ;
     rdfs:domain esi:Country ;
     rdfs:range xsd:positiveInteger ;
     rdfs:comment
     "An internationally-agreed-to integer that identifies a
     particular country, for the purpose of routing telephone calls."
     .

esi:CustomerID rdf:type owl:DatatypeProperty ;
     rdfs:domain esi:Customer ;
     rdfs:range xsd:positiveInteger ;
     rdfs:comment
     "A system-generated integer that uniquely identifies each
     instance of Customer." .

esi:CustomerName rdf:type owl:DatatypeProperty ;
     rdfs:domain esi:Customer ;
     rdfs:range xsd:string ;
     rdfs:comment
     "Text which labels or identifies an instance of Customer." .

esi:CustomerStreetAddress rdf:type owl:DatatypeProperty ;
     rdfs:domain esi:Customer ;
     rdfs:range xsd:string ;
     rdfs:comment
     "The street and number of a Customer's address--or, as an
     alternative, a post office box number." .

esi:HoursRequired rdf:type owl:DatatypeProperty ;
     rdfs:domain esi:SalesLineItem ;
```

```
        rdfs:range xsd:decimal ;
        rdfs:comment
        "The amount of time required to perform the work promised by a
        Service." .

   esi:name rdf:type owl:DatatypeProperty ;
        rdfs:domain esi:GeographicArea ;
        rdfs:range xsd:string ;
        rdfs:comment
        "A label or identifier of instances of a GeographicArea" .

   esi:POCompletedDate rdf:type owl:DatatypeProperty ;
        rdfs:domain esi:PurchaseOrder ;
        rdfs:range xsd:dateTime ;
        rdfs:comment
        "The point in time when the last instance of an ordered Product
        Type has been delivered in support of a PurchaseOrderLineItem." .

   esi:POIssuedDate rdf:type owl:DatatypeProperty ;
        rdfs:domain esi:PurchaseOrder ;
        rdfs:range xsd:dateTime ;
        rdfs:comment
        "The point in time when a PurchaseOrder has been issued." .

   esi:POLineNumber rdf:type owl:DatatypeProperty ;
        rdfs:domain esi:PurchaseOrderLineItem ;
        rdfs:range integer ;
        rdfs:comment
        "A system-generated integer that uniquely identifies instances of
        a POLineNumber, in the context of the PurchaseOrder that this
        POLineNumber is partOf" .

   esi:PONumber rdf:type owl:DatatypeProperty ;
        rdfs:domain esi:PurchaseOrder ;
        rdfs:range xsd:string ;
        rdfs:comment
        "A system-generated integer that uniquely
        identifies instances of a PurchaseOrder." .

   esi:PricePerHour rdf:type owl:DatatypeProperty ;
        rdfs:domain esi:Service ;
        rdfs:range xsd:decimal ;
        rdfs:comment
        "The monetary amount charged for each hour of a Service." .

   esi:ProductModelNumber rdf:type owl:DatatypeProperty ;
        rdfs:domain esi:ProductType ;
        rdfs:range xsd:string ;
        rdfs:comment "The designator specified by a manufacturer that
        uniquely identifies each instance of a ProductType." .

   esi:ProductTypeName rdf:type owl:DatatypeProperty ;
        rdfs:domain esi:ProductType ;
        rdfs:range xsd:string ;
        rdfs:comment
        "Text that labels and/or identifies an instance of ProductType."
        .

   esi:QuantityOrdered rdf:type owl:DatatypeProperty ;
```

```
        rdfs:domain esi:PurchasOrderLineItem ;
        rdfs:range xsd:decimal ;
        rdfs:comment "The amount of a particular ProductType that is
        being ordered in a particular PurchaseOrder." .

esi:SOCompletedDate rdf:type owl:DatatypeProperty ;
        rdfs:domain esi:SalesOrder ;
        rdfs:range xsd:dateTime ;
        rdfs:label
        "The point in time when all the activities delivered under a
        Sales Order are complete." .

esi:SOIssuedDate rdf:type owl:DatatypeProperty ;
        rdfs:domain esi:SalesOrder ;
        rdfs:range xsd:dateTime ;
        rdfs:comment
        "The point in time when a Sales Order is agreed to." .

esi:SOLineNumber rdf:type owl:DatatypeProperty ;
        rdfs:subPropertyOf owl:topDataProperty ;
        rdfs:domain esi:SalesLineItem ;
        rdfs:range xsd:positiveInteger ;
        rdfs:comment
        "A system-generated integer that uniquely identifies each
        instance of SalesLineItem, within the context of the SalesOrder
        that it is part of." .

esi:SONumber rdf:type owl:DatatypeProperty ;
        rdfs:domain esi:SalesOrder ;
        rdfs:range xsd:positiveInteger ;
        rdfs:comment
        "A system-generated integer that uniquely identifies all Sales
        Orders." .

esi:ServiceID rdf:type owl:DatatypeProperty ;
        rdfs:domain esi:Service ;
        rdfs:range xsd:integer ,
        xsd:positiveInteger ;
        rdfs:comment
        "A system-generated integer that uniquely identifies each
        instance of a Service." .

esi:ServiceName rdf:type owl:DatatypeProperty ;
        rdfs:domain esi:Service ;
        rdfs:range xsd:string ;
        rdfs:comment "Text that labels and/or uniquely identifies a
        particular Service." .

esi:StandardUnitPrice rdf:type owl:DatatypeProperty ;
        rdfs:domain esi:ProductType ;
        rdfs:range xsd:decimal ;
        rdfs:comment
        "The monetary value for a unit of a ProductType." .

esi:VendorId rdf:type owl:DatatypeProperty ;
        rdfs:domain esi:Vendor ;
        rdfs:range xsd:positiveInteger ;
        rdfs:comment "A system-generated integer that uniquely identifies
        an instance of a Vendor." .
```

```
esi:VendorName rdf:type owl:DatatypeProperty ;
    rdfs:domain esi:Vendor ;
    rdfs:range xsd:string ;
    rdfs:comment
    "Text that labels and/or identifies an instance of a Vendor." .

esi:VendorStreetAddress rdf:type owl:DatatypeProperty ;
    rdfs:domain esi:Vendor ;
    rdfs:range xsd:string ;
    rdfs:comment
    "The number and street name identifying the location of a
    Vendor." .

esi:c_TotalCost rdf:type owl:DatatypeProperty ;
    rdfs:domain esi:SalesLineItem ;
    rdfs:range xsd:decimal ;
    rdfs:comment
    "Derived as hoursRequired * INFER-
    THRU(toSell,Service,PricePerHour)" .

esi:c_TotalPrice rdf:type owl:DatatypeProperty ;
    rdfs:domain esi:PurchasOrderLineItem ;
    rdfs:range xsd:decimal ;
    rdfs:comment "Derived as Quantity * INFER-THRU
    (toBuy,ProductType, StandardUnitPrice" .
```

Object Properties

Script 3 shows each *relationship* from Figure 20 (page 61, above) as a semantic web *object property*. For each case also, the *domain* is the class (also called *entity type*) of which it is a property. In each case, the *range* is the class the domain class is *related to*.

Thus, in the example, the entity/relationship model relationship "Each **Contract** must be *from* one and only one **Party**" is in OWL, esi:from—an owl:**ObjectProperty** with a *domain* of esi:**Contract** and a *range* of esi:**Party**.

It is possible to specify the specific cardinality as "1". The same outcome however, is accomplished by specifying "must be one and only one" as simply a *functional* property. Thus, in Script 3, esi:toBuyfrom, esi:toSellTo, esi:part of, esi:toSell, and esi:toBuy are all owl:functional properties.

Script 3: Semantic Web Object Properties

```
esi:basedIn rdf:type owl:ObjectProperty ;
    rdfs:subPropertyOf owl:topObjectProperty ;
    owl:inverseOf esi:theSiteOf ;
    rdf:type owl:FunctionalProperty ;
    rdfs:domain esi:Vendor ;
    rdfs:range esi:City .

esi:boughtVia rdf:type owl:ObjectProperty ;
    owl:inverseOf esi:toBuy ;
    rdf:type owl:FunctionalProperty .

esi:buyerIn rdf:type owl:ObjectProperty ;
    owl:inverseOf esi:toSellTo .
```

```
esi:composedOf rdf:type owl:ObjectProperty ;
    owl:inverseOf esi:partOf .

esi:homeOf rdf:type owl:ObjectProperty ;
    owl:inverseOf esi:toBeFoundIn .

esi:locatedIn rdf:type owl:ObjectProperty ,
    owl:FunctionalProperty ,
    owl:TransitiveProperty ;
    rdfs:comment
    "Looking for classes that have \"locatedIn\" as an object
    property." .

esi:partOf rdf:type owl:ObjectProperty ,
    owl:FunctionalProperty ;
 rdfs:comment
    "Looking for classes that have \"partOf\" as an object property."

esi:sellerIn rdf:type owl:ObjectProperty ;
    owl:inverseOf esi:toBuyFrom .

esi:soldVia rdf:type owl:ObjectProperty ;
    owl:inverseOf esi:toSell .

esi:theLocationOf rdf:type owl:ObjectProperty .

esi:theSiteOf rdf:type owl:ObjectProperty .

esi:toBeFoundIn rdf:type owl:ObjectProperty ;
    rdfs:subPropertyOf owl:topObjectProperty ;
    rdf:type owl:FunctionalProperty ;
    rdfs:domain esi:Customer ;
    rdfs:range esi:City .

esi:toBuy rdf:type owl:ObjectProperty,
    owl:FunctionalProperty;
    rdfs:domain esi:PurchaseOrderLineItem ;
    rdfs:range esi:ProductType .

esi:toBuyFrom rdf:type owl:ObjectProperty ,
    owl:FunctionalProperty ;
    rdfs:domain esi:PurchaseOrder ;
    rdfs:range esi:Vendor .

esi:toSell rdf:type owl:ObjectProperty ,
    owl:FunctionalProperty ;
    rdfs:domain esi:SalesLineItem ;
    rdfs:range esi:Service .

esi:toSellTo rdf:type owl:ObjectProperty ;
    rdfs:subPropertyOf owl:topObjectProperty ;
    rdf:type owl:FunctionalProperty ;
    rdfs:domain esi:SalesOrder ;
    rdfs:range esi:Customer .
```

Logical inferences

OWL greatly extends RDF and RDFS by its ability to make logical inferences. This is covered in greater detail by several books listed in the bibliography, but here is one example (demonstrated above in Script 3):

First, you have `esi:toBuy`, which is a relationship from `esi:PurchaseOrderLineItem` (its `domain`), to `esi:ProductType` (its `range`).

Then, you have `esi:boughtVia`, which is the `owl:inverseOf` `esi:toBuy`. Note that neither domain nor range are specified. This is because it is possible to invoke a piece of software called an *inference engine*, which will *infer* the fact that (for the object property `esi:boughtVia`), the `rdfs:domain` must be `esi:ProductType` and the `rdfs:range` must be `esi:PurchaseOrderLineItem`.

Multiple inheritance

In the world of entity/relationship modeling and database design, the issue of "multiple inheritance" is very controversial. Note that this is because while the the logic behind sub-typing in the data world is to capture **Aristotle's** "essential" categories: every instance of the sub-type is *necessarily* an instance of one and only one super-type. An automobile is essentially of the class "four-wheeled vehicles". A particular kind of wall is essentially of the class "structural walls".

In The Semantic Web, on the other hand, you can also capture **Aristotle's** "accidental characteristics". (That is to say, "accidental super-categories") "Redness", for example, is *not* a fundamental characteristic of a car that is essential to its definition.. It is simply a category. Similarly, "redness" is not essential to the definition of a wall that happens to be red. The set of "red things" can be a super-category to both car and structural wall, but automobile is also fundementally of the class "Four-wheeled vehicle", and the wall in question is also fundamentally of the class "Structural Walls".♠

Duplicate property names

Note that each property is defined in terms of a single **domain**. This means that the same property cannot be used more than once. For example, if the object property `esi:locationOf` has as its domain `esi:City`, it cannot (as would be implied by the entity/relationship model in Figure 21) also have as its domain `esi:State`. Addressing this discrepancy requires viewing the assignment from a different perspective.

The list in Script 4 shows the semantic web approach. First, define the object property (e.g. "located in"), without any domain or range. Then identify the set of those classes which are "located in" somewhere. This set of classes is called a **restriction**. Then specify that each **domain** class is a *sub-class* of that restriction set.

In the example shown, both **City** and **State** are subclasses of that abstract class.

♠   Your author's son, when he was about two years old, once set out to collect all the "red things" in the house. The set wound up including, in addition to two of his mother's lipsticks, three magic markers, a ball point pen, three books, one "Master of the Universe" action figure, and three of his sister's toys.

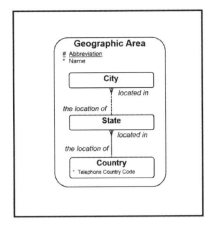

Figure 21: Duplicate Object Properties

Script 4: Dealing with Duplicated properties

➤ First, define the object property, "esi:located in":

```
esi:locatedIn a owl:ObjectProperty ,
     owl:FunctionalProperty ,
     owl:TransitiveProperty ;
     rdfs:comment "Looking for classes that have "esi:located in" as
     an object property." .
```

➤ Then specify the classes that comprise the set of things with that object property:

✓ First City:

```
esi:City a owl:Class ;
   rdfs:subClassOf a owl:Restriction
       owl:onProperty :locatedIn ;
       owl:qualifiedCardinality "1"^^xsd:nonNegativeInteger ;
       owl:onClass esi:State .
   rdfs:subClassOf esi:GeographicArea ,
esi:City
   rdfs:comment """
   1. A large, important town
   2. In the United States, an incorporated municipality, whose
   boundaries and powers of self-government are defined by a charter
   from the State in which it is located.
   3. In Canada, a municipality of the highest rank.
   4. In Great Britain, a borough or town with a royal charter.
   [ Webster's New World Dictionary. 1964. \"City\". (New York:
   World Publishing Company). p. 267.]"""
```

✓ Then State:

```
esi:State a owl:Class ;
rdfs:subClassOf owl:Restriction ;
   owl:onProperty esi:locatedIn ;
   owl:qualifiedCardinality "1"^^xsd:nonNegativeInteger ;
   owl:onClass esi:Country .
rdfs:subClassOf esi:GeographicArea
```

```
esi:State rdfs:comment
"""One of the territorial and political units constituting a federal
government, as in the United States.

[ Webster's New World Dictionary. 1964. \"State\". (New York: World
Publishing Company). p. 1424.]""" .
```

The same approach can be taken where there is a need to duplicate attributes (rdfs:DataTypeProperty).

Disjoint Classes

In the Barker/Ellis version of entity/relationship diagramming, there is the controversial assertion that all *sub-types* must be **disjoint**. That is, an instance of a **City** cannot also be an instance of a **State** or a **Country**. Interestingly enough, however, all other entity types—in any entity/relationship notation—are also *assumed to be disjoint*. It is obvious (I hear you say) that a **Sales Order** cannot be a **ProductType**. In the world of the Semantic Web, however, no such assumptions can be made. It is necessary, therefore, to make all such disjointed associations *explicit*.

To accomplish that, define an abstract class that describes the set of all disjoint classes. Script 5 shows two examples of this.

Script 5: Disjoint Classes

```
[ rdf:type owl:AllDisjointClasses ;
 owl:members ( esi:City
 esi:Country
 esi:State
 )
] .


[ rdf:type owl:AllDisjointClasses ;
 owl:members ( esi:Customer
 esi:GeographicArea
 esi:ProductType
 esi:PurchasOrderLineItem
 esi:PurchaseOrder
 esi:SalesLineItem
 esi:SalesOrder
 esi:Service
 esi:Vendor
 )
] .
```

The Essential Data Model

Where the *semantic model* describes the language of the business in detail, it is difficult to design a system around such a complex model. Instead, designers must address that complexity by identifying patterns and by using more abstract terms. This creates an **essential data model** that allows a complex domain to be described more simply. The overall structure of the essential model should have many fewer pieces than the corresponding semantic model. The result is called an "integrated" or *convergent model*.

This is a model of the things of significance to the enterprise that define its *essential* or *fundamental* nature. Note that the Oxford English Dictionary's definition of "ontology" is "that department of metaphysics that relates to the being *or essence* of things, or to being in the abstract."[125] [italics in the original]

The notation of choice is the Messrs. Barker's and Ellis's entity/relationship model, described above. (See Pages 35ff.)

Ockham's Razor

William of Ockham was a 14th century logician and friar, whose works of philosophy were concerned with cutting through the theological pontification of his era. While not directly written by him, attributed to his thinking is a maxim called "Occam's Razor". ♦

> **"Entia non sunt multiplicanda praeter necessitatem"**

Huh?

Coincidentally—and fortunately for us— this translates into English as:

> **"Entities must not be multiplied beyond necessity"**

Yes, even in the 14th century, people were concerned with complexity, as described in terms of the number of entities. The move to **essential data models** is based on the assumption that using *simpler* models as the basis for design will yield systems that are

➢ Easier to build

➢ Easier to test and validate

➢ Easier to change

➢ Less likely to need changing in the first place

➢ Easier to operate without making mistakes

Unnecessarily *complex* designs, on the other hand, yield systems that are

➢ Difficult to build correctly

➢ Difficult to operate

➢ Prone to error

Thus, it is true that...

> **Complexity is the enemy of Data Quality**

---

125 Various Editors. 1971. The Compact Edition of the Oxford English Dictionary. (Glasgow: Oxford University Press).

♦ Presumably, William of Ockham was in fact from the English town of Ockham, outside London, but his "razor" is typically called "Occam's".

The question for Friar Ockham, then, is this: How complex is "unnecessarily complex"? Or, from the other point of view, how simple is *too* simple?

As Albert Einstein put it, "Everything should be as simple as it can be, but not simpler."[126]

Unfortunately, Einstein's observation doesn't really answer either question. It turns out, however, that…

> **Determining *that* is at the heart of
> our jobs as
> Data Architects.**

It's *our* job to defeat *unnecessary* complexity.

This is the objective of the *essential* model.

Use of Patterns

Reviewing the detailed definitions of the *semantic model* allows you to identify patterns. You will find different terms that mean the same thing, or, more commonly, you will recognize that different terms describe concepts that are in fact *sub-types* of a more general concept. This *abstraction* of terms removes details to broaden the applicability of the model to a wider class of situations, while preserving the important properties of the more detailed situations.

You can make this abstraction either *inductively* or *deductively*:

Induction

The **inductive approach** involves examining various semantic models and identifying patterns.

A good example of such a semantic model is from our discussion of semantic entity/relationship diagrams from the chapter on Semantic Models, reproduced here as Figure 22.

Note the separate, similar-looking shapes describing the purchase and sales orders. They each consist of one or more **…Line Items**, each describing the things bought or sold. Several issues arise from this version of the model:

➢ **Vendors** and **Customers** are shown as different entity types. But how can you handle the situation where we are buying and selling to the same business entities?

➢ **Vendor** and **Customer** aren't really "things" of significance. One isn't born a customer. Rather, these are **Persons** and **Organizations** that are playing roles. An Enterprise is a "customer" only by virtue of its buying something from us.

➢ In the case of the **Sales Order**, the company being modeled is itself playing the role of "vendor", and in the case of the **Purchase Order**, this company is playing the role of "customer".

---

[126] Quoted in many places but the most definitive one seems to be Louis Zukofsky. June, 1950 "'Poetry, Reviews", Poetry in a Modern Age. [Review of the volume "William Carlos Williams" by Vivienne Koch (The Makers of Modern Literature Series)], Page 180, Volume 76, Number 3, Modern Poetry Association.

➢ In this view, the company is buying **Product Types** and selling **Services**. That is a very specialized company. In most companies, they both buy and sell both Products and Services.

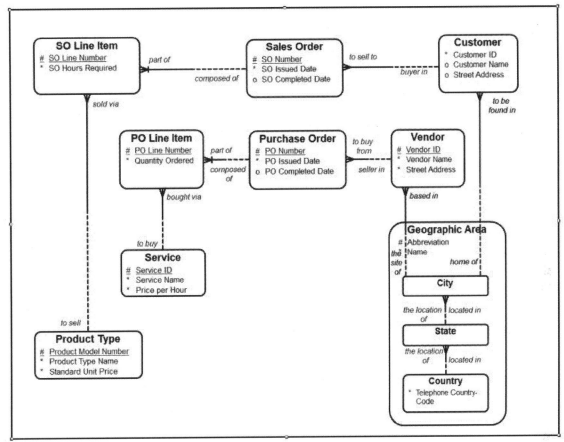

Figure 22: Semantic Entity/Relationship Diagram

This suggests that the patterns should be merged, into something like that shown in Figure 23. Several things have happened here:

➢ **Purchase Order** and **Sales Order** have been replaced by the more general concept of **Contract.**♦ In this context, a "Contract" is "an agreement between two parties whereby one will provide a specified set of products and/or services in exchange for remuneration from the other".

➢ **Vendor** and **Customer** have been replaced by **Person** and **Organization**. "Person" is any human being of interest to the company, and "Organization" is a collection of Persons brought together for a specified purpose. Note that an Organization must be either:
  ✓ A Company
  ✓ An **Internal Enterprise** (such as a "Department")
  ✓ A **Government** (such as that governing The United States or London)
  ✓ A **Government Agency** (such as the US Environmental Protection Agency)

♦ Or, depending on the company's industry or other preferences, this could be called "Order", "Agreement", or something similar.

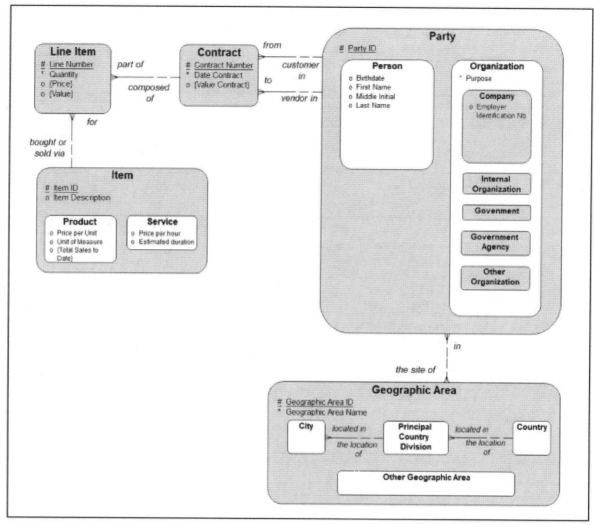

Figure 23: The Result of Pattern Usage

These categories are considered *sub-types* of Organization.

For purposes of understanding, **Contract**, **Person** and **Organization** have been gathered together under an abstraction called **Party**. Here, "Party" simply means "a person or enterprise that is of interest." **Party** has no physical existence by itself. It is, however, useful because often (as in contracting) it is helpful to address all Persons and Enterprises as a single set. ♥

Person and **Organization** are then *sub-types* of **Party**.

Note the definition of **Contract** is "an agreement between two *parties*..." Thus:

- Each **Contract** must be *from* one and only one **Party**.
  (Each **Party** may be *a customer in* one or more **Contracts**.)
- Each **Contract** must be *to* one and only one **Party**.
  (Each **Party** may be *a vendor in* one or more **Contracts.**)

♥ Note that the concept "customer" is now defined as a role (relationship). It is defined as "a **Party** that is the customer in a Contract that we are vendor in." Similarly, "vendor" is now defined as a role (relationship). It is defined as "a **Party** that is the vendor in a Contract that we are customer in."

➢ **Purchase Line Item** and **Sales Line Item** are now combined into **Line Item**, each of which must be *part of* one and only one of what is now **Contract**.

➢ The **Services** we sell (and may now buy), along with the **Product Types** we buy (and may now sell), are combined into (again an abstraction) **Item**. Thus
   – Each **Line Item** must be *for* one and only one **Item**.
   (Each **Item** may be *bought or sold via* one or more **Line Items**.)

The result of this exercise is that we now have a model that is…

   – … more widely applicable,
   – … a more accurate representation of the underlying nature (essence) of the enterprise, and
   – … simpler.

Deduction

The **deductive approach** makes use of one of the published data model patterns available. Looking at a particular business situation, you can conclude that is similar to one of the available published patterns. That is, keep in mind a set of patterns and *deduce* that one or more of them applies. Among them are (by date):

➢ **Business-oriented**
   ✓ David C. Hay. 1995. *Data Model Patterns: Conventions of Thought.*
   ✓ Len Silverston, W. H. Inmon, K. Graziano. 1997. *The Data Model Resource Book: A Library of Logical Data Models and Data Warehouse Designs.*
   ✓ Len Silverston. 2001. *The Data Model Resource Book (Revised Edition): Volume 1 - A Library of Universal Data Models for all Enterprises.*
   ✓ _____. 2001. *The Data Model Resource Book (Revised Edition): Volume 2 - A Library of Universal Data Models by Industry Types [sic].*
   ✓ _____, P. Agnew. 2009. *The Data Model Resource Book: Volume 3—Universal Patterns for Data Modeling.*
   ✓ David C. Hay. 2011. *Enterprise Model Patterns: Describing the World.*

➢ **Object-oriented**
   ✓ Martin Fowler. 1997. *Analysis Patterns: Reusable Object Models.*
   ✓ Craig Larman. 1998. *Applying UML and Patterns.*
   ✓ Blaha, Michael. 2010. *Patterns of Data Modeling.*

➢ **Event-oriented**
   ✓ Pavel Hruby. 2006. *Model Driven Design Using Business Patterns.*

Note that Messrs. Fowler, Larman, and Blaha use UML to show patterns oriented toward the systems development. Messrs. Hay and Silverston provide more business-oriented (essential) models in the Barker/Ellis format. (It is true that Hay's latest book, *Enterprise Model Patterns:…*, makes use of the UML syntax, but it still enforces the Barker/Ellis rules.)[127] Mr. Hruby, on the other hand, while using the UML notation, focuses his patterns on an evaluation of *events*, which is a different approach altogether.

---

[127] Hay. 2011. *UML… op. cit.*

Some Enterprise Patterns

In your Author's latest book on the subject,[128] he catalogues patterns in terms of *levels of abstraction*:

➤ **Level 1: The Generic Enterprise Model**
  - ✓ People and Enterprises
  - ✓ Geographic Locations
  - ✓ Physical Assets
  - ✓ Activities and Events
  - ✓ Time

➤ **Level 0: Three elements**
  This provides an additional level of abstraction. It includes one template and two "meta" models:
  - ✓ A Template for the first four Level 1 models.
    (**Thing** and **Thing Type**, for example.)
  - ✓ A Pattern Segment describing *Accounting*.
    Accounting (double-entry bookkeeping, that is) is itself a model of the enterprise, so it must be treated separately.
  - ✓ A Pattern Segment describing *Document*.
    Each Document (or other ***information resource***—such a magazine, e-mail, photograph, etc.) is typically *about* something else in the enterprise. That is, it may be linked to anything else in the model.

➤ **Level 2: Functional Model Segments**
  Each of these is an assembly of Level 1 components to address a particular functional area in a typical enterprise:
  - ✓ Facilities
  - ✓ Contracts
  - ✓ Marketing and Communications
  - ✓ Manufacturing
  - ✓ Laboratories

Note that, while the Level 2 model fragments are more specialized, the still apply to a wide variety of industries

Industry Patterns

Both Silverston (Silverston. 2001. ...*Industry types.*), and Hay (Hay. 2011. *Enterprise*... Part 5), have published some models targeting particular industries.

For example, in your author's *Essential Model Patterns: Describing the World*,[129] a third level of abstraction is:
  - ✓ Criminal Justice
  - ✓ Microbiology
  - ✓ Banking
  - ✓ Oil Production

---

[128] Hay. 2011. Enterprise... op. cit.

[129] Hay. 2011. Enterprise... op. cit.

  ✓ Highway Design

In Len Silverston's *Data Model Resource Book Revised Edition*, his *Volume 2: A Library of Universal Data Models by Industry Types*[130] includes:

  ✓ Manufacturing
  ✓ Telecommunications
  ✓ Health Care
  ✓ Insurance
  ✓ Financial Services
  ✓ Professional Services
  ✓ Travel
  ✓ E-Commerce

In addition, various industrial enterprises have set out to define their own. These industry patterns are sold by different vendors. Notable are oil and gas, banking and insurance, among others.

Some Basic Patterns

In addition to patterns derived from the meanings of portions of the model, some are more technical, and apply no matter the subject matter:

Identifying Instances

The logic for identifying instances of tables is an important part of relational theory, so the particulars for doing it in a relational database will be described below. It is certainly not of interest for either the *Overview* or the *Semantic* models. **Unique identifiers** for entity types is of interest for the Essential Model, however:

In the Essential Model, instances of an entity type may be identified by:

➢ **Instances of one or more *attributes***

➢ **Instances of one or more *relationships***

➢ *Combinations* **of the two.**

In the Barker / Ellis model, **identifying attributes** are displayed alongside an octothorpe symbol (#). **Identifying relationships** are displayed with a mark across the relationship line at the end next to the identified entity type.

Note that Figure 24 is again, a copy of Figure 7 (from page 40), which shows identifiers labeled.

Specifically:

- **Party** is identified by the attribute "Party ID".

- **Geographic Area** is identified by the attribute "Geographic Area ID".

- **Item** is identified by the attribute "Item ID".

- **Contract** is identified by the attribute "Contract Number".

---

130 Len Silverston. 2001. The Data Model Resource Book Revised Edition: Volume 2 A Library of Universal Data Model by Industry Types. (New York: Wiley Computer Publishing).

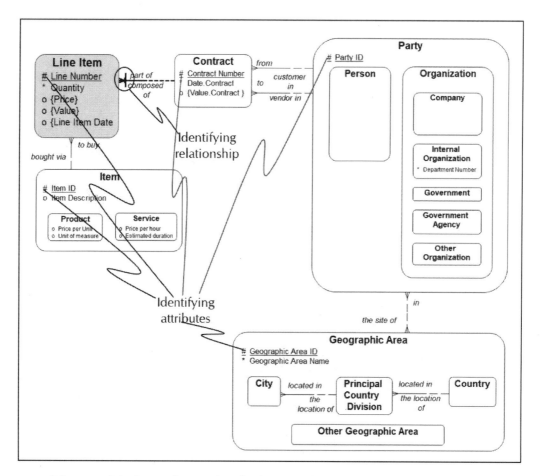

Figure 24: Sample entity/relationship Diagram (Identifiers)

However:

- **Line Item** is identified by the attribute "Line Number", <u>plus</u>

- **Line Item** is <u>also</u> identified by the relationship *part of* **Contract**.

That means that, for a given Contract, the first line number is unique to that Contract. It is identified by the "Line Number" plus the "Contract Number".

Note that the "…ID", for **Party**, **Geographic Area**, and **Item** are examples of **surrogate identifiers**, meaning that they are automatically generated as integer numbers, to guarantee uniqueness. "Line Number" in **Line Item** is a special case of surrogate identifier, in that line number sequences are within the context of a particular **Contract**. That is, while "Party ID" will be unique throughout a designated system's boundaries, **Line Number** is only unique within the context of a particular **Contract**. That is, "Line Number" "1" will be repeated for all **Contracts**.

Understand that Your Author makes use of the following conventions:

➤ **Reference entity types** have no dependent entity types These represent real, tangible things. Each of these is usually uniquely identified by a surrogate identifier, even though alternative identifiers made up of other attributes may also be recognized.

➤ **Intersect entity types** have mandatory relationships with other entity types. These usually represent transactions. Each of these is identified by a combination of relationships connecting each of the related entity types. To allow for duplications (such as a **Person** working for a **Project** during two different time periods), the "Effective Date" is added to the identifier.

Many-to-many Relationships

Figure 25 shows that:

- Each **Party** may be *based in* one or more **Geographic Locations**, and
- Each **Geographic Location** may be *the site of* one or more **Parties.**

Because the relationship is *many-to-many*, it obscures important information about each instance of a **Party** being *based in* a **Geographic Area**. If you are capturing semantics, the information about the nature of each instance of a relationship is important. So, for some *Semantic Models* and for all *Essential Models*, it is valuable to define specifically the nature of any many-to-many relationships.

In the *Overview Model*, many-to-many relationships are common. Since there are relatively few entity types involved, many-to-many relationships may provide sufficient detail for the Overview Model..

By convention, in more detailed entity/relationship diagrams, an ***intersect entity type*** is used to provide these details. This entity type has two "many-to-one" relationships, one with each of the two related things.

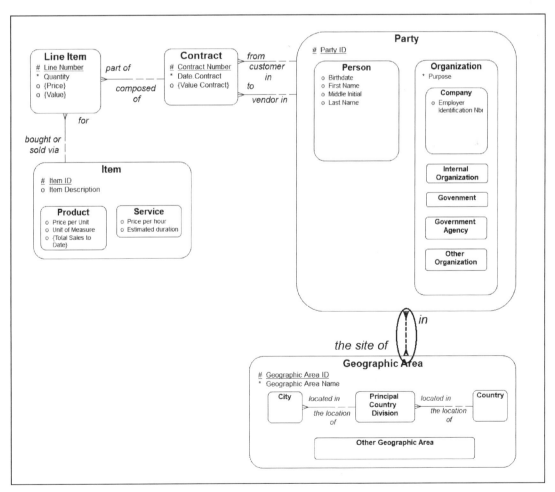

Figure 25: The Many-to-many Problem

The result for this example is shown in Figure 26. The entity type **Geographic Placement** is defined as "the fact that a particular **Party** is located for a specified period of time in a particular **Geographic Location**." The period of time is defined by the attributes "Effective Date" and "Until Date". Note that each **Geographic Placement** is also *an example of* one and only one **Geographic Placement Type**, such as "Headquarters", "Home Address", etc.

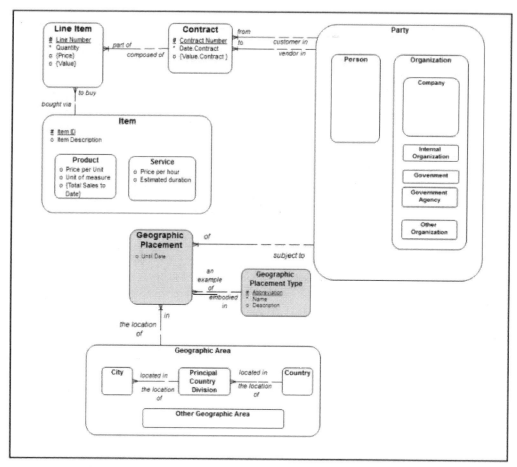

Figure 26: Resolving Many-to-Many Relationships

Roles

Looking at Figures 23-26 again shows our sample model of a **Contract** and its associated entity types. Note that in this version, "each **Contract** must be *from* one and only one **Party**, and that each **Contract** must also be *to* one and only one **Party**. This, however implies a constraint. A **Contract** must be between only *two* **Parties**, each of them playing a specified role.

In the case of financial institutions, however, this isn't a true representation of the facts. There could easily be *from* at least two customers (such as a husband and wife), or it could be *to* several companies (as in a consortium of banks). That is, there could be more than one **Party** involved with each side of this **Contract** (which might be called "account" instead).

This means that the annotation on those two relationships is incorrect. This is corrected in Figure 27:

- Each **Contract** may be *from* at least one or more **Parties**.

- Each **Contract** may be *to* at least one or more **Parties**.

This, however, introduces two many-to-many relationships. Moreover, this raises another question:

Are the various related **Parties** only "customer" and "vendor"? Moreover, what attributes might describe each occurrence of this relationship ?

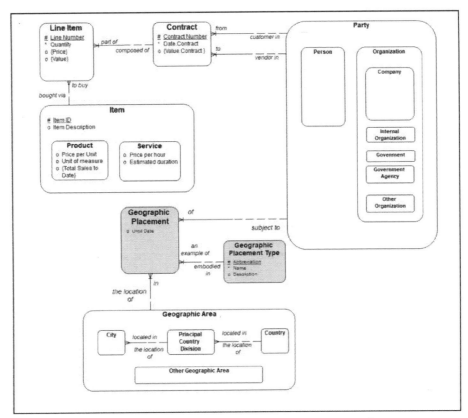

Figure 27: Many Customers and Vendors

In the case of Figure 27, there were in fact two relationships between **Contract** and **Party**. These could be addressed by two intersect entities, but since what differentiates them is the kinds of roles they play, this can be addressed with a single intersect entity, as shown in Figure 28.

Contract Role, then, is defined as the fact that a particular **Party** (that is, a **Person** or an **Enterprise**) is concerned with the creation, servicing, management, and/or termination of a particular **Contract**.

Two relationships further define the entity type **Contract Role:**

- Each **Contract Role** must be *played by* one and only one **Party**. (Each **Party** may be *player of* one or more **Contract Roles**), and

- Each **Contract Role** must be *played for* one and only one **Contract**. (Each **Party** may be *managed via* one or more **Contract Roles**.)

This raises the question as to what exactly is the *nature* of the **Contract Role**? There are three *alternative* ways to represent the answer to this question, all of which are all represented on Figure 28:

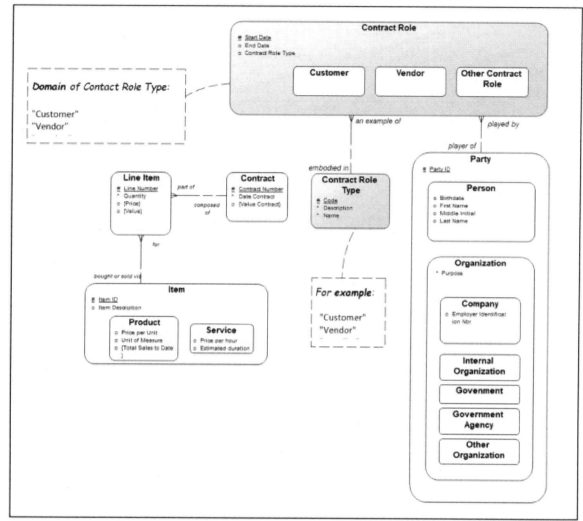

Figure 28: Contract Roles

➤ **Version 1: Sub-types**

If the two principal roles are indeed *customer in* and *vendor in*, iusing sub-types of Contract Role, Customer, and Vendor can work.

This has the advantage of presenting the situation graphically, but managing the "other" contract role types could be problematic.

➤ **Version 2: Attributes**

Alternatively, an attribute (in this case, "Contract Role Type") can be used, provided a domain is defined with the list of possible values. Of course, "customer" and "vendor" would be part of such a domain, but others might be included as well, such as "supplier", "attorney of record", and so forth.

This has the advantage of providing more flexibility, but it does mean that managing the domains will remain the job of the data modeler. It would be better for that information to be the responsibility of the user community

➤ **Version 3: "Type" Entity Type**

The third way to defining the meaning of each Contract Role is accommodated by adding the entity type **Contract Role**. That is:

- Each **Contract Role** must be *an example of* one and only one **Contract Role Type**. (Each **Contract Role Type** may be *embodied in* one or more **Contract Roles**.)

Here, the list of possible Contract Role Types is in the hands of the user (i.e. the data manager). The examples shown could be expanded to include, for instance:

- "Customer"
- "Vendor"
- "Supplier"
- "Attorney of Record"
- Etc.

It falls to the **data stewards** or their representatives to maintain this list.

Note that this sample model shows the three different approaches to managing the meaning of a **Contract Role.** In a particular model, only one will be used.

Note also that the model no longer constrains a **Contract** to be *from* one **Party** and *to* another **Party.** There is nothing in this model that requires any roles to be played at all. There is nothing to prevent there being three customers and no vendors, or vice-versa. If such constraints are required, they are in the domain of **business rules**, and must be managed separately from the structural data ("class") model.

Recursive Relationships

In conceptual models, most relationships are **binary**. That is, they are always between instances of exactly two entity types. And indeed, we've seen that it is preferable to keep them of the "one-to-many" variety. It is possible, however to have **unary** relationships between multiple instances of the same entity type. These are called "recursive" or "self-referencing". ♥

A one-to-many recursive relationship describes a **hierarchy**, whereas a many-to-many recursive relationship describes a **network**.

Hierarchy

Representations of the world are often **hierarchical**. In the eighteenth century, Carl Linnaeus published an original view of life, organizing a set of categories into a hierarchy. This was an early example of the field called ***taxonomy:*** "classification, esp. in regard to general laws and principles".[131] For Carl Linnaeus, there were three kingdoms, each divided into multiple classes, and they, in turn, each into orders, families, genera (singular: genus), and species (singular: species), with no rank lower than species. Figure 29 shows the hierarchy that is Linnaeus' taxonomy. Each of these is an example of what is here labeled a "Life Category". To the left of it is a symbolic set of instances.

Figure 30 shows how, if all his categories were treated together, Linnaeus' view of the world might be represented in an entity/relationship diagram.

- Each **Life Category** (for example, an instance of "Kingdom") may be *composed of* one or more (other) **Life Categories** (for example instances of "Phylum"); this **Life Category** (for

---

♥   Not in the Oxford English Dictionary (or any other): recursion – (n) (See recursion.)

131   Compact Oxford English Dictionary. 1971. op. cit.

example, instances of "Phylum") in turn may be *composed of* one or more (other) **Life Categories** (for example, instances of "Class").

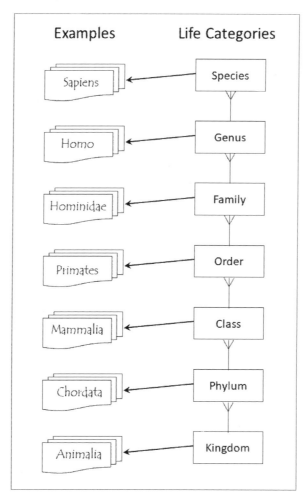

Figure 29: Linnaeus' Taxonomy

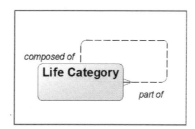

Figure 30: Recursion – Hierarchy

- Each **Life Category** (for example an instance of "Phylum") may be *part of* one and only one (other) **Life Category** (for example, an instance of "Kingdom").

This models what are basically **hierarchical** data. That is, each "parent" has one or more "children", but each "child" can have *only one* "parent". Note that it is optional in both directions. "Kingdom" is not *part of* any other **Life Category**. "Species" is not *composed of* any other **Life Categories.**

Network

Figure 31 shows a diagram of the structure of a fictional bicycle. Note that the bicycle consists of a frame, a crank and chain assembly, a front wheel, and a back wheel. Each of these components in turn are composed of various sub-components.

If we were talking about the structure of an actual bicycle, the structure would indeed be hierarchical—a particular tire can only be part of one wheel in one bicycle. This however is about a *model* of a bicycle, as a product manufactured from standardized parts. The "SXY Tire" is in fact used in both the front and rear wheel for this model bicycle.

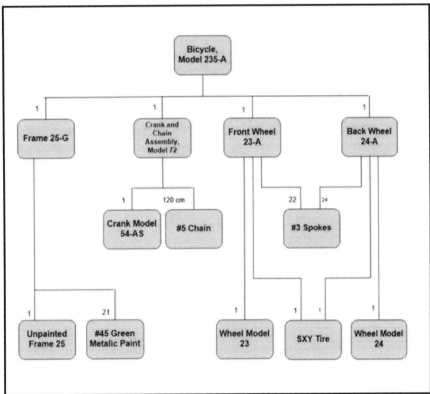

Figure 31: A Sample Product Structure[132]

This is in fact a **network**—with many-to-many relationships. The crows' feet will have to be both ends of the diagram, as shown in Figure 32. The two ends of the relationship then read as:

- Each **Product Component** (for example, "Front Wheel-23A") may be *composed of* <u>one or more </u>(other) **Product Components** (for example "spokes" <u>and</u> "SXY Tire");

- Each **Product Component** (for example "SXY Tire") may be *part of* <u>one or more</u> (other) **Product Components** (for example "Front Wheel 23-A" <u>and</u> "Back Wheel 24-A").

You may now notice that the Network model has a modeling problem: We have a **many-to-many relationship**. As a starting point, that is acceptable. But it raises a flag that more must be done.

---

132 From David C. Hay. 2011. Enterprise Model Patterns: Describing the World. (Westfield, NJ: Technics Publications). Page 138. (Diagram Copyright © Essential Strategies International. Used with permission.)

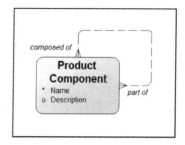

Figure 32: Recursion – Network

As it happens, we know what to do: add an **intersect entity type**. This gives you the model in Figure 33. In this case, the intersect is shown as **Product Structure.** Since database management systems started with the problem of managing manufacturing product structures back in the 1960s, this is a classic form. While it is the obvious solution to the many-to-many modeling problem, some people have difficulty internalizing the concept.

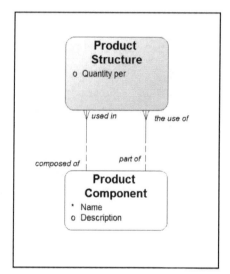

Figure 33: Product Structure

Product Structure is defined as "<u>the fact that</u> a particular **Product Component** is <u>part of</u> a particular other **Product Component.**" That is, each **Product Structure** must be *the use of* one **Product Component** and *the use in* another **Product Component**.

If you look at the network shown above in Figure 31, each round-cornered *box* is an instance of a **Product Component.** Each *line* is an instance of a link between two product components. These lines are represented in Figure 33 instances of **Product Structure.** Thus:

- Each **Product Component** (parent) may be *composed of* one or more **Product Structures,** <u>each of which</u> must be *the use of* one and only one (other) **Product Component.**

- Each **Product Component** (child) may be *part of* one or more **Product Structures,** <u>each of which</u> must be *used in* one and only one (other) **Product Component.**

Note that, as with all intersect entity types, attributes include start date ("Effective Date") and end date ("Until Date"), which allows for structures to change over time. Also, in this case note the attribute "Quantity Per", which allows us to record specifically (for example) how many "Spokes" are included in the "Front Wheel 23-A" (24) and how many are included in the "Back Wheel 24-A" (only 22). These are not values of either **Spoke** entity type nor either **Wheel** entity type. Rather they are attributes of the links between them. This is why the intersect entity is important.

While this model started in the world of manufacturing in the 1960s, the structure has turned out to be widely adopted. See the works of Len Silverston,[133] David Hay,[134] and the team of Graeme Simsion and Graham Witt[135] for many examples.

Notice by the way, two <u>constraints</u> on this model:

1. Both ends of both the hierarchical version and the network version are *optional*: Among others, "Unpainted Frame 25" has no components. Similarly, the "Bicycle Model 235-A" is not part of anything else.

2. Neither the hierarchical nor the network relationships can connect an instance of an entity type to *itself*. ♥

Ternary Relationships

The Barker/Ellis notation does not permit more than two participating entity types in a relationship. The one conceptual modeling notation that does is the **Object Role Model (ORM)** approach. (The concept of **n-ary relationships**, however, is supported by ORM and UML.)

Attributes and Characteristics

Taking a look at existing systems often reveals tables that have *a lot* of columns. A mild sample of this is shown in Figure 34. The **Person** and **Enterprise** tables are featured, and these reveal some problems:

First, some of the columns are actually multi-valued over time. The best they can store with this structure is "*Current* Salary", "*Current* Credit Score", "*Current* Annual Revenue", and "*Current* Profit". In addition, there is no guarantee that this is the definitive list. What if, in addition to "Height" for a **Person**, you wanted to add "Weight". (Both of these suffer from the "current" problem.) Indeed, if you wanted to get progressive and change "Wife's Name" to "Spouse's Name"[♣], that would require a change to the file structure.

As it happens, the list of attributes, which are ***metadata*** that describe an aspect of the model, could in fact be managed by a human as ***data***. This can be accomplished by making the Essential Model look like Figure 35.

First, you have a new entity type, **Party Characteristic.** This is defined as "a reference to an aspect, quality, or measurement of a **Party**".

Instances include (for example, on the model in Figure 34) "Birthdate", "First Name", "Official Name", "Purpose", etc.

---

[133]   Len Silverston. 2001. *Data Model Resource Book, Revised Edition*. (John Wiley and Sons).

[134]   Hay. 2011. Enterprise Model Patterns... Op. cit.

[135]   Graham C. Simsion and G. C. Witt. 2005. *Data Modeling Essentials, Third Edition*. (Amsterdam: Morgan Kaufmann.)

♥   Note, by the way, that in entity / relationship modeling, connecting an instance of an entity type to itself is <u>not</u> prohibited. This business rule constraint would have to be invoked via software. It (and many other constraints) <u>can</u> be explicitly described in the Object Role Modeling (ORM) notation. (See ORM description, above, on pages 54-61).

♣   Or even "Current Spouse's Name", if you want to be truly modern...

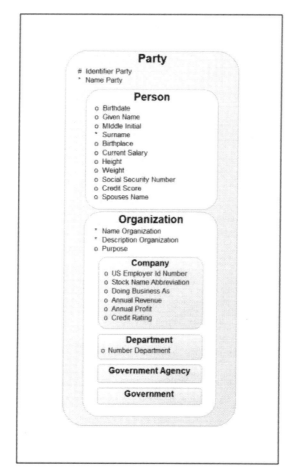

Figure 34: Party Attributes

Then, to assign a *value* of a **Party Characteristic** *to* a particular **Party** (that Is, a **Person** or an **Enterprise**), you need instances of **Party Characteristic Value**—the fact that a particular Party has a specified value for a particular **Party Characteristic**.

Each **Party Characteristic Value**, then, must be...

— *... to describe* one **Party**. (Each **Party** may be *described by* one or more **Party Characteristic Values**), and

— *... for* one **Party Characteristic**. (Each **Party Characteristic** may be *used as* one or more **Party Characteristic Values**).

That is, Party Characteristic Value is defined as the fact that a particular Party has a particular "Value" for a particular Party Characteristic at a particular time ("Effective Date" through "Until Date").

Careful observation will reveal that there is an additional relationship between Party Characteristic Value and Party:

☐   Each Party Characteristic Value may be issued by one and only one Party. (Each Party may be the issuer of one or more Party Characteristic Values.)

Since the concept of Party is being evaluated, it is useful to be able to identify just who is providing values for the Party.

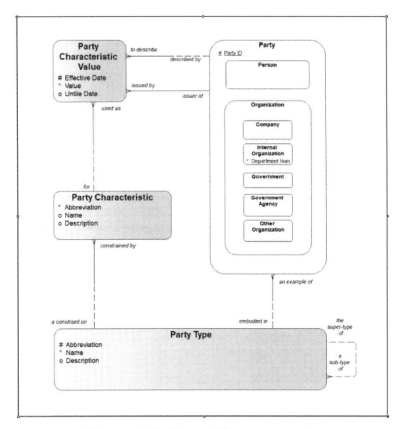

Figure 35: Party Characteristics

You may have noticed that while capturing values for both **Person** and various kinds of **Organization**, we cannot assure that values for each attribute/characteristic are assigned to the right kind of **Party**. One problem with this more general approach is that it loses some business rules that are hard-coded in the semantic version, including:

- "Birthdate" can only be an attribute of **Person**.
- "Purpose" can only be an attribute of **Enterprise**.
- Etc.

This issue can be addressed partially by recognizing more formally the structure of **Party** sub-types. This is done by introducing the concept **Party Type**, where each **Party** must be *an example of* one and only one **Party Type**. That is, **Party Type** is a way of describing a fundamental classification scheme for **Party**.

But wait! (I hear you say…) Isn't that already accomplished by the use of sub-types?

Actually, it is. Adding an entity type to describe types of **Parties** is slightly redundant. Indeed, instances of it are:

- "Person"
- "Enterprise"
- "Internal Enterprise"
- "Company"
- "Government"
- "Government Agency"
- "Other Enterprise"

The graphical sub-type structure and the categorical structure are linked by the relationship:

- Each **Party** must be *an example of* one and only one **Party Type**. (Each **Party Type** may be *embodied in* one or more **Party**.)

If data describing "Julia Roberts" constitutes an instance of the entity (sub-) type **Person**, it must also be the case that *that instance* is *an example of* the **Party Type** with the "Name" evaluated as "Person". Notice that the sub-type structure of the various party "types" is represented by the additional relationship:

- Each **Party Type** may be *the super-type of* one or more (other) **Party Types**. (Each **Party Type** may be *the sub-type of* one and only one (other) **Party Type**.)

This exactly reproduces the structure shown in the diagram of super-types and sub-types.

Having the same information conveyed in two ways has advantages. First of all, the sub-types shown graphically are easier to understand. Representing the sub-type structures as instances in another entity type, however, make it possible to express a business rule, to be shown below. Thus, in Figure 35, we can assert that:

- Each **Party Characteristic** (like "Height") must be *constrained by* one and only one **Party Type** (like "Person"). (Each **Party Type** may be *a constraint on* one or more **Party Characteristics.**)

This means that each **Party Characteristic** is constrained to apply to only one **Party Type**. Another way to describe this is as a business rule.

Business Rule

- Any **Party Characteristic Value** that is to describe a particular **Party** <u>must be</u> *for* a **Party Characteristic** that is *constrained by* the **Party Type** that is *embodied in* that **Party**.

This rule is expressed by the values shown in Table 3. This table shows what *instances* of the **Party Characteristic** entity type shown in Figure 35 would be if that entity type were to represent the attributes of the various Party (and sub-type) entity types shown in Figure 34.

Table 3: Party Characteristic Entity Type

Party Characteristic ("Name")	Party Type ("Name")
Birthdate	Person
First Name	Person
Middle Initial	Person
Last Name	Person
Birthplace	Person
Current Salary	Person
Birthplace	Person
Social Security Number	Person
Credit Score	Person
Height	Person
Purpose	Organization
Official Name	Company
Nickname	Company
Employer Identification Number	Company
Stock Abbreviation	Company
Doing Business As	Company
Annual Revenue	Company
Annual Profit	Company
Credit Rating	Company

NOTE: this structure allows us to *express* the business rule above. It does *not* actually *enforce* the rule *per se*. That must be carried out by application code associated with updating each **Party Characteristic Value.**

You may be interested to know that back in 1989, your author developed a model to describe clinical research which adopted exactly this approach. The Clinical research studies involved provided each patient with a medication and observed over time the patient's response. The medication would be a studied pharmaceutical or a placebo. The goal was to determine whether the medication had a greater effect than the placebo.

In the course of the this study, each patient visited a physician numerous times; the physician recorded observations of the h'[*] condition on a "Case Report Form". This CRF, as it was called, was always a paper form; it comprised a variable number of boxes, each of which could contain one or more numbers and/or textual annotations. Designing a database to capture each and every study was a formidable task.

Parke Davis called on Oracle Corporation to come up with a better, automated, solution. After working out the modeling, the solution turned out to be similar to what was described above. Each **Person's** identity was recorded, but not available to analysts. The data, however, were available. The patient made one or more **Visits**, where one or more **Data Elements** were captured, grouped by topic. Each **Data Element** was identified by the **Patient/Visit** and by a **Parameter**. This had a "value". The **Data Elements** entity type converted to a very long, skinny table. But the **Parameters** were grouped by topic (**Parameter Type**), so a utility could rotate the night's batch and sort by topic, producing one table per **Parameter Type**, with one row per **Visit**, with the **Parameters** defining the columns. The statistical software could readily work on those tables.[♦]

Rather than use the clumsiness "his or her", or the grammatically incorect "their", this is an abreviation that should solve the problem. Also "he or she" is covered by 'e.

[♦] Your author left Oracle Corporation after the model was finished, and sadly, the project team was not able to complete the system. Several years later, however, Oracle returned to offer Parke Davis its "Oracle Clinical" packaged software. My former client examined its underlying model—and it was the one developed for Parke Davis!

This exercise also was the source of the section "Variable Format Forms" in my *Data Model Patterns: Conventions of Thought.*

CHAPTER 5:
DETAILS – TECHNOLOGICAL

Once *Essential Models* of the enterprise have been developed, they can be converted to *Logical Models* that are oriented toward particular data management technologies.

Logical Model [136]♦

A **Logical Data Model** is a detailed representation of *business data requirements*, specifically organized in terms of a particular *database management architecture*. While logical data models do each reflect a particular modeling approach, these are still independent of any specific implementation constraints. A logical data model often begins as an extension of a conceptual data model.

NOTE: Because there are different underlying data management technologies available, there are as many different kinds of logical models.

Originally, the ANSI/SPARC vision of data "management" only envisioned choices for the "internal" schema to be "Hierarchical", "Network", and "Flat files". That was in 1975. Oracle, the first relational database management system, was first released in 1979[137], and eventually dominated the field. As databases became larger and more complex, the limitations to the relational approach became apparent. Johan Oskarsson, then a developer at Last.fm, introduced the term NoSQL in early 2009 when he organized an event to discuss "open source, distributed, non-relational databases".[138] Since then a number of database approaches have been developed to address the issues of very large databases, as well as dealing with unstructured data.

As of 2018, the most significant logical model approaches include:

> **Relational**
> This is the representation of entity types and attributes, with their identifiers, as **tables** and **columns** with **primary keys**. It further represents each relationship between pairs of tables as a set of **foreign key** columns in one table, corresponding to **primary key** columns in the related table.

> **Dimensional**
> A model in relational terms, but organized for efficient access, in terms of **dimensions** (structured keys) and *facts* (underlying information).

> **Hierarchical**
> This recognizes that some things can be linked in hierachies, with multiple "branches" for each "root". This makes retrieval of high level elements very fast, but retrieval of categories

---

♦ NOTE: It is common practice to develop logical models first – that is, designing databases – without first examining thoroughly the business being served. While this may speed development of small (i.e., "agile") projects, the approach can cause problems when additional "apps" are built that do not connect well to each other. Logical models (designs) will be much more sound if they are based on sound essential models. – DCH Editorial.

137   Paulo Ferriera. 2015. "The History of Oracle". *Oracle Tips*. (Burlson Consulting). Retrieved 4/18/2018 from *http://www.dba-oracle.com/t_history_oracle.htm*.

138   "NoSQL 2009". Blog.sym-link.com. 12 May 2009. Retrieved 29 March 2010.

of lower level elements very slow.[*] The eighteenth century Swedish biologist Carl Linnaeus devised the first scheme for organizing kinds of life forms, and found that the nomenclature lent itself to a hierarchical form. Based on his work, this came to be known as a **taxonomy**. "Organisms are grouped together into **taxa** (singular: taxon) and these groups are given a **taxonomic rank**; groups of a given rank can be aggregated to form a super-group of higher rank, thus creating a **taxonomic hierarchy**."[139]

In modern times, the term "taxonomy" refers to any hierarchical structure. The most common language to approach the world hierachically in 2018 is XML. It's primary structure is high-level terms successively composed of lower-level terms. In those cases where the taxonomy is violated, it is possible to define an association with a different branch.

> ➤ **Object-oriented**
>
> A model oriented towards object-oriented programming, where entity types are implemented as **object classes** and relationships are **associations**.

> ➤ **XML Schema**
>
> Not a graphic model, but an organization of XML to represent classes. It is expressed in terms of **element** (the definition of an XML term or "tag") plus **simpleType** (a class definition with simple restrictions) and **complexType** (a class definition that encompasses multiple other elements).

> ➤ **NoSQL**
>
> An approach to very large databases (**big data**) that is "Not only SQL". Instead of taking a business subject and breaking it up into multiple relational structures, NoSQL databases frequently store the business subject in a structure called a document. There are four versions of this:
>
> ✓ **Document** – a piece of (typically) JavaScript Object Notation (JSON) code.
>
> ✓ **Key-value** – an application which stores its data in only two columns (*key* and *value*). More complex information may be stored within the "value" columns. (It's not limited to one value.)
>
> ✓ **Column-oriented** – databases that can work with more complex data types including unformatted text and imagery. These data can also be defined when they are entered.
>
> ✓ **Graph** – for data whose relations are well represented as a set of nodes with a variable number of connections between these nodes.

---

[*] Your author's experience goes back to the early 1970s, when he developed a market research database using an early hierarchical DBMS called "RAMIS". This included a lovely user-oriented language. In this case, he organized the data source, with various categories down the branches, to the brand of product at the bottom. The data were very easy to load in batches on the database maintained by a commercial time-sharing company. This company charged by the minute. All was lovely until the first time someone wanted a report by brand. The three hour query wound up costing the client $3000. In those days, that was a lot of money.

Your author was strongly encouraged to take a different approach.

[139] Wikipedia. "Taxonomy". (Retrieved February, 2018.)

Relational Data Model

First articulated by Dr. Edward Codd in 1970[140], relational theory provides a systematic way to organize data so that they reflect their meaning. This approach has the additional effect of reducing redundancy in data storage. While there are no hidden links between elements, the one redundancy required is to explicitly describe such links. Codd's insight was that data could most effectively be managed in terms of two-dimensional *relations*. The term "relation" was derived from the mathematics (set theory) upon which his approach was based. In practice, each relation is implemented by a two-dimensional table.

The implementation of relational database management systems didn't follow until the late 1970s. For a detailed description of relational technology, see C. J. Date's book, originally written in 1975. The most current version was published in 2003.[141]

The design objectives for the relational model are it exactly represents business data and each fact is in only one place.

The two most common notations to express the association between entities in relational modeling are **Information Engineering (IE)** and **Integration Definition for Information Modeling (IDEF1X).** The most common form is IE syntax, with its familiar tridents or "crow's feet" to depict cardinality. Figure 36 shows the automated conversion of a sample Barker/Ellis Essential Model (Figure 23, page 76, above) into a Logical Model diagram. (This was done using the SAP tool, PowerDesigner.)

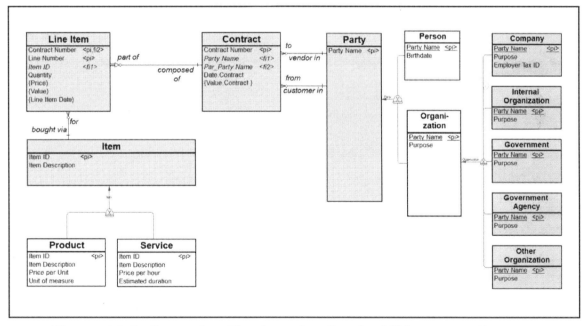

Figure 36: Information Engineering Logical Diagram – Contracts

---

[140]   Edward F. Codd, 1970, "A Relational Model of Data for Large Shared Data Banks". *Communications of the ACM,* 13, No. 6 (June).

[141]   C. J. Date. 2003. An Introduction to Database Systems (8th Edition). (Pearson).

Entity Types to Tables

Tables are created from the entity types found in the Essential Model. While the round-cornered boxes from the essential model represented entity types, the square-cornered boxes shown here represent relational **tables**. The attributes of the entity types are shown here as relational *columns*.

Note that, while they are derived from entity types, they do not have to have exactly the same names. A convention followed by some Oracle users is to have the table names be plural. The idea is that while an entity type represents a *concept*, it is appropriate for it to be singular. Since a table is fundamentally a collection of instances, it can be rendered in the plural form.

This is but one convention, not followed in this example. Others may be followed—provided that they are followed *consistently*.

Sub-type boxes

… here are separated from their super-types. The SAP PowerDesigner software that created this diagram shows that the super-type attributes are all inherited as columns by the sub-types. That is, the example shown in Figure 36 reflects the *assumption* that each sub-type will be implemented as a *separate table*.

NOTE

One of the tasks to be done before converting it to a physical relational database structure will be to **challenge** the assumption of separate tables. It may be more reasonable to implement the structure as a single table—or as a combination of the two approaches.

The process of deciding how to render sub-type ("inheritance") structures in a two-dimensional relational data structure is described in detail in Chapter 6 (page 143).

Each relationship

… is rendered as a **foreign key** in the **child table**. That is, when each instance of one table is related to one or more instances of another table, the first is called a *parent table* and the second is called a **child table**. The set of columns playing the role of *foreign* key corresponds to the set of columns that are the **primary key** in the **parent table.**

For example, in Figure 36, **Line Item** (ItemID) is identified as a "<fk>", which means that it replicates Item ID from the **Item** table.

Notice that the two relationships from Contract to Party cause the generation of two foreign keys. They are:

- **Party_Name <fk>**
- **Par_Party_Name <fk>**

To clarify this—if you are working from the essential model—you can rename one of the columns "**To_Party_Name**" and the other one "**From_Party_Name**". ♦

♦ The SAP PowerDesigner tool, when it converts from what it calls a "conceptual" model to a "logical" model, preserves the spaces between words. Before it becomes a physical model, though, the spaces will have to be removed. In the relational world, that means substituting underscores for them. In this one example, that was done here.

Also remember that in the Essential Model, the relationship between entity types **Line Item** and **Contract** was part of the former's *identifier*. In the relational Logical Model, the *foreign key* that implements that relationship (**Line Item**(Contract Number)) is now part of the *primary key* of the Line Items table, along with the column **Line Items**(Line Number).

Dependent Table

Because part of the table's identifier is a foreign key pointing to another table, the first table is called a **dependent table**. The other tables are **independent tables**. If this were in the IDEF1X notation, dependent tables are shown with a different notation. (The corners are rounded.) See "Appendix C – Kinds of Notations", for details.

About Primary keys

In describing the essential model above, the concept of instance *unique identifier* was brought up. It is useful to describe this to add meaning to the entity/relationship model. In the conceptual model, however, unique identifiers do not always have to be shown. . To the extent that these identifiers *were* specified in the essential entity/relationship model, however, they are converted to **primary keys** in the relational logical model. Here, the identifying columns are identified with the symbols "<pk>". Identifying relationships are identified by the modified "crow's foot" ("=>").

By the time that a database is being designed, primary keys and their cousins, foreign keys, must be specified. As shown, each row in a table is identified by the values of one or more **primary keys.**

> **Simple key**
> This is one column that uniquely identifies a table instance. Universal Product Codes (UPCs) and Vehicle Identification Numbers (VIN codes) are examples of simple keys.

> **Surrogate key**
> This is a kind of simple key. A surrogate key is a unique identifier for a table. In the case of long tables, like Product or Person, it could be a system-generated integer. If it is a short "type" table with only a handful of instances, it could be a human-assigned abbreviation. Surrogate keys serve technical functions and typically are not be visible to end users of a database. They remain behind the scenes to help maintain uniqueness, allow for more efficient navigation across structures, and facilitate integration across applications.

> **Compound key**
> This is a set of two or more columns that together uniquely identify a table instance. Examples are US phone number (area code + exchange + local number) and credit card number (issuer ID + account ID + check digit).

> **Composite key**
> This contains one compound key and at least one other simple or compound key or non-key column. An example is a key on a multi-dimensional fact table, which may contain several compound keys, simple keys, and maybe a load timestamp.

> **Candidate key**
> This is any set of columns that uniquely identify a row in the table. A candidate key is a minimal set of one or more columns (i.e., a simple or compound key) that identifies the table instance to which it belongs. This is also known as a *natural primary key*.

> Minimal means that no subset of the candidate key uniquely identifies the table instance. A table may have multiple candidate keys. Examples of candidate keys for a customer table are email address, cell phone number, and customer account number. Candidate keys can be business keys (sometimes called natural keys). A business key is one or more columns that a

business professional would use to retrieve a single table instance. Business keys and surrogate keys are mutually exclusive.

> **Alternative Key**[*]
> An alternative key is a candidate key that, although unique, was not chosen as the primary key. Even though a table may contain more than one candidate key, only one candidate key can serve as the primary key for a table. An alternative key can still be used to find specific table instances. Often the primary key is a surrogate key and the alternative keys are business keys.

Normalization

Normalization is the process of applying rules to organize business complexity into stable data structures. The basic goal of normalization is to keep each attribute in only one place, to eliminate redundancy (and the inconsistencies that redundancy brings). The process requires a deep understanding of each attribute and the ability to see each attribute in relation to every other attribute.

Note that, if you followed the logic behind creating an Essential Model, you would have taken care to make sure that every attribute in fact uniquely described it entity type. Thus, when you converted it to a relational logical model, you would find that it is already in 5th Normal form. Dr. Codd, however, used relational algebra to use a systematic *process* to arrive at a *"normalized"* structure.

Normalization rules sort attributes according to primary and foreign keys. Normalization rules sort into levels, with each level applying granularity and specificity in search of the correct primary and foreign keys. Each level comprises a separate normal form.[♣]

Normalization levels include:

Zeroth normal form (0NF):

This determines that tables are, in fact, relational tables. Figure 37 shows a sample table (called TEST), which represents a collection of chemical tests that might be taken from sample materials in one's backyard. Shown are:

- ✓ Sample Date – locating the collection of the sample in time
- ✓ Material Code – a unique identifier describing the kind of material sampled
- ✓ Material Description – text describing the kind of material sampled
- ✓ Test <n> – a set of several tests conducted on the sample. Each consists of:
  - – (Test)**Date** – Test Date
  - – (Test)**#** - Test Number
  - – (Test)*Type* – a code identifying the kind of test
  - – (Test)*Description* – text characterizing the kind of test
  - – (Test)**pH** – the value derived from the test

---

[*] Some would call this an "alternate key", but it does not go back and forth like alternating current. Rather, it is an alternative to other possible keys.

[♣] Contrary to what some may claim, by the way, it is not true that Dr. Codd's discussions of "normalization of relations" are somehow related to President Nixon's efforts to "normalize relations" with China. His trip to China didn't happen until 1972—two years after Dr. Codd published his paper. And the President was not a mathematician.

This table meets the first set of restrictions:

1. Data shall be organized into tables, each of which is defined by a set of unduplicated columns.

2. The sequence of rows in a table is not significant.

3. Each row is uniquely identified by a set of columns called a **primary key**. ("Unique identifier" in the corresponding *conceptual data model*.)

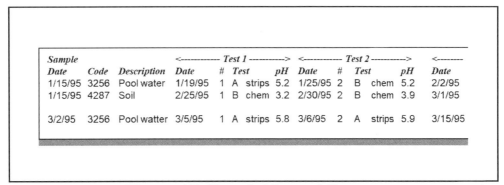

Figure 37: Zeroth Normal Form

First normal form (1NF):

Ensures each table has a valid primary key, and every column depends on the primary key; removes repeating groups, and ensures each column is atomic (not multi-valued). 1NF includes the resolution of many-to-many relationships by adding rows for each of the elements of the repeating group.

The sequence of columns is not significant.

Every column may have only *one value* for a *row* in a table.

Figure 38 shows that the table, **TEST**— derived from Figure 37—has been re-worked to follow this constraint. Here the multiple "Test…" entries now each get their own instances in **TEST**. In this case, "Test#" has now become part of the primary key, in combination with columns "Sample Date" and "Material Code".

There is, however, an anomaly in this table: Values for "Material Description" are dependent only on "Material Code", not the whole key. Indeed this means that values for "Material Description" are duplicated whenever "Material Code" appears. This introduces the opportunity for errors— such as "Pool Watter".

Second normal form (2NF):

This ensures each table has the minimal primary key and that every column depends on the complete primary key.

The value of each column must be dependent on the entire primary key.

Figure 39 shows introduction of a second table **MATERIAL**. This is an example of an **intersect table**. The primary key of the new table is "Material Code". This is repeated as a foreign key column in **TEST**. Now each material, no matter how many times it is tested, gets just one instance in the **MATERIAL** table.

TEST no longer has any columns dependent on only part of the primary key.

There remains one anomaly, however: values for "Test Desc'n" exactly correspond to those for "Test Type". That is, apparently, "Test Desc'n" is dependent on "Test Type". This leads us to the next form.

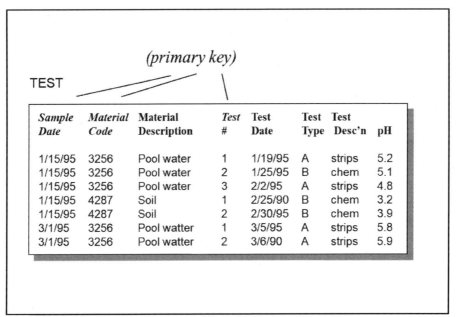

Figure 38: First Normal Form

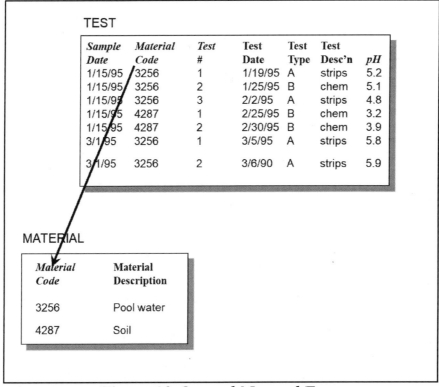

Figure 39: Second Normal Form

Third normal form (3NF):

Ensures each table has no hidden primary keys and that each column depends on no columns outside the key ("the key, the whole key and nothing but the key"♥).

Each column must be dependent on *only* the primary key.

Figure 40 shows how this constraint may be met by separating out a third table for **TEST—TEST TYPE**. Its primary key is "Test Type", which is identical to the foreign key Column "Test Type" in **TEST**.

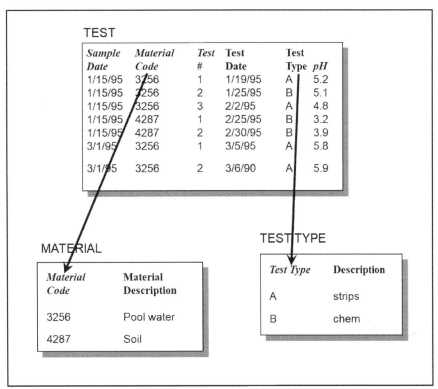

Figure 40: Third Normal Form

The process of normalization provides a systematic way to arrive at the least redundant design. It is the case, however, that the result is exactly the same as that arrived at it by an entity/relationship modeler who understands what the meaning of each "thing of significance" is. From there, it is easy to see what is truly a column describing that thing. The result of the exercise should have been arrived at from the problem being properly modeled, as shown in Figure 41.

There are some more arcane "Normal Forms" as well.

Boyce / Codd normal form (BCNF):

Figure 42 adds to our example the concept of "Location"—the place where the test was conducted. In addition, for this example, "Sample Date" and "Test Date" have been combined into "Date", under the assumption that both events always happen on the same day.

Boyce/Codd normal form resolves overlapping composite candidate keys. A candidate key is either a primary or an alternative key. *Composite* means more than one (e.g. two or more columns in an entity's primary or alternate keys), and *overlapping* refers to hidden business rules between the keys.

♥   … so help me Codd." (Sorry, couldn't resist…)

In Figure 42, the columns "Mat'l Type", "Test Type" and "Location" would appear to be primary keys. What is not clear initially is that there is *a correlation between* "Test Type" and "Location". Only Test Type "A" is conducted in the "Yard". Only Test Type "B" happens in the "Lab". It's unclear from this sample whether the "Yard" can only conduct tests of Test Type "A". Either way, **TEST** is not in **Boyce-Codd Normal Form.**

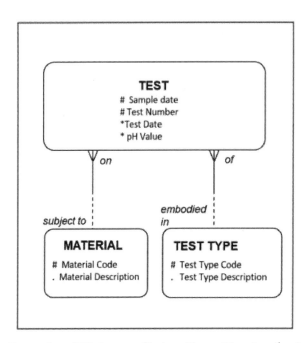

Figure 41: The Result of "Normalizing" an Entity/relationship Model

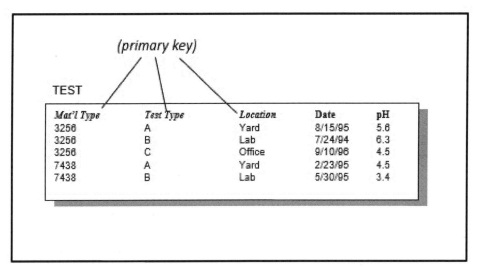

Figure 42: Boyce-Codd Setup

No key column may be dependent on another key column.

You can see in Figure 43 that there is not a single answer. A single table is spun off to describe the correlation between "Location" and "Test Type". But it doesn't matter whether the "Test Type" foreign key or the "Location" foreign key appears in the **TEST** table.

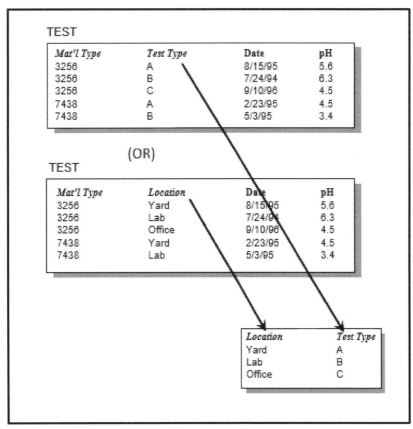

Figure 43: Boyce-Codd Normal Form

Fourth normal form (4NF):

Resolves all many-to-many-to-many relationships (and beyond) in pairs until they cannot be broken down into any smaller pieces.

C.J Date has compiled very thorough definitions of all the normal forms up through and including fifth normal form.[142] Unfortunately, they are defined in technical terms that make—for the purposes of this book—the last ones particularly difficult to understand.

In particular, the criteria for whether something is in fifth normal form is not internal. It concerns whether the model describes what is actually going on. If it does, it's in fifth normal form. If not, then it is not.

Figure 44(a) shows a variation on our example, renaming **TEST** to **POTENTIAL TEST**, and adding the column that shows each test be *by* someone.

There may be no independent sets of dependencies within a primary key.

If there is no correlation between any of the primary key columns, it is in fourth normal form. In Figure 44(a), this suggests that there is no correlation between "Test Type" and "Conducted By".

On the other hand, if there is a correlation, separate tables (in Figure 44(b)) show **CONDUCTORS** (who conducts the tests for each "Test Type"), and **TEST LOCATIONS** (where each "Test Type" is conducted).

---

142   Date, C.J, Darwen, Hugh. 2000. *Foundation for Future Database System: The Third Manifesto.* (Reading, MA: Addison-Wesley).

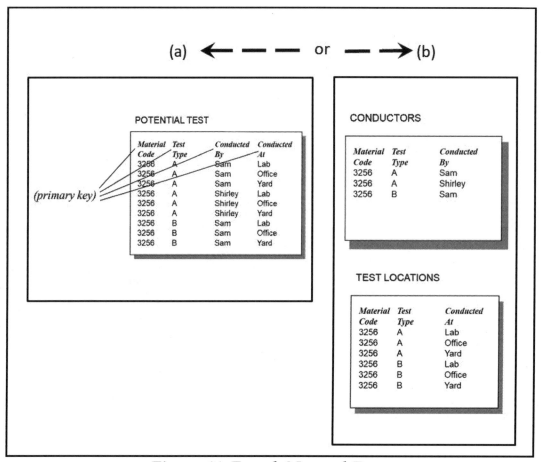

Figure 44: Fourth Normal Form

Fifth normal form (5NF):

Resolves inter-table dependencies into basic pairs, and all join dependencies use parts of primary keys.

Figures 45 and 45 show two configurations of three "reference tables"—**MATERIAL TYPE**, **TEST TYPE**, and **LOCATION**—plus the intersect tables that link each pair together.

In one case— where there are instances linking *all three* of the reference tables—you have the super-intersect table, **TEST MATERIAL LOCATION**.

Note that this is not a characteristic of the data structure, but rather the extent to which the drawing corresponds to the real world.

Version 2 (Figure 45), on the other hand, does contain instances of three-way intersects. For example, **MATERIAL TYPE** "4287" had conducted a **TEST TYPE** B at **LOCATION TYPE** "14", despite the fact that the standard **LOCATION TYPE** of **TEST TYPE** B is "18". Indeed, the standard **LOCATION TYPE** for **MATERIAL** "4287" is also "18".

In Version 2 (Figure46) there is no situation that requires the three-way intersect. There is no case where a particular **MATERIAL TYPE** / **LOCATION TYPE** / **TEST TYPE** would have any instances.

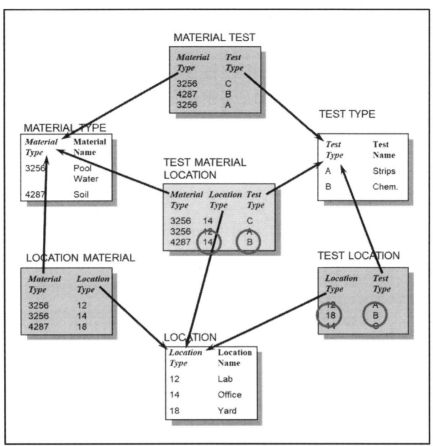

Figure 45: Fifth Normal Form Alternative 1

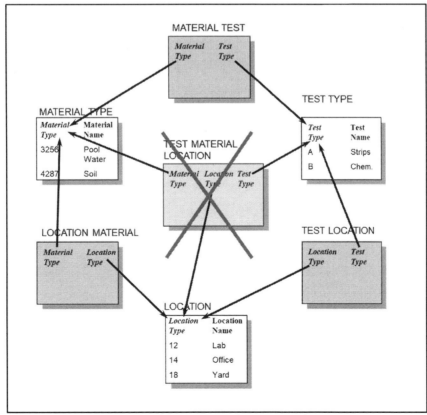

Figure 46: Fifth Normal Form Alternative 2

The term *normalized model* usually means the data is in 3NF. Situations requiring BCNF, 4NF, and 5NF occur rarely.

Denormalization

Denormalization is the deliberate transformation of normalized logical data model entities into physical tables with redundant or duplicate data structures. In other words, denormalization intentionally puts one attribute in multiple places. It actually happens in three stages, beginning with the creation of the *logical* (or at least *relational*) model:

> ➢ **Default Database design (essential to logical model)**

> If an essential model has been prepared on a computerized modeling (*CASE)* tool, a utility can convert it to a first-draft logical (relational) model:

> ✓ Entity types are converted to table definitions

> ✓ Attributes are converted to column definitions

> ✓ Sub-types are generated as separate, related tables.

While these are steps that modify the logical model, there are other steps that can be taken when the physical model is generated. These will be described in "Step Two Denormalization" (page 129).

Step One Denormalization

At this point, the database designer must make some design decisions, based on expectations of how the data will be used. These are among the **engineering trade-offs** that a designer must make to accomplish system objectives in the face of physical limitations. The idealized essential model probably won't fit in a real computerized system without some modifications. This is described in more detail in the "Create Logical Models" section of Chapter 6, "The Development Process"(pages 143ff). In brief, though, the important decisions are summarized here:

> ✓ **Sub-type decisions**

> These concern default logic prepared one table for each sub-type. That is, all of the resulting tables inherit any common attributes from the parent, but otherwise are different. This is appropriate if there are many attributes that are different from sub-type to sub-type, or if the various tables are to be used by different people. Moreover, some sub-typed tables may have relationships to other tables that others do not.

> This approach means that all attributes of (and relationships to) the super-type must be replicated in each sub-type table implementation.

> However, if there is little variation among sub-types (or if most of the prospective users are from the same population), a single, combined table with sub-type attributes as optional columns might be ideal.

> A column called "<table> Type" is added whose value for each instance of the combined table is an indicator of the sub-type entity it came from[*]. Any attributes that were mandatory in the sub-type cannot be made mandatory in this table. Such "mandatoriness" must be implemented via software business rules.

---

[*] This presumes that the sub-types within the super-type were all constrained to be mutually exclusive. This is the assumption in the Barker/Ellis approach.

✓ **Derived attribute/column decisions**

If the components of derived attributes/columns are stable, and they are queried frequently, it is best to compute and store values when they are entered. If they are more dynamic, it's better to compute when they are retrieved.

1. **Calculated and stored on input** - Queries can be much faster, but if the components change, there is maintenance required to update the stored fields. Assuming components are relatively stable, derived columns that are inferred from parents (like "{Price}" in a **Line Item** inferred from the "List Price" stored in the parent table **Product Type**) should be derived and stored when the data are entered.

2. **Calculated when retrieved** - The retrieved value is always current—by definition—but it can add considerable processing time to the queries. As an example, if a derived column is summarized in a parent table from data in child tables (such as "Total Value" for a **Contract** summarized across all component **Line Items**), this should not be stored, but derived only when requested.

➢ **Parameter/Attribute Decisions**

Where characteristics describing entity types were separated into **Characteristic**, **Parameter**, or **Type** entity types, queries against databases with this structure can be very time-consuming indeed. In certain cases, specific parameters (like "Birthdate" for a Person) are relatively well-defined and relatively stable. These then could revert to being stored as columns in their respective table. Others—especially those that change over time—should be left in their **...Parameter** or **...Type** tables.

> **WARNING:**
>
> Any decision to optimize performance for a particular process will *cost* performance in *some other process*. These are the *trade-offs* that are fundamental to the design process.
>
> Each decision should be tested overall to ensure that the benefit is actually received.
>
> *Moreover* each decision should be *documented*, so that subsequent designers will know exactly *why* that particular design was made—
>
> … and how to *back out of it* when the physical conditions have *changed*.

Dimensional Model

A **Dimensional Model** is a database structure that is optimized for online queries—specifically in the case of data warehousing applications. It is composed of **fact tables** and **dimension tables**. It can be either normalized or de-normalized.[143]

A "fact" is a numeric value that a business wishes to count or sum. A "dimension" is essentially an entry point for getting at the fact. Dimensions are hierarchical expressions of things of interest to the business.

---

[143] This section is derived from the DAMA International. 2017. *DMBOK: Data Management Body of Knowledge.* (Technics Publications). Pp. 138-140.

Star Schema

Dimensional data models capture business definitions in terms of facts. Figure 47 shows an example of a dimensional model, called a **star schema** . This version is denormalized to one level. A sales report could be organized by quarter, product group, and state. If the numbers for a state called for further analysis, one could "drill down" to see individual stores. Alternatively, if a particular quarter looked problematic, one could drill down to month or even a day.[*]

The diagramming notation used to build this model—the axis technique—can be a very effective communication tool for those who prefer not to read traditional data modeling syntax.

This example only shows dimensions for "when", "where", and "what". Other dimensions could be added identifying "who" (e.g., customers and customer groups) and "why" (e.g., marketing approaches).

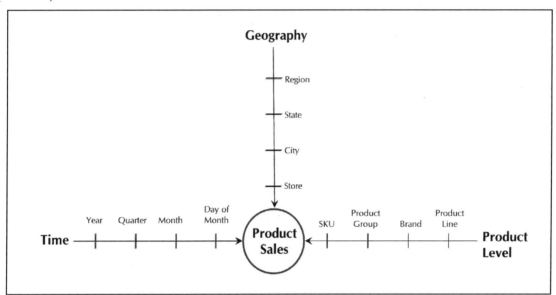

Figure 47: Axis Technique for Dimensional Models

In dimensional data modeling, denormalization is called "collapsing" or "combining". If each dimension is collapsed into a single structure, the resulting data model is also called a **Star Schema**. Figure 48 illustrates a dimensional logical star schema data model with "tables" for **Time**, **Geography**, and **Product**, in addition to **Product Sales**. Note that there is one table for each dimension).

This physical model is based on the Logical Dimensional Model shown above in Figure 47). Each of the dimension bars shown there is a table here. Note that all of the tick marks show up as attributes in each of the dimensional tables.

---

[*] Lest the reader thinks that times have really changed, 'e should be advised that this example is from one of your author's very first projects. It was for Bird's Eye Vegetables and it nicely solved a problem they had with understanding vegetable sales across the country. Mind you, this was done in 1971! It used a computer time-sharing facility, where the user interface was a 10 character-per-second teletype machine. (Reports were via a dot-matrix printer.) Moreover, it was all done in the Basic language! It is reasonable to assume that it was your author who first came up with the terms "dimensions" and "drill-down". These were the terms he invented to present this facility to his audiences.

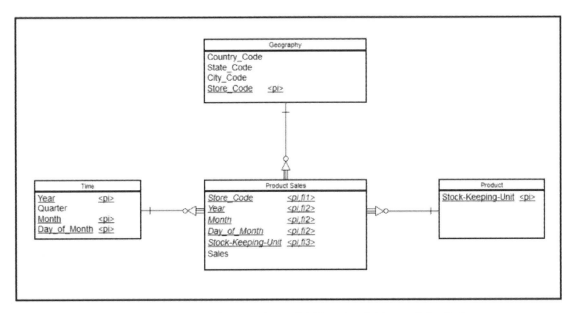

Figure 48: Dimensional Physical Data Model

Fact Tables

Within a dimensional scheme, the rows of a **fact table** each correspond to a particular measurement and are numeric, such as amounts, quantities, or counts. Some measurements are the results of algorithms, in which cases metadata documentation is critical to proper understanding and usage. Fact tables take up the most space in the database (90% is a reasonable rule of thumb), and tend to have a large number of rows. The *fact table* in Figure 47 is for **Product Sales.**

The "Sales" number in the example is the most atomic value for a particular date, stock-keeping-unit, and store.

Dimension Tables

A **dimension table** consists of a hierarchy of the classes that constitute the structure of the business. Each of the tick marks in Figure 47 represents a short table listing the values for each. These contain mostly textual descriptions. Queries can accumulate totals along one or more of the dimensions; for example, these might provide totals for the quarter, the city, and/or the product line.

In this star schema example, the dimensions are highly de-normalized. Dimensions must have a unique identifier for each row. Typically, the rows are identified by surrogate keys. In the case of relatively short lists, such as **Product Group,** these keys could be human-assigned abbreviations.

Dimensions also have attributes that change at different rates. Slowly changing dimensions (SCDs) manage changes based on the rate and type of change. The three main types of change are:

➢ **Overwrite (Type 1):**
The new value overwrites the old value in place.

➢ **New Row (Type 2):**
The new values are written in a new row, and the old row is marked as not current.

> ➢ **New Column (Type 3):**

Multiple instances of a value are listed in columns on the same row, and a new value means writing the values in the series one spot down to make space at the front for the new value. The last value is discarded.

Snowflake Schema

Where the star schema is de-normalized to provide some performance benefits, the **snowflake schema** is for those who want a schema closer to the normalized version. Taking the dimensions described above and splitting them out into their component tables provides a scheme that looks more like a **snowflake.** This is shown in Figure 49.

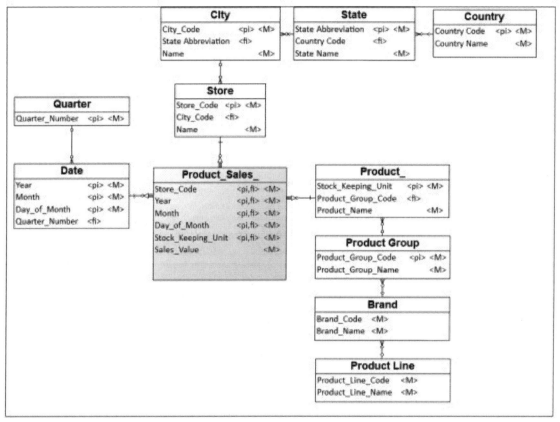

Figure 49: Snowflake Schema

Conformed Dimensions

Conformed dimensions are shared across multiple data marts or fact tables. It is important for the row headers from any answer sets from conformed dimensions must match exactly.

When data are gathered from multiple sources, the dimensions must be reconciled across the sources and with internally generated data. For products, product categories from syndicated data sources must be matched to those managed internally, time units must match, and so forth. The geographic tables above (**Country**, **State**, and **City**) should in fact already exist elsewhere in the database—with these values.[144]

---

144   Ralph Kimball. 1996. *The Data Warehouse Toolkit.* (John Wiley & Sons).

Conformed Facts

Conformed facts use standardized definitions of terms across individual marts. Different business users may use the same term in different ways. "Customer additions" may be different from "gross additions" or "adjusted additions." Developers must be keenly aware of things that may be named similarly but actually represent different concepts across enterprises, and of things that are named differently but are actually the same concept.

In other words, the **Product Value** ("Sales") value (for the specified Date, SKU, and Store) should exist elsewhere in the data warehouse—and mean exactly the same thing.

Object-oriented Model (UML)

The Unified Modeling Language (UML) is a graphical language for modeling software. The UML has a variety of notations of which one (the *class model*) concerns databases. The UML class model specifies classes (analogous to entity types) and their associations (analogous to relationships).[145] Figure 49 illustrates characteristics of a UML Class Model. The notation is described more completely in Appendix C.

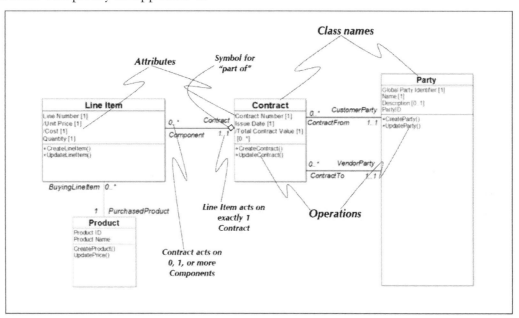

Figure 50 UML Class Model

UML and entity/relationship modeling

A class diagram is analogous to an entity/relationship diagram except for both:

> ➤ **The Operations or Methods section**
> This section exists in UML models but is not present in an entity/relationship model. An operation is a specification of how a class might be manipulated.[146] A method is the process that implements the operation.[147] Methods appear in UML classes.

---

[145]   Michael Blaha. 2014. *UML Database Modeling Workbook.* (Technics Publications).

[146]   James Rumbaugh, Ivar Jacobson, Grady Booch. 1999. *The Unified Modeling Language Reference Manual.* (Addison-Wesley). P. 369.

➢ **Associations / Relationships**

In either an essential entity/relationship model or in a relational database design, each *relationship* represents *two structural assertions* about two elements. By definition, the whole relationship is about the two of them as a set. The relationship names are constructed to produce the two clear assertion sentences. For example, in Figure 7 (page 40), it was asserted that "each **Contract** may be *composed of* one or more **Line Items**," and "each **Line Item** must be *part of* one and only one **Contract**."

A UML *association*, on the other hand, describes the *processing* necessary to get from one to the other. Each is described on each end by the *rolename* the target class played in processing.[148] Thus, in Figure 50, it can only assert that each **Contract** acts upon 0, 1, or more instances of the class playing the role *component*. Stated differently, the "behavior" doesn't even *see* the second *class* (in this case, **Line Item**); it can only act on the *role* (*component*). In UML, the association is a property of a class, as are its attributes. The uniqueness of all of these is assured because the class defines a *namespace*. Since the related class is *itself* a namespace, it cannot be part of the semantics of named assocation. Thus, the Barker/Ellis approach to naming relationships cannot apply to these particular cases. (Without some tweaking, that is. See your author's book on *UML and Data Modeling: A Reconciliation*[149] for details on how to do it.)

Note that UML does provide the ability to document a relationship with an *association class*. That is, this is a class that describes properties of the association that are not particular to each associated class. This provides exactly the same funcionality as an *intersect entity* in an entity/relationship model—with the exeption that in the UML model, you cannot have more than one instance of an association class. For example, if an intersect entity, such as **Project assignment,** could assign one **Project** to one **Person**. If this is described with an attribute such as the "Effective Date", added to the intersect entity's identifier, a **Person** (for example, "Sarah") could be assigned to a **Project** (such as "Project X") more than once. If it is described by an association class, the class is only identified by the two associated classes. You cannot have more than one instance of that class between the specified associated classes.

➢ **Sub-types**

As in an essential (entity/relationship) model, a sub-type in UML represents a sub-set of the instances of one super-type class. The concept of inheritance, while it is very important in Essential Models, *cannot* be directly implemented in a relational database. Ironically, it *is* covered well by a UML model. Understand that a UML model *does* have an ability to describe an association as a sub-type of another association. ♦

➢ **Attributes**

In UML, attribute types (Date, String, etc.) are expressed in the implementable application code language, not in physical DB implementable terminology.

The presentation of attributes in UML is more descriptive in UML than in entity/relationship diagrams:

---

[147] *Ibid.* p. 346.

[148] *Ibid.* p. 414.

[149] Hay, 2011. *UML... op. cit.*

♦ This is a feature that is sorely missing from entity / relationship modeling.

✓ Default values can optionally be shown.

✓ That an attribute is derived can optionally be shown.

The original goal of UML class modeling was to support object-oriented *programming*. The differences between relational database design and object-oriented class design, it didn't lend itself to modeling in the relational (or even conceptual) world. By modifying its assumptions, however, and imposing good modeling practices, the UML notation was adapted to present essential (conceptual) models for your author's book *Enterprise Model Patterns: Describing the World.* [150] The adaptation was described in a second book *UML and Data Modeling: A Reconciliation.*[151]

Time-Based Model – Data Vault

Data Vault originated as an approach to modeling the structure of a data warehouse. Data Vault 2.0 has expanded beyond that original scope, becoming a "system of business intelligence containing the necessary components needed to accomplish enterprise vision in Data Warehousing and Information Delivery. Data Vault 2.0 – is truly a solution, comprising Architecture, Methodology, Modeling, and implementation. A company can use the Data Vault model by itself, but will only gain about 15% to 20% of the overall benefits." [152]

The definitions presented here are from Daniel Linstedt's 2016 book, *Building a Scalable Data Warehouse with Data Vault 2.0.* [153]

Data Vault models have at their core three kinds of entity types:

➢ **Hub**
A *hub* is a unique list of business keys where each key points to an underlying thing of significance to the enterprise. The set of hubs in a data vault comprise the keys to all reference entity types. "The purpose of a hub entity is to store the business keys of [a] business object along with some other information, which is called the metadata."

➢ **Link**
A *link* is a unique list of relationships, each of which is among two or more business keys. The relationships each represent the transactions by which business is conducted. "Business objects are connected to each other through the operational business processes that use business objects in the execution of their tasks."[154] These correspond to the intersect entity types in the essential model.

➢ **Satellite**
A *satellite* is a collection of the columns that describe either a hub or a link. A satellite stores "the columns that belong to either a business key (in a hub), [a] relationship or a transaction (in a link)."[155]

---

[150] Hay. 2011. Enterprise Model Patterns. op. cit.

[151] Hay. 2011. UML and … op. cit.

[152] Daniel Linstedt. 2018. Correspondence with your author.

[153] Daniel Linstedt and Michel Olschimke. 2016. *Building a Scalable Data Warehouse with Data Vault 2.0.* (Morgan Kaufmann). pp. 91.

[154] Ibid.

[155] Ibid.

The essential data model "Contract Roles" (Figure 28, page 84), is reintroduced here as a default logical model in Figure 51.

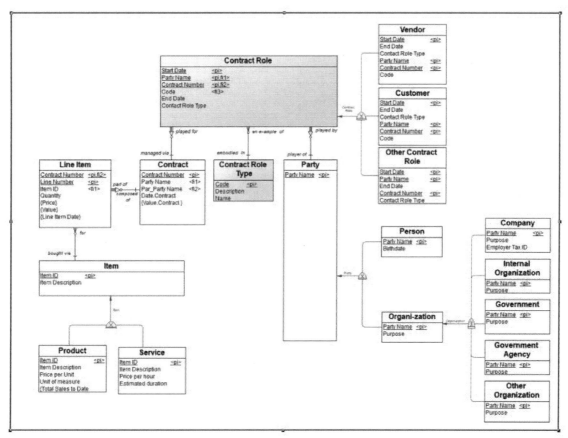

Figure 51: Information Engineering Logical Diagram – Contract Roles

Note that the PowerDesigner utility that generated this logical diagram made the assumption that each sub-type would be created as a separate table. This can be modified in the physical model, as it has been in the satellites of the Data Vault model shown in Figure 52.

The Data Vault example shown here, however, first addresses references **Party** and **Contract,** plus the relationship between them called **Contract Role**. Specifically, it includes[156]:

> **Hub**
>
> The reference tables **Party** and **Contract** here become hubs:

✓ HUB_PARTY

✓ HUB_CONTRACT

Note that they both have the same columns:
- HUB_PARTY_KEY – A system generated unique identifier for each instance of **HUB_CONTRACT** (the *hash key*).
- <Local Identifier> – one or more natural keys as alternative identifiers for each instance of **HUB_CONTRACT** (the *business key*).
- HUB_load_DTS – The date each instance of **HUB_CONTRACT** was loaded.
- HUB_load_SRC – The source system for each instance of **HUB_CONTRACT**.

---

156 Ibid.

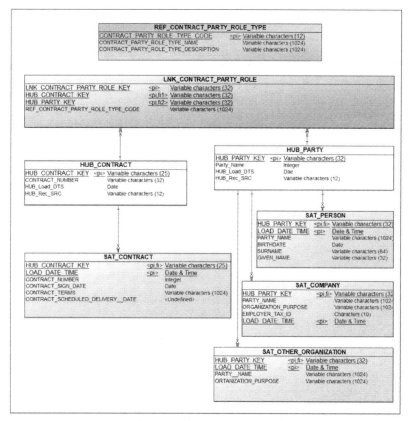

Figure 52: Data Vault

Note that the ***hash key*** is a system-generated unique identifier for a hub. In the past, hash keys have been generated by an industry standard algorithm, such as "MD5". The MD5 algorithm is a popular hash function that produces a 128 bit hash value.[157] The hash key logic is now optional, though, based on whether the platform supports internal hashing of the business keys.

All other columns for these "things of significance" are contained in associated satellites, described below.

Note that each hub has what may be called a ***business key***. This is the set of columns that uniquely identify this business object in its source system. Since the uniqueness of a key may be only in the context of the source system, a ***hash key*** may also be generated. Queries can use the hash key to avoid joining all the business key columns in a query.[158]

➢ **Link**

In the logical model, the entity type **Contract Role** can be rendered in the data vault as:

✓ LINK_CONTRACT_PARTY_ROLE

Its columns are simply the foreign keys to the two linked hubs, plus a link identifier:

– LINK_CONTRACT_PARTY_ROLE_KEY – A system generated unique identifier for each instance of the link table.
– HUB_CONTRACT_KEY – a foreign key pointing to the **Contract** hub.
– HUB_PARTY_KEY – a foreign key pointing to the **Party** hub.

---

157   Wikipedia. 2017. MD5. (Retrieved October 8, 2017 from *https://en.wikipedia.org/wiki/MD5*).

158   Ibid, p. 98.

➤ **Satellite**

These are the columns that describe the hubs. A satellite's columns consist of a foreign key to the related hub table, plus the descriptive columns from the hub's source entity type. For example:

✓ SAT_CONTRACT
 – <u>HUB_CONTRACT_KEY</u> – the foreign key linking this satellite to its hub, **Contract**.
 – <u>LOAD_DATE_TIME</u> – for each instance, the data and time it was loaded into this data vault.

 The remaining columns are specific to each instance of **Contract.**
 – contract_date
 – contract_number
 – contract_terms
 – contract_delivery_date

Transforming the logical model into a physical model requires us to address the sub-types. For our purposes here, we will assume that **Person** and **Company** will be tables, with all other **Organization** instances grouped into **Other Organization**. The following satellites accomplish this. The columns include some inherited from **Party**, and others specific to the sub-type.

✓ SAT_PERSON
 – *HUB_PARTY_KEY* – the foreign key linking this satellite to its hub, **Party**.
 – LOAD_DATE_TIME – for each instance, the data and time it was loaded into this data vault.

 The remaining columns are specific to each instance of **Person**
 – party_name
 – birthdate
 – given_name
 – surname

✓ SAT_COMPANY
 – <u>HUB_PARTY_KEY</u> – the foreign key linking this satellite to its hub, **Party**.
 – <u>LOAD_DATE_TIME</u> – for each instance, the data and time it was loaded into this data vault.

 The remaining columns are specific to each instance of **Company**
 – party_name
 – organization_purpose
 – employer_tax_id
 – company_name

✓ SAT_OTHER ORGANIZATION
 – <u>*HUB_PARTY_KEY*</u> – the foreign key linking this satellite to its hub, **Party**.
 – <u>LOAD_DATE_TIME</u> – for each instance, the data and time it was loaded into this data vault.

The remaining columns are those inherited from super-types **Party** and **Organization**. If the other sub-types of **Organization** had unique columns, they would appear in **SAT_Other_Organization** as well.
- – party_name
- – organization_purpose

➢ **Reference Data**

Contains a table of a kind that is not in the above list. Indeed it is only tangentially referred to in Messrs Linstedt and Olschimke's book.[159]

✓ REF_CONTRACT_PARTY_ROLE_TYPE.

This is a convenient way of dealing with the fact that LINK_CONTRACT_PARTY_ROLES may be classified. That is, this entity type recognizes that the role played by a Contract Party Role may be "Customer" or "Vendor". More significantly, an instance of REF_CONTRACT_PARTY_ROLE_TYPE could be another role, such as "Distributor", "Wholesaler", etc.

The table's coluns are:
- – CONTRACT_PARTY_ROLE_TYPE_CODE – a probably user-assigned abbreviation used to identify each instance of **REF_CONTRACT_PARTY_ROLE_TYPE.**
- – CONTRACT_PARTY_ROLE_TYPE_NAME – a short name labeling and/or identifying each instance of **CONTRACT_PARTY_ROLE_TYPE.**
- – CONTRACT_PARTY_ROLE_TYPE_DESCRIPTION – a long text characterizing the nature of each instance of **CONTRACT_PARTY_ROLE_TYPE.**

Note the addition of a "foreign key" column to **LNK_CONTRACT_PARTY_ROLE:**
- – ref_contract_party_role_type_code

XML Schema

XML is a language developed to support data communications. It consists of **tags** that encapsulate pieces of data hierarchically. Script 6 shows a sample. Here are some things to observe in Script 6:

1. Tags always appear in pairs. For example, `<product>` begins the script, and `</product>` ends it.

2. A tag can contain a string of characters (as in `<number>` and `<size>`, or it can contain a complex set of statements (as in `<product>`).

3. Sometimes a tag can have an "attribute" (as in `effDate="2001-04-02"`).

Script 6: Sample XML Script[160]

```
<product effDate="2001-04-02">

    <number>557</number>

    <size>10</size>

</product>
```

---

159   Linstedt & Olschimke. 2016. *Op. cit. Pp. 618-619.*

160   Walmsley, P.2002. *Definitive XML Schema.* (Prentice Hall).

Note that the tag names are all defined by the application. None of the ones shown are in "XML language". As such, we need a mechanism for defining those tags. This is achieved by a kind of XML called ***XML Schema***.

Script 7 shows the schema behind the bit of XML shown in Script 6. This reveals several things:

1. This script is dominated by tags defined specifically for XML Schema. These are all preceded by `<xsd:…>`.

2. All XML Schema scripts begin with `<xsd:schema…>` and end with `</xsd:schema>`, as seen in Script 7.

Script 7: Sample XML Schema[161]

```
<xsd:schema xmlns:xsd="http://ww.w3.org/2001/XMLSchema>

    <xsd:element name="product" type="ProductType"/>

    <xsd:complexType name="ProductType">

        <xsd:sequence>

            <xsd:element name="number" type="xsd:integer"/>

            <xsd:element name="size" type="SizeType"/>

        </xsd:sequence>

        <xsd:attribute name="effDate" type="xsd:date"/>

        </xsd:complexType>

    <xsd:simpleType name="SizeType">

        <xsd:restriction base="xsd:integer">

            <xsd:minInclusive value="2"/>

            <xsd:maxInclusive value="18"/>

        <xsd:restriction/>

    </xsd:simpleType>

</xsd:schema>
```

3. The XML tag `<product>` is represented in XML Schema as an **xsd:element**. It is defined with attributes `name="product"`, and `type="Product Type"`.

4. In this case, the "/" character is at the end of this line, so there is no need for a separate termination tag at the end.

5. `Product Type`, in turn, is represented as an **xsd:complexType**. It is "complex" because it consists of an `xsd:sequence` consisting of other `xsd:elements`— specifically, defining "`number`" and "`size`", as seen in the original script.

6. The `xsd:element` with the `name` "`number`" itself has a `type`— in this case "`xsd:integer`". Since it is a recognized "`xsd:`" term, this completes the definition.

---

[161] Ibid.

7. The `xsd:element` with the name "size", on the other hand has a `type` ("SizeType") which itself must be further defined.

8. Thus **xsd:SimpleType**, with name="SizeType", is an `xsd:simpleType` because it consists simply of an `xsd: restriction`. The restriction has three components:

   ✓ <xsd: restriction base="xsd:integer">   ... the format of the variable

   ✓ <xsd:minInclusive value="2"/>   ... The minimum value it can take

   ✓ <xsd:maxInclusive value="18"/>   ... The maximum value it can take

NoSQL

NoSQL is the name for a category of very large (*big data*) databases built on non-relational technology. NoSQL is not a good name for what it represents as it is less about how to query the database (which is where SQL comes in), than it is about how the data are stored (non-relational structures). Even Carlo Surozzes, who chose the name in 1998 for his lightweight, open-source relational database , suggests that "NoREL" would have been a better name than NoSQL.[162]

The definitions in this section are derived from Dan Sullivan's 2015 book, *NoSQL for Mere Mortals*.[163] The reader is strongly encouraged to consult that book for more details on each of the concepts described here.

There are four main types of NoSQL databases: document, key-value, column-oriented, and graph.

Document

Instead of taking a business subject and breaking it up into multiple relational structures, document databases frequently store the business subject in one structure called a *document*. For example, instead of storing Student, Course, and Registration information in three distinct relational structures, properties from all three will exist in a single document called Registration. Document-oriented models are generally application focused, whereas table-oriented models are more data focused.

Documents contain both structure information and data. The name in a name-value pair indicates an attribute and the value in a name-value pair is the data assigned to that attribute. JSON and XML are two formats commonly used to define documents.

Collections can be thought of as lists of documents. Document database designers optimize document databases to quickly add, remove, update, and search for documents. They are also designed for scalability, so as your document collection grows, you can add more servers to your cluster to keep up with demands for your database.

Key-value

One kind of database is a *key-value database.* This allows an application to store its data in only two columns ("key" and "value"), with more complex information sometimes stored within the

---

162 Wikipedia. (Retrieved 3/7/2018 from *https://en.wikipedia.org/wiki/NoSQL*).

163 Dan Sullivan. 2015. *NoSQL for Mere Mortals*. (Addison Wesley Professional).

"value" columns. A ***key*** is a reference to a value. Keys in key-value databases are similarly not values but are ways of finding and manipulating values. A ***value*** is an object, typically described in a set of bytes, which has been associated with a key. Values can be integers, floating-point numbers, strings of characters, binary large objects (BLOBs), semi-structured constructs such as JSON-defined objects, images, audio, and just about any other data type you can represent as a series of bytes.

Column-oriented

Out of the four types of NoSQL databases, ***column-oriented database*** is closest to the relational structure. Both have an analogous way of looking at data as rows and values. The difference, though, is that RDBMSs work with a predefined structure and simple data types, such as string, number, and date, whereas column-oriented databases, such as Cassandra, can work with more complex data types including unformatted text, collections, and imagery. This data can also be defined on the fly. A column-oriented database is defined in terms of:

> ➤ **Keyspace –** the top-level data structure in a column family database. It is top level in the sense that all other data structures you would create as a database designer are contained within a keyspace. A keyspace is analogous to a schema in a relational database. Typically, you will have one keyspace for each of your applications.

> ➤ **Row Key -** uniquely identifies a row in a column family. It serves some of the same purposes as a primary key in a relational database. Row keys are one of the components used to uniquely identify values stored in a database. The others are column family names, column names, and a version ordering mechanism, such as a time stamp. Row keys are one of the components used to uniquely identify values stored in a database. The others are column family names, column names, and a version ordering mechanism, such as a time stamp.

> ➤ **Column -** the data structure for storing a single value in a database. Depending on the type of column family database you are using, you might find values are represented simply as strings of bytes. This minimizes the overhead on the database because it does not validate data types. HBase takes this approach.

> In other cases, you might be able to specify data types ranging from integers and strings to lists and maps. Cassandra's Query Language (CQL) offers almost 20 different data types. Values can vary in length. For example, a value could be as simple as a single integer, such as 12, or as complex as a highly structured XML document.

> Columns are members of column family databases. Database designers define column families when they create a database. However, developers can add columns any time after that. Just as you can insert data into a relational table, you can create new columns in column family databases.

> Note that, unlike in relational databases, a column may have multiple values. (See Figure 53.)

> Columns have three parts:

> ✓ A column name

> ✓ One or more values

> ✓ A time stamp or other version stamp for each value

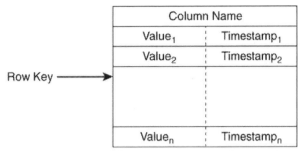

Figure 53: Column with Row Key and Versioned Values

➤ **Column Family** - Column families are collections of related columns. Columns that are frequently used together should be grouped into the same column family. For example, a customer's address information, such as street, city, state, and zip code, should be grouped together in a single column family. (See Figure 54.)

Street	City	State	Province	Zip	Postal Code	Country
178 Main St.	Boise	ID		83701		U.S.
89 Woodridge	Baltimore	MD		21218		U.S.
293 Archer St.	Ottawa		ON		K1A 2C5	Canada
8713 Alberta DR	Vancouver		BC		VSK 0AI	Canada

Figure 54: Column Family

Column families are stored in a keyspace. Each row in a column family is uniquely identified by a row key. This makes a column family analogous to a table in a relational database. There are important differences, however. Data in relational database tables is not necessarily maintained in a predefined order. Rows in relational tables are not versioned the way they are in column family databases.

Perhaps most importantly, columns in a relational database table are not as dynamic as in column family databases. Adding a column in a relational database requires changing its schema definition. Adding a column in a column family database just requires making a reference to it from a client application, for example, inserting a value to a column name.

Graph

A *graph database* is designed for data whose relations are well represented as a set of nodes with an undetermined number of connections between these nodes. Examples where a graph database can work best are social relations (where nodes are people), public transport links (where nodes could be bus or train stations), or roadmaps (where nodes could be street intersections or highway exits). Often requirements lead to traversing the graph to find the shortest routes, nearest neighbors, etc., all of which can be complex and time consuming to navigate with a traditional RDMBS. Graph databases in 2018 include Neo4J, Allegro, and Virtuoso.

Note that essential data models also are graphs. Here, however, the nodes are always *classes (entity types)*, not instances of those classes. The idea is to represent a domain in conceptual terms, describing it in terms of its fundamental entity types and relationships. If it is directly implemented as a relational database, however, querying that database may be difficult.

Figure 55 reproduces the Essential model presented in Figure 23, on page 76. Note that the nodes in this diagram are classes of things of significance, not instances.

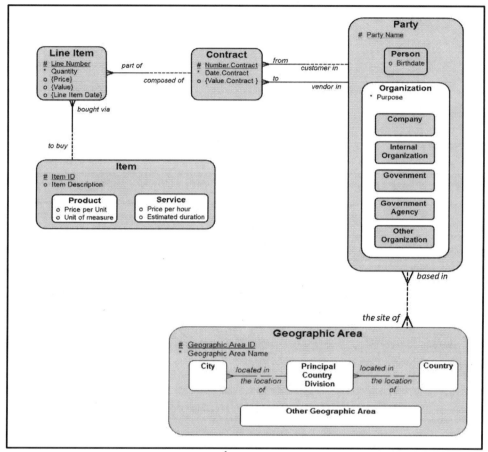

Figure 55: E/R Domain: Orders

Figure 56 shows a relational design that is a logical model derived from the above essential model. This is a ***third normal form*** version, that minimizes redundancy and, like the essential model, reflects the underlying structure of the enterprise. It does not, however, represent instances (rows) of any of the tables. Constructing queries to retrieve, for example, "Alice's order for "strawberry ice cream" would involve at least 5 joins. This could be mitigated somewhat by "denormalizing" the structure, but to do that for one kind of query would invariably do damage to other kinds of queries.

Note that any **Person** involved is actually a sub-type of **Party**, and any **Product** ordered is a sub-type of **Item**.

While constructing the essential model is the right first step in understanding the nature of the data, storing the data according to that model (i.e., relationally) is not always appropriate.

Figure 57 shows the graphic structure of several examples of **orders**. This was constructed from the interview sentences, "Alice placed orders on August 8, 2012 for strawberry ice cream, Brussels sprouts, and espresso beans." "Then on August 16, she also ordered more espresso beans." Specifically, the model in Figure 57 was created by Ian Robinson, Jim Webber, and Emil Eifram, and is reproduced from their book, *Graph Databases: New Opportunities for Connected Data.* [164]

---

[164] Ian Robinson, Jim Webber, & Emil Eifram. 2015. *Graph Databases: New Opportunities for Connected Data.* (O'Reilly

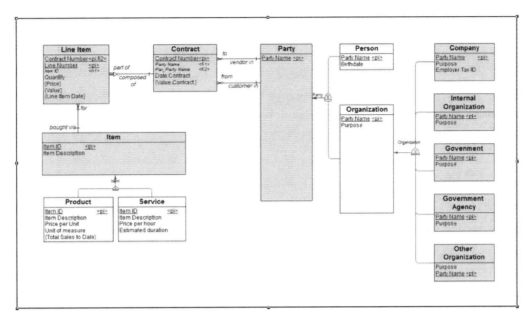

Figure 56: Relational Design: Orders

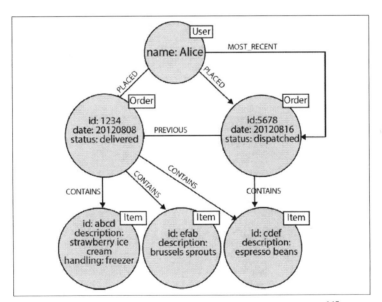

Figure 57: Graphic Version: Orders[165]

The resulting **Graph Model** consists of **nodes** (the circles with rectangular annotations) and **ridges** (the lines). Each of these is an *instance* of something encountered in the world. Each node includes a kind of classification; in the conceptual model, this would be called an ***entity type***. Here, this is represented by a box with the category name attached to the node circle.

The modelers who created this did not have the benefit of having first developed an essential model of the world. But when they asserted that there existed an "Alice: user" and an "Order1234:order", they were describing the **metadata** which corresponded to the entity types shown in Figure 55.

Media).

[165]   Drawing Copyright © 2015 Neo Technology, Inc., from Ian Robinson, etc. al. ibid.

Specifically, **User** is a category of significance—represented in the essential model as **Person** (a kind of **Party**). **Order** in the essential model shows up as **Contract**.

This is significant, because it is extremely likely that as the model expands, there will be a call to describe other people and other kinds of orders. These people won't necessarily be "users". Some might appear as "customers", while someone else might appear simply as a "hungry person". As the model becomes more and more complex, it will become important to ensure that, for example, the roles of all the people placing orders are consistent. Recognizing that Alice is a "person" would be a good start.

The texts in the process of developing a graph model could also be used to create a ***Resource Definition Framework (RDF)*** script in the context of the Semantic Web (see pages 57*ff*). This approach is similar to RDF's "subject", "predicate" and "object", where the predicate is an "edge", and the "subject" and "object" are "nodes".

The relationship names are rather casual as well, which provides some semantic problems. For example, while the dates of the orders make it clear that "Order 5678" was placed *after* "Order 1234", adding this relationship adds the opportunity for it to be wrong. Specifically (the arrow head is hidden, but it appears to be on the left), to say that "Order 5678" is *previous* to "Order 1234" is simply incorrect.

While is worthy to name nodes and lines so they can be easily read, applying some Barker/Ellis entity/relationship rules to these graphs can also be very beneficial.

Your author's version is shown in Figure 58.

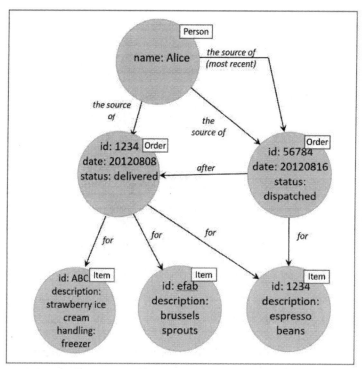

Figure 58: Graphic Version (DCH) Orders

Note that the relationship names are similar to those used in the Barker/Ellis approach[*]:

➢ Alice PLACED Order 5678 becomes Alice is *the source of* Order 5678.

➢ Order 5678 PREVIOUS Order 1234 becomes Order 5678 is *after* Order 1234.

➢ Order 1234 CONTAINS Item abcd becomes Order 1234 is *for* Item abcd.

➢ Alice is no longer a **User** but a **Person**.

➢ **Order** is a reasonable synonym for **Contract**, so that wasn't changed.

➢ **Item** is exactly the same as in the essential model.

In your author's version of the Neo4j language, *Cypher*, the resulting statements are shown in Script 8.

Script 8: Cypher Statements for Order Graph Model

```
CREATE     (alice:Person {name:Alice}),

           (order1234:Order {id:1234, date:20120808,status:delivered}),

           (order5678:Order {id:5678, date:20120816, status:dispatched}),

           (icecream:Item {id:abcd, description:strawberry ice Cream,
           handling:freezer}),

           (bsprouts:Item {id:efab, description:brussels sprouts}),

           (ebeans:Item {id:cdef, description:espresso beans}),

           (alice)-[:source_of]->(order1234),

           (alice)-[:source_of]->(order5678),

           (alice)-[:source_of(most-recent)]->(order5678),

           (order5678)-[:after]->(order1234),

           (order1234)-[:for]->(icecream),

           (order1234)-[:for]->(bsprouts),

           (order1234)-[:is_for]->(ebeans),

           (order5678)-[:is_for]->(ebeans).
```

Physical Model

The physical "data model" is typically not graphical at all. Its specific shape will depend on the technology being used. Until recent years, the design of a database focused on the design of a single, relational database. This entailed defining how the data might be organized in terms of groups called **tablespaces**.

A **tablespace** is a storage location where the actual data underlying database objects can be kept. It provides a layer of abstraction between physical and logical data, and allocates storage for all DBMS managed segments.[166]

---

[*]   Also note that the typography is gentler.

[166]   Wikipedia. Retrieved 2018, from https://en.wikipedia.org/wiki/Tablespace.

For a relational database, the "model" is represented by **Data Definition Language (DDL)** statements; these statements contain specifications for defining the columns in a single **server**, or set of tables. The statements may be generic, but most frequently they contain instructions for features specific to the particular kind of database management system that is its target. The most common targets (in 2018) are Oracle, DB2, and SQL Server.

The relational databases effectively address the qualities **atomicity**, **consistency**, **isolation**, and **durability** (together known as **ACID**). These qualities describe required database behavior when addressing transactions:[167] Specifically, they are:

> ➤ **Atomicity** – All steps in a transaction must be complete for the transaction to be considered complete.

> ➤ **Consistency** – A transaction may not leave data violating database integrity constraints.

> ➤ **Isolation** – Data manipulated by a transaction must not be seen by other transactions until the first one is complete.

> ➤ **Durability** – Once a transaction is completed, its results remain consistent, even if there is a power failure.

Relational database management systems have always been able to embody all four of these characteristics.

Life gets much more complex when the database is distributed over multiple servers in a **database network**. For most of their history, relational databases have been *distributed* across multiple severs as **partitions.** This has always incurred additional expense in both hardware and networks, however, and affected response time for online enquiries.

In the world of networked servers, it's possible for one server to go down, while the others are expected to carry on. With enough expenses covered, even a large networked system can still address the ACID characteristics. If the database size falls into what is currently called very **big data**, however, response time requirements may make it prohibitively expensive to implement a network with many servers.

On the other hand, with the kinds of applications that use large quantities of data, the rules can sometimes be relaxed. The acronym for this environment is not **ACID** but **BASE**♦, which represents:

> ➤ **Basically Available** – Some parts of a distributed system may fail, but the rest will continue to function.

> ➤ **Soft State** – Data will expire if not refreshed. Data may be overwritten with more recent data. This has to be dealt with in the final design.

> ➤ **Eventually Consistent** – There may be times when not all copies are updated simultaneously. At some later time, though, all will be consistent.

If a query is made to a collection of servers, the transaction will involve compareing values to ensure consistencey. If most of them match and a few do not, a *quorum* rule will determine the number that must agree in order to return a value.

---

[167] Sullivan. 2015. *Op. cit.* p.54.

♦ There were chemical engineers in the room that came up with this?

Relaxing the ACID transaction rules can improve response time significantly. The decision to do so is one more of the **engineering trade-offs** that designers must make. This change in the underlying architecture also affects the kinds of models seen by developers. This was the origin of the phenomenon of **No SQL**, described above (pages 121-127).

Again, detailed information about physical database design is beyond the scope of this book. For that, you are advised to view C.J. Date's latest version of *An Introduction to Database Systems*[168].

For tips on network design in a NoSQL distributed world, see the Dan Sullivan book *NoSQL for Mere Mortals*.[169]

Step Two Denormalization

Here follows some further principles of denormalization and optimization for performance. The discussion of the Relational Logical model also presented the first steps in denormalizing the database design. (See pages 108-109 above.) That was the first round of **engineering trade-offs** required to accommodate physical constraints on processing in order to address certain requirements derived from the essential model. That covered design decisions to be made about sub-type definitions, how to deal with derived columns, and how to model attributes as parameters.

The second part of the denormalization process happens when the Data Definition Language is created to generate the actual relational tables. The decisions made here deal with the final assessments about performance, based on the physical characteristics of the expected data.

Split Tables

Final issues of system performance can be dealt with by dividing the resulting database into smaller pieces, either horizontally or vertically.

> **Horizontal Denormalization (by instance)**
> Here one recognizes that an entire portion of a table applies only to one subject area, while others apply to different ones. (For example, the division might be by department, geographic region, time, etc.) Because instances come from (and are used in) different places, it is appropriate to put them in different tables.

> **Vertical Denormalization (by column)**
> If the **Persons** data (for example) can be categorized by whether they are "employment information", "Sales data", and/or some other category, it may be appropriate to define different tables for each kind of **Persons** data.
>
> Note, by the way, that if the columns are in fact implemented as **Person Characteristics**, this is simpler to do.

Address Physical Storage Issues

Depending on the DBMS vendor, there are many options for organizing databases to improve processing speeds. Among these are:

> **Index for performance**
> **Add attribute details**
> **Define partitions and tablespaces**

---

[168] C. J. Date. 2003. An Introduction to Database Systems (8th Edition). (London: Pearson)

[169] Sullivan. 2015. *Op. cit.*

Figure 59 illustrates a relational de-normalized data model.

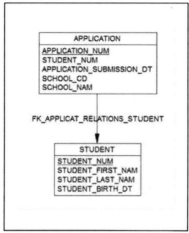

Figure 59: Relational De-normalized Data Model

In this example, structures of STUDENT and APPLICATION have been combined (denormalized) to improve retrieval performance.

Script 9 shows the contents of the Data Definition Language file generated from the de-normalized model shown in Figure 59. This was generated by the SAP tool PowerDesigner; indexes have been added. The foreign key is defined as a "constraint". Notably, the **APPLICATION** table can be neither updated nor deleted if the related instance of **STUDENT** exists.

Script 9: Data Definition Language Script for a Physical Database

```
/* DBMS name: SAP SQL Anywhere 16 */

/* Created on: 4/14/2017 10:34:06 AM */


if exists(select 1 from sys.sysforeignkey where
role='FK_APPLICAT_RELATIONS_STUDENT') then

 alter table APPLICATION

 delete foreign key FK_APPLICAT_RELATIONS_STUDENT

end if;

drop index if exists APPLICATION.Relationship_14_FK;

drop index if exists APPLICATION.APPLICATION_PK;

drop table if exists APPLICATION;

drop index if exists STUDENT.STUDENT_PK;

drop table if exists STUDENT;


/*==============================================*/

/* Table: APPLICATION */

/*==============================================*/

create table APPLICATION

(
```

```
 APPLICATION_NUM char(256) not null,
 STUDENT_NUM integer null,
 APPLICATION_SUBMISSION_DT date not null,
 SCHOOL_CD integer not null,
 SCHOOL_NAM char(256) not null,
 constraint PK_APPLICATION primary key clustered (APPLICATION_NUM)
);


/*==============================================*/
/* Index: APPLICATION_PK */
/*==============================================*/
create unique clustered index APPLICATION_PK on APPLICATION (
APPLICATION_NUM ASC );


/*==============================================*/
/* Index: Relationship_14_FK */
/*==============================================*/
create index Relationship_14_FK on APPLICATION (
STUDENT_NUM ASC
);
/*==============================================*/
/* Table: STUDENT */
/*==============================================*/
create table STUDENT
(
 STUDENT_NUM integer not null,
 STUDENT_FIRST_NAM char(256) not null,
 STUDENT_LAST_NAM char(256) not null,
 STUDENT_BIRTH_DT date not null,
 constraint PK_STUDENT primary key clustered (STUDENT_NUM)
);


/*==============================================*/
/* Index: STUDENT_PK */
/*==============================================*/
create unique clustered index STUDENT_PK on STUDENT (
STUDENT_NUM ASC
);
```

```
alter table APPLICATION

add    constraint    FK_APPLICAT_RELATIONS_STUDENT    foreign    key
(STUDENT_NUM)

references STUDENT (STUDENT_NUM)

on update restrict

on delete restrict;
```

Note that this book is *not* the place to discuss the finer points of physical database design. Each of the vendors has ample current documentation for that topic. For example, Oracle has updated *Oracle: The Complete Reference* frequently since 1997.[170]

---

[170]   Bob Bryla, Kevin Loney. 2013. *Oracle Database 12c The Complete Reference (Oracle Press) 1st Edition.* (McGraw-Hill Education).

CHAPTER 6:
THE DEVELOPMENT PROCESS

As with other topics covered in this book, you will not find here a comprehensive guide to planning systems projects. Rather, here are some key concepts to be kept in mind when planning such projects, with particular emphasis on the modeling steps. The basic organization is similar to that of the book as a whole:

1. Dispose of the pressures to begin by reverse engineering current systems.
2. Lay out a plan for the conceptual part of the project
3. Gather information
4. Build and deliver the conceptual data models (overview, semantic, essential)

This is followed by addressing the development of the database system to carry out the objectives of the project. Planning this is beyond the scope of this book, but it will involve the following steps, at least:

1. Create one or more logical models from conceptual (semantic or essential) models.
2. Create one or more physical database structures from each logical model.

Reverse Engineering

Sometimes the assignment is to simply take an existing system and upgrade it.

This effort involves "reverse engineering", or documenting an existing database in terms that allow it to be improved. Reverse engineering of the *physical data model* is completed first to understand the technical design of an existing system. Then some sort of *logical data model* is created to document the business solution met by the existing system.

Most data modeling tools support reverse engineering into some sort of graphical form, from a variety of databases. Creating a readable layout of the model elements, however, still requires a modeler. There are several common layouts (e.g., orthogonal, dimensional, hierarchical) that can be automated by tools, but identifying and dealing with the enterprise context (e.g., grouping tables/entities by subject area or function) is still largely a manual process.

Even so, consider the following. :

When the original system was created,

1. The client had an *original idea* of what it should be.
2. The client communicated this original idea to one or more systems analysts.
3. Based on their understanding of this original idea, the systems analysts evaluated the technologies that were available (*at that time*) and converted the idea into statements of *requirements* for developing a system.
4. These *requirements* were then handed over to the designers.
5. Based on their understanding of the requirements (plus their understanding of the technologies that were available *at that time*) the designers created the appropriate coding and database *design*.
6. This *design* was then handed over to developers.

7. Based on their understanding of the design (plus their knowledge of the technologies that were available *at that time*), they *implemented the system* that is being evaluated for this project.♥

Over time, the current system was patched and changed, thanks to clarification of requirements, technological changes, and political fortunes. With luck, it finally improved enough to be basically useful. Even so, how well will a system based on the constraints and technologies of the past serve the future?

Figure 60 shows how well reverse engineering worked in the 19th century. At that time, carriages were the standard means for "mass" transportation. When railroads were introduced, initially they adapted existing technology. The designers didn't understand that things had, well, changed. Simply adding carriage bodies to railroad wheels was not going to work in the long term.

The objective of any new data management effort is to *improve the quality of data being used in the business*. Reverse engineering by itself is *unlikely* to be useful. Certainly, if you check out the "Gather Information" step below, you can see that data archeology is part of the assignment. There is important information to be drawn from looking at existing, functional systems, but *do not* imagine that the computer will translate an existing system into a new one.

B & O Railroad Museum

Figure 60: Reverse Engineering Carriages to Become Railcars

Create Conceptual (Overview, S emantic, Essential) Models

A **plan** for a conceptual data modeling effort at least includes the following deliverables:

➢ Estimate of **overall scope**, in terms of business objectives, functions and data requirements.

➢ Identification of **participants**.

♥ Many readers who were born in the last century played a game which, back then, was called "telephone". It began with one person writing down a message and storing it away. 'E then whispered the message to a second person. This person then relayed it to a third. And so forth, until the last person wrote down h' version of the message, and they were compared. If there were more than about five children involved, comparing the final message with the first one was, shall we say, amusing.

➤ Schedule of steps (**Project Plan**). For example:
  o Define (approximate) scope (functions *and* data) and objectives.
  o Identify participants.
  o Gather information.
  o Select modeling tools.
  o Create models.
  o Define requirements.
  o Present models to participants to obtain feedback, and finally acceptance.
  o Publish models in formal sense.

Define overall scope, in terms of objectives, functions, and data requirements.

When the project was undertaken, presumably there were some basic statements of scope. An initial planning meeting will be responsible for laying out this scope in more detail, along with explicit definitions of objectives, functions, and data requirements.

Will these be **enterprise models**, describing as much of the entire enterprise as possible? Or will the effort be limited to a particular area of the business? Might the project be to support only a single new **app** or service? The chosen scope affects both the number of people involved, the expertise required of each, and the overall sophistication required for the effort.

Moreover, do not simply assume that everyone knows the project's objectives. Begin with hypothetical statements of the objectives and the scope of the overall project. Then, for each of the component modeling efforts, refine its objectives and scope, In each case, the final statement should include brief descriptions of the business problems being addressed. These descriptions are *not* of detailed requirements; they will come later. This is simply an expression of the problem(s) that motivated the effort in the first place.

Understand that, while the Overview modeling effort will probably address as much of the enterprise as possible, the scopes of each subsequent modeling effort will also be defined inside that one, as a result of the Overview modeling effort.

Author's Opinion

"Agile systems development" has become the rage in recent years. The idea is that relatively small products are developed quickly, taking advantage of close participation with the prospective users. In the method's early days, this bypassed the whole modeling process altogether. The problem with that was that, in the absence of an overall architecture, many small systems combined to create a total that was a complete (how to put this delicately?) mess. The secret to success is to first develop a large scope (if not for the entire enterprise) model that will link together all of the agile projects. Thus, whenever one system must "interface" with another, the data connections will have already been defined. Each project can then proceed quickly—but only when the context is already well understood.

Identify Participants

There are basically three groups of people who should actively participate in the model development process:

➤ **Top Management**

In overview meetings, these people will define the scope of subsequent projects. They provide statements of how the mission of this project is related to the mission of the enterprise. They will participate in the modeling activity to the extent that they can offer suggestions for the most important concepts that run the business. They will be introduced to the modeling activities as they see the facilitator sketch the results of their suggestions on a white board. This will (ideally) involve a lot of erasing and re-drawing, until everyone in the room agrees that they are correct.

➢ **Middle Management and Staff**
These are the people who manage the day-to-day activities of the enterprise. They will participate both in the initial interviews (and/or modeling sessions) and in the feedback sessions. In these, they will validate both the semantic model, and eventually, the essential model as well.

➢ **Other Subject Matter Experts**
These are the individuals who may not be managers, but who are responsible for the day-to-day activities of the enterprise. Many of them are in the management category cited above, but others may be accountants, engineers, or other specialists who have unique knowledge of how things work. They too will participate both in the initial interviews (and/or modeling sessions) and in the feedback sessions. In these sessions, they will validate both the semantic model and, eventually, the essential model.

Specifically, depending on the modeling level, the following business roles will be involved:

➢ **Overview Model**
  ✓ Management – Relatively high-level. They help identify other participants.

➢ **Semantic Model**
  ✓ **Management** –Middle managers.

  ✓ **Subject matter experts** – The people who know how things really work. These may be accountants, engineers, shop supervisors, etc.

➢ **Essential Model**
  ✓ **Management** – Both staff and executive levels.

  ✓ **Subject Matter Experts** – Specialists, who know how things really work.

  ✓ **Database Designers** – Those responsible for designing the future data structures.

  ✓ **Enterprise Architects** – Those working to update the enterprise architecture alongside this effort.

➢ **Logical / Physical models**
  ✓ **Data Administrators** – Those responsible for managing database software.

  ✓ **Database Administrators** – Those responsible for designing and building the future data structures.

Gather Information

There are many ways to gather the necessary information from all parties involved. Most efforts to gather information involve one or more of the following techniques:

1. Conduct Interviews

Schedule and meet with a dozen representatives of the enterprise. Meet people from as many different departments (within the project's scope) as possible. Interviews should be done by two people–one who asks the questions, and one who takes notes. Instead of asking broad questions like "What would you like to see systems do?", it's better to focus on the person's job by asking questions like "What information do *you* use?" or "Who do you send your results to?" After getting this person's unique viewpoint, you may ask more pointed questions, like "Do you see any problems with the data you use?"

WARNING:
DO NOT begin with the question,
"What would you like to see systems do?"

You will get either:
- "Gee, I don't know. What do you suggest?" or
- A lie.

RATHER, focus on the person's job:
"What do you do here?"
"What information do you use?"
"Where do you get that information?"
"What do you do with it?"
"Who do you send the results to?"

Only *AFTER* you've discussed these things for a while can you ask:
"Do you see any problems with the data you are working with?"

Be sure to obtain from your participants *their* definitions for all specialized words, acronyms, and jargon

2. Conduct Modeling Sessions (known in the IBM world as Joint Applications Development Sessions or JADs)

Rather than starting with interviews (or after a few of them have provided the "lay of the land"), you may conduct introductory modeling sessions with a few managers and other subject matter experts. If you have some patterns in mind, begin by sketching out elements on the whiteboard. Most significantly, solicit ideas from the audience. Add the relationships necessary (with proper names, so that they can be read as simple—assertive—sentences).♠

Continue obtaining from your participants *their* definitions for all terms.

3. Review Existing Documentation

This effort is like archeology. It entails digging into existing models, database designs, and other documentation, in order to find clues about how the business really works. Sources could include:

Existing reports –
Beware of these. They carry a lot of history with revisions and tweaks. It may not be clear what is the real structure is of the data being captured.

Existing models –

♠   Before you get here, be sure you have internalized the rules for reading relationship names—see page 50, above.

If these were developed without paying attention to the aesthetic standard described in this document (see page 157), this will be tough. Lines will migrate all over the page, linking things that are nowhere near each other. If possible, rearrange the boxes on the drawing to provide a workspace where you can at least get a sense of the meanings of the relationships. On the other hand, if they are readable, reverse engineer them as a starting point for the semantic and the essential models.

Patterns –
These are useful for identifying meaningful structures, recognizing, on the existing models, that there is probably a lot of visual noise to be cleared away to arrive at an understanding of what is there.

Existing databases –
How these are used depends on what you find. At least, table names (translated into English) can provide clues to the vocabulary. In some cases, tables and columns may even have definitions associated with them. Many of them, however, will not be well-documented and will not directly correlate to real-world things.

Do *not* spend a lot of time looking at the current database. Your time is better spent talking to the people who actually use the data.

> **NOTE:**
> If the business people who will be responsible for the data are *not available*, give serious consideration to the question of whether this project should continue at all.

Select Modeling Tools

Over the years, modeling tools have evolved. Known as *Computer-aided System Engineering (CASE)* tools, some are very simple while others are more sophisticated. At the very least, to accommodate the kinds of modeling described in this document, look for:

➢ The ability to produce **Barker/Ellis** models.

➢ The ability to produce **Information Engineering** models.

➢ The ability to convert one to another.

➢ Depending on the development environment, the ability to produce **UML**, **IDEF1X**, and/or **XML Schema** models

➢ The ability to generate data definition language (DDL)

➢ The ability to capture all entity and attribute **definitions**. This includes the ability to convert them to table and column definitions.

➢ *Flexibility* in being able to **generate reports** on the models. At the very least, the ability to report (by subject area) entities with definitions, attributes with definitions, and relationship sentences.

➢ Ideally, the ability to produce a **glossary**, where the terms defined include both entity types and other terms added by the user.

➢ Ideally, the ability to capture **design decisions.**

This whole process—from selecting which software is right for your team, to obtaining and installing it—can be very *time-consuming*. Remember, if this software will be used by many, and installed with a central repository, there are serious organizational issues to be addressed as well. What roles will have to be defined, and who will play them? A month or more should be planned for, in order to carry out this step.

Build and Deliver the Conceptual Data Model

Modeling is a very iterative process. Modelers draft the model, then return to business professionals and business analysts to clarify terms and business rules. They then update the model and ask more questions. This iterative process is shown in Figure 61.

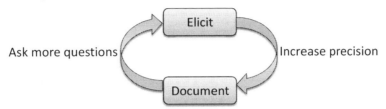

Figure 61: Modeling is iterative[171]

The overview model will have very few entity types, with mostly many-to-many relationships. Only a few attributes will be shown. If used, the semantic entity/relationship model will have many entity types, ideally grouped by subject-area. There will be some many-to-many relationships, and many attributes. The entity type names will be business terms. The essential model will be smaller than the semantic one, since it will take advantage of abstraction and patterns.

In all three cases, the process for the modeling team is the same:

> ➢ Sketch out the model on a whiteboard.

> ➢ Criticize the names of *entity types*.

> ➢ Criticize the names of *relationships*.

> ➢ *Erase* and *redraw* as necessary.

> ➢ Enter the full model into a *modeling tool* by subject area (no more than 15 boxes each).

Define requirements

To identify **business information requirements**, one must first identify information needed in the context of one or more business functions and/or processes. While conducting the interviews for the overview model, include conversations that identify **business functions**. A "business function" is an activity that carries out an objective of the enterprise. It describes what it is to accomplish, without regard to the technology used to carry it out. An example of a function is "order material". This is represented in a **function hierarchy.**"[172]

Business functions are also described without reference to time or dependency on other business functions at the same level in the hierarchy.

The detailed interviews used to develop the *semantic model* can also be useful in defining the lower levels of the function hierarchy. In some situations, it is also useful to develop a more detailed **process model** (or its predecessor, a **data flow diagram** or **DFD**). The DFD is concerned with

---

[171]   Steve Hoberman 2014. *Data Modeling for MongoDB*. (Technics Publications).

[172]   Richard Barker, Cliff Longman. 1992. *CASE*Method: Function and Process Modelling*. (Addison-Wesley).

how data move between processes in time, and how they are transformed by those processes. It consists of **processes** (the activities performed to convert input data to output data), **external entities** (that constitute the environment), **data stores** (that keep data temporarily), and **data flows** (connecting them together). DFDs are also organized on multiple levels. DFDs generally start at a lower level of detail than the basic corporate functions.

At the lowest level of detail, an **essential data flow diagram** organizes the smallest process fragments in terms of the **external events** that cause the enterprise to do what it does[173].

Once processes and/or functions have been properly identified, the next task is to relate them to the essential data model. This is typically done via a matrix that relates each function to the entity types that it uses. Specifically, for each function/entity type combination, indicate whether the data described by the entity type is **c**reated, **r**etrieved, **u**pdated or **d**eleted by the function. Colloquially, this is called the **"CRUD" matrix.** Then, if the interviewee calls this particular kind of data unreliable (e.g., inaccurate, late), you have the beginning of a requirement specification.

Requirements, then, are expressed in terms both of functions (or processes) as well as data entity types.[174]

Many enterprises have a formal requirements management disciplines to guide drafting and refining formal requirement statements. For instance, statements might begin with "The system shall …". Written data requirement specification documents may be maintained using requirements management tools.

The specifications gathered through the contents of any such documentation should carefully synchronize with the requirements captured with data models. This will make it possible to answer questions like "Which parts of my data models represent or implement Requirement X?" or "Why is this entity here?"

Prepare and present models to participants

Present the slide show created from the model to a group of subject matter experts. See the section titled "Prepare an Interesting Presentation"(page 161) for a complete description of how to do this. The standards presented there are important.

Step 1: Prepare Slides

1. Organize the model *by* **subject area** (a collection of related topics that are appropriate as a *sub-section* of an **enterprise data model.**)*,* with no more than 15 or so entity types on each (A4 / 8½x11) page.

2. Print out a copy and determine which entity types will be presented at each step. Circle each group and number them 1 to n. There should be no more that 5-6 slides, but there could be up to 10.

3. Bring up another copy and save it as <subject>.<highest slide number>.

4. Highlight the entity types that were to be presented during this step.

5. Save it.

---

[173] Steve McMenamin and John Palmer. 1984. *Essential Systems Analysis.* (Yourdon Press).

[174] For an overview of how to use the data modeling processes described here to support requirements analysis, see Hay. 2003. *Requirements… Op. cit.*

6. Now save it again as <subject><next highest slide number>.

7. Delete the entity types that were previously highlighted.

IMPORTANT:

Delete the entity types *in the drawing only*.

Do not delete any entity types from the *data modeling tool repository*.

---

8. Repeat steps 4-7 until you've reached step 1 of the presentation.

Print each of the step drawings, and sort from step 1 through the end for presentation.

Step 2: Present the Model.

1. *Introduce yourself:*

2. *Review the interviewing process.*

3. *Explain why a data model is important:*
   ✓ To clarify how things really work.
   ✓ To provide a coherent view of the enterprise to system and database designers.

4. *Optionally, present a function hierarchy:*
   ✓ At least through 2-3 levels
   ✓ Provides a context for the model presentation schedule

5. *Present the schedule for the day, by subject area.*

6. *Present the first slide, with only a few highlighted entity types:*
   ✓ Agree on definition of each term.
   ✓ If present, read relationship sentences and get agreement on them.
   ✓ In all cases, you are making assertions about the nature of the enterprise. Are these assertions true or false?
   ✓ The model is simply a way to take notes. It is not necessary for the participants to know anything about data modeling. As long as your sentences are doing nothing other than describing the business, participants should have no difficulty following you.
   ✓ Where necessary, mark up the slide with corrections.

7. *Present the second slide, with only new entity types highlighted:*
   ✓ Agree on definition of each term.
   ✓ If present, read relationship sentences and get agreement on them.
   ✓ Where necessary, mark up slide with corrections.

8. *Repeat Step 3 until finished.* [*]

9. *Be sure to have collected everyone's telephone number and e-mail address, so you can follow up with any questions.*

---

[*] To see an example of how this is done, check out Hay. 2011. *Enterprise Model... Op. cit.*

10. *If there are too many unresolved issues, it may be necessary to get together again.*

IMPORTANT NOTICE:

Your assignment is <u>*not*</u> to impress your audience with your cleverness and get a pat on the back. Your assignment is TO BE WRONG!

➤ Where you are wrong in this presentation, it is a *simple* matter to mark up the slides, *correct the model*, and *proceed*.

➤ If you misunderstood something, and it wasn't discovered until people were trying to design a database/system, it will be a <u>*bit more expensive*</u> to fix then.

➤ If it isn't discovered until someone is trying to construct the database/system, it will definitely be **more expensive** to fix.

➤ If it isn't discovered until people are trying to install the database/system, it will be ***much more expensive to*** fix.

➤ If it isn't discovered until the system is implemented, it will be ***VERY EXPENSIVE TO FIX*** indeed.

Get all misunderstandings resolved now.

Publish the models formally

Subsequently, update the model to accommodate all the changes, and produce a document that includes it, along with a narrative that is much like what was presented at the feedback session. The idea is that the business reader can look at the drawings if interested, but the narrative should be understandable enough for the reader to accept the contents. Components should include:

➤ **The set of slides**
   … accompanied by a text narrative describing each. This includes both definition of each entity type, but also every relationship sentence ("Each … must be…").

➤ **Articulation**
   … of what requirements have been identified, along with recommendations for future steps.

➤ **Appendix one**
   … a glossary-type report from the CASE tool, with every entity type and other business term not in the model, plus its definitions.

➤ **Appendix two**
   … a detailed report from a CASE tool describing, for each entity, its definition, all of its attributes, and all of its relationships described as structured sentences (at least the mandatory ones).

Create Logical Models

Given an **essential model** that comprehensively describes the enterprise and defines its requirements for new systems, the next step is to create one or more *logical models* (appropriate to those requirements and the operating environment). In the relational world, for example, this process might involve the following steps:

Step 1: Roll Over Essential Model into "default" Logical (Relational) Model.

Use a CASE tool utility to generate a first draft Logical (Relational) Model:

1. Each **entity type** becomes a **table**.

2. Each **attribute** becomes a **column**.

3. Each **unique identifier** becomes a **primary key**.

4. Each **relationship** becomes a **foreign key** in the table on the "many" side, referring to a **primary key** of the table on the "one" side.

5. Each **super-type** and each **sub-type** becomes a *separate* **table**. The **inherited attributes** are duplicated in the **sub-types**. Each **relationship inheritance** generates appropriate **foreign keys**. By default, each sub-type also has a foreign key pointing to the super-type table.

Step 2: Modify Default Logical (Relational) Model

Some preliminary steps require design decisions to move from the Essential Model to complete the relational version of a Logical Model. These involve **engineering trade-offs**, in order for a designer to meet system objectives in a constrained physical environment.:

Resolve sub-types

In the logic for the default relational design, each sub-type becomes a table, with inherited attributes and relationships, and with a foreign key pointing to the super-type. This can become very complex—especially if a lot of super-type relationships are involved.

An alternative approach creates a single table from the super-type, with all the attributes and relationships from all the sub-types included as attributes of and relationships to the super-type. This produces a smaller structure, but the values of the attributes can no longer be controlled.

Figure 62 shows an example from an Essential Model, showing **Party** and its sub-types **Person** and **Organization.** In this case, we've chosen to implement the main sub-type **Person** and the first sub-type of **Organization** (**Company**) as separate tables. The rest of **Organization**, subsuming **Department**, **Government Agency**, and **Government** will be collected into one table.

The result is shown below in Figure 63. All three tables inherited from **Party**, with "Party ID" as a primary key (underlined). In addition, both **Company** and **Other Organization** inherited from **Organization** "Official Name", "Nickname", and "Purpose".

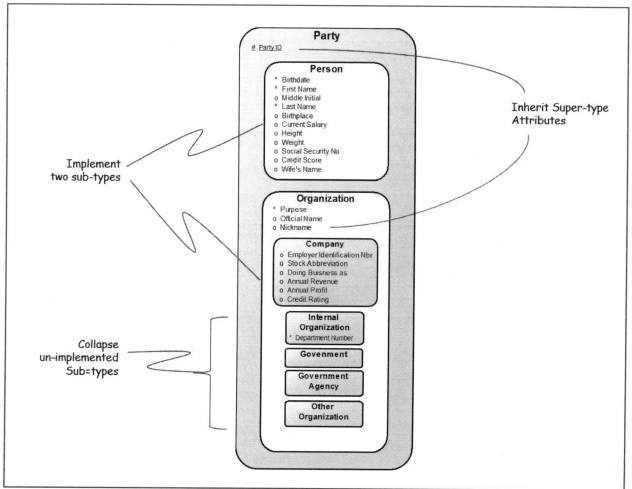

Figure 62: Resolving Sub-types – Step 1

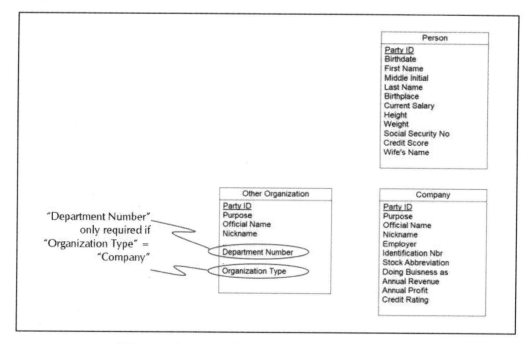

Figure 63: Resolving Sub-types – Step 2

What **criteria** are involved in choosing the best approach to resolve sub-types?

✓ Relative *frequency* of sub-type *retrieval?*
If it's high, then the sub-type should be a separate table. If it's low, the sub-type should be corporated into the super-type..

✓ Target *audience?*
  – Different populations?
    Different departments may produce different amounts of traffic for each sub-type. When this is the case, they should be separate. If many people preferthe same sub-types, it may be worthwhile to implement the collection as single table.
  – Different timings?
    One of the sub-types is updated daily. Others only weekly or monthly. This argues for them being in separate tables. Different populations will update the separately.

✓ Different *relationships?*
Some sub-types have relationships with tables not referred to by others.

Design derived columns

As described previously, while this makes the essential model not strictly in third normal form, it is often useful for the Essential Model to indicate that some attributes may be derived from others. This can be indicated in three ways:

✓ Derived from a *simple formula* based on attributes in the same table.
✓ *Inferred from* a parent table into a child table.
✓ *Summarized* from child table into a parent table.

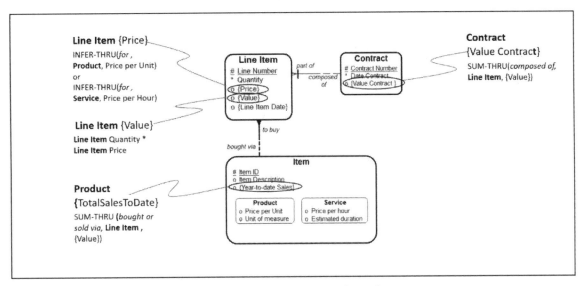

Figure 64: Sample Derived Columns

Note that it is desirable to calculate some values dynamically. This means that queried values are always current. Unfortunately, this process is very time-consuming. Alternatively, the values of computed columns may be calculated when the data are input. This makes querying faster, but adds to the cost of maintaing accurate data. Thus, the designer must choose one of the following options:

✓ Have the calculation done *when* the data originally *are captured?*
  – No further calculations are required upon retrieval.

- Appropriate for relatively stable sources of derivation.
- However, if the incoming data change, any resulting columns must be recalculated.
- High ratio of writes to reads.

✓ Have the calculations done *dynamically*, when *retrieved?*
- The output is always current.
- Appropriate when underlying data change frequently.
- However, there are performance implications.
- High ratio of reads to writes.

Figure 65 shows examples of each of these strategies, as implemented:

✓ Computed on input and *stored*
- **Line Item** {Price}
- **Line Item** {Value}
- **Contract** {Value Contract}

✓ Computed on *query*
- Product {Total Sales to Date}

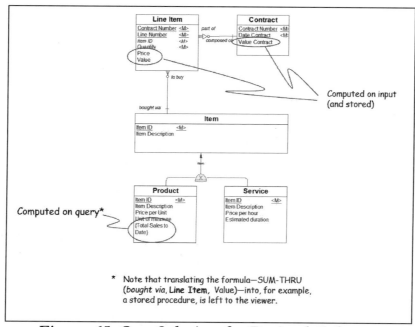

Figure 65: One Solution for Derived Columns

Deal with characteristics

Figure 66 reproduces Figure 35 from page 91 91). This figure demonstrated that many columns discovered in legacy systems could better be managed (in this example) as **Party Characteristic.** This provides maximum flexibility. On the other hand, there are advantages to storing some of those characteristics as columns in their appropriate tables. This is where the designer has to use judgement.

Figure 63 (page 144, above, reproduced below as Figure 67), showed creation of the logical models, with attributes for **Person**, **Company**, and **Other Organization**, before they were assigned as **Party Characteristics.**

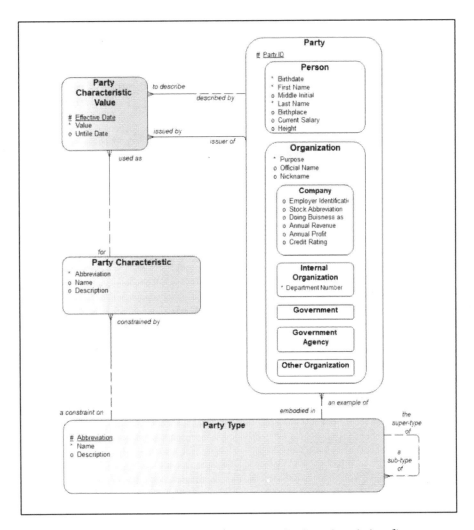

Figure 66: Party Characteristics (revisited)

Table 4 shows a prototype set of Person and Company characteristics, including the Party Type of each. The table also identifies whether each attribute is a **dynamic attribute** or not. Once a value for the attribute is assigned to an instance, will there be many opportunities to change it? If not, it is *not* dynamic (a **static attribute**). For example "Birthdate", "Birthplace" and "Social Security" are static, so their values can be captured as columns in **Party**. If, on the other hand, values for an instance change over time, and multiple instances are required to deal with that, then they *are* *dynamic*. "Current Salary", "Credit Score", and "Height" are examples of dynamic columns.

Dynamic attributes are candidates for inclusion as instances of **Party Characteristic,** while the others are candidates to appear as hard-coded columns in the **Person** and **Company** tables. Figure 68 shows instances of the five tables involved.

Party Characteristic shows the **dynamic attributes** ("Current Salary", "Credit Score", etc.), as instances. Each may then be *evaluated as* one or more instances of **Party Characteristic Value**. Each value is shown with a "Start Date" and an "Until Date". Each **Party Characteristic Value** must be *for* exactly one **Party**, which in turn must be an instance of one of the sub-type tables, **Person** or **Company**.

The **static attributes**, on the other hand ("Given Name", Birthdate", etc. for **Person**, and "Employer Identification Number", "Official Name", etc. for **Company**), appear as hard-coded columns describing the **Person** or the **Company** table. These are typically evaluated when an instance of the appropriate table is created.

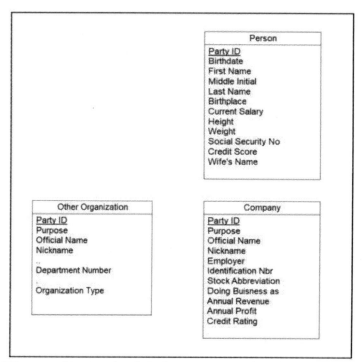

Figure 67: Logical Sub-types With All Columns

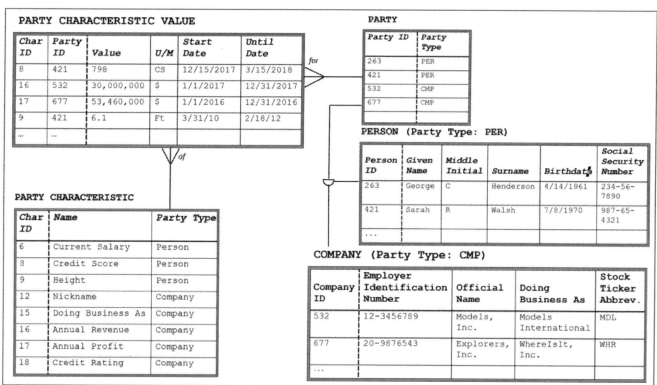

Figure 68: Characteristics and Columns

Table: 4: Party Characteristic Prototype

ID	Party Characteristic Name	Party Type Name	Dynamic?
1	Birthdate	Person	No
2	First Name	Person	No?
3	Middle Initial	Person	No?
4	Last Name	Person	No?
5	Birthplace	Person	No
6	Current Salary	Person	Yes
7	Social Security Number	Person	No
8	Credit Score	Person	Yes
9	Height	Person	Yes
10	Purpose	Organization	No
11	Official Name	Company	No
12	Nickname	Company	Yes
13	Employer Identification Number	Company	No
14	Stock Abbreviation	Company	No
15	Doing Business As	Company	Yes
16	Annual Revenue	Company	Yes
17	Annual Profit	Company	Yes
18	Credit Rating	Company	Yes

Create Physical Models

The first set of design decisions required to denormalize and move to a physical model were described above as being carried out to tweak the *logical model*. More may be required before generating the **data definition language** script for creating a **relational database.**

One of the best sources for information on how to create a physical database is C.J. Date's *An Introduction to Database Systems.*[175]

---

175 C. J. Date. 2003. op. cit.

Denormalize as necessary

In some circumstances, denormalizing (or adding redundancy) can improve performance to outweigh the cost of duplicate storage and synchronization processing. Dimensional structures are the main implementations of denormalization.

To the extent that computed columns have already defined inferences, the first step to denormalization has already occurred. We've already decided how to treat inferred and summarized columns . In addition, the decisions about characteristics and sub-types already addressed many of the performance issues that cause denormalization. The designer of the physical database must also choose how to split tables—either horizontally or vertically

Split tables horizontally (by instance)

Horizontal denormalization is recognition that an entire portion of a candidate table applies to only one geographic area (or department, or year, etc.), while other portions apply to other geographic areas. When instances come from different places, it is appropriate to put them in different tables.

Split tables vertically (by column)

Vertical denormalization is recognition that if the **Persons** data (for example) is categorized as "employment information", "sales performance", etc. it may be appropriate to define different tables for each kind of **Persons** data.

Note that, to the extent that the "columns" are in fact implemented as **Person Characteristics,** this division is simpler to do.

Address physical storage issues[176]

Depending on the DBMS vendor, there are many options for organizing the physical database.

Index for Performance

An index is an alternate path for accessing data in the database to optimize query (data retrieval) performance. Indexing can improve query performance in many cases. The database administrator or database developer must select and define appropriate indexes for database tables. Major RDBMS products support many types of indexes. Indexes can be unique or non-unique, clustered or non-clustered, partitioned or non-partitioned, single column or multi-column, b-tree or bitmap or hashed. Without an appropriate index, the DBMS will revert to reading every row in the table (table scan) to retrieve any data. On large tables, this is very costly. Try to build indexes on large tables to support the most frequently run queries, using the most frequently referenced columns, particularly keys (primary, alternate, and foreign).

Partition for Performance

Great consideration must be given to the partitioning strategy of the overall data model especially when facts contain many optional **dimensional** keys (sparse). Ideally, partitioning on a date key is recommended; when this is not possible, a study is required based on profiled results and workload analysis to propose and refine the subsequent partitioning model.

---

176 C. J. Date. Database Design. Op. cit.

Add Attribute Details

Add details to the physical model, such as the technical name of each table and column (**relational** databases), or file and field (non-relational databases), or schema and element (**XML** databases).

Define the physical domain, physical data type, and length of each column or field. Add appropriate constraints, such as nullability and default values for columns or fields, especially for NOT NULL constraints.

Add Metadata columns

In some database environments, the metadata repository maintains data about who is updating each datum and when. As an alternative approach, the following columns may be added to each table in the database proper:

➤ Person who created the row.

➤ Person who updated it last.

➤ Creation date.

➤ Last update date.

Maintenance of the database should also then involve the processes required to update these columns.

Assign Surrogate Keys

In some cases, **surrogate keys** were already added to **entity types** that were the source of the tables now being addressed. If not, you may want to assign them here. This is an optional step; its inclusion depends primarily on whether the natural key is large and/or compound, and whether its attributes are assigned values that could change over time.

If a surrogate key is assigned to be the primary key of a table, make sure there is an **alternative key** on the original primary key. For example, if on the logical data model the primary key for **Student** was "Student First Name", "Student Last Name", and "Student Birth Date" (i.e. a compound primary key), on the physical data model, the primary key for **Student** may be the surrogate key "Student ID". Defining this does not negate the use of an alternative key defined on the original primary key ("Student First Name", "Student Last Name", and "Student Birth Date").

Generate and run DDL Script

Assuming all of these mechanisms were taking place in a corporate metadata repository, the next step is to run the utility that generates the code that will update the physical database.

Script 10 is a copy of the sample DDL shown in the "Physical Data Model" section on page 130.

Script 10: Sample Data Definition Language Script

```
/*=================================================*/
/* DBMS name: SAP SQL Anywhere 16 */
/* Created on: 4/14/2017 10:34:06 AM */
/*=================================================*/
```

```
if exists(select 1 from sys.sysforeignkey where role='FK_APPLICAT_RELATIONS_STUDENT')
then

 alter table APPLICATION

 delete foreign key FK_APPLICAT_RELATIONS_STUDENT

end if;


drop index if exists APPLICATION.Relationship_14_FK;

drop index if exists APPLICATION.APPLICATION_PK;

drop table if exists APPLICATION;

drop index if exists STUDENT.STUDENT_PK;

drop table if exists STUDENT;


/*=========================================================*/
/* Table: APPLICATION */
/*=========================================================*/
create table APPLICATION

(

 APPLICATION_NUM char(256) not null,

 STUDENT_NUM integer null,

 APPLICATION_SUBMISSION_DT date not null,

 SCHOOL_CD integer not null,

 SCHOOL_NAM char(256) not null,

 constraint PK_APPLICATION primary key clustered (APPLICATION_NUM)

);


/*=========================================================*/
/* Index: APPLICATION_PK */
/*=========================================================*/
create unique clustered index APPLICATION_PK on APPLICATION (

APPLICATION_NUM ASC

);


/*=========================================================*/
/* Index: Relationship_14_FK */
/*=========================================================*/
```

```
create index Relationship_14_FK on APPLICATION (
STUDENT_NUM ASC
);


/*========================================================*/
/* Table: STUDENT */
/*========================================================*/
create table STUDENT
(
STUDENT_NUM integer not null,
STUDENT_FIRST_NAM char(256) not null,
STUDENT_LAST_NAM char(256) not null,
STUDENT_BIRTH_DT date not null,
constraint PK_STUDENT primary key clustered (STUDENT_NUM)
);


/*========================================================*/
/* Index: STUDENT_PK */
/*========================================================*/
create unique clustered index STUDENT_PK on STUDENT (
STUDENT_NUM ASC
);


alter table APPLICATION
add constraint FK_APPLICAT_RELATIONS_STUDENT foreign key (STUDENT_NUM)
references STUDENT (STUDENT_NUM)
on update restrict
on delete restrict;
```

CHAPTER 7:
BEST PRACTICES

Introduction

Several authors have published criteria for good data models. There are variations, but the basic ones include readability, truth, and form correctness.

In 1994, **Michael Reingruber** and **William Gregory** wrote *The Data Modeling Handbook: A Best-practice Approach to Building Quality Data Models,* a detailed book with guidelines for entities, attributes, relationships, generalization hierarchies, data model views, and normalization. [177] In the introduction, they cite some general characteristics for a "quality data model":

> **Embodies business plans, policies, and strategies.**
> "Understand and use business plans and rules to drive your data modeling efforts".

> **Uses recognized set of [modeling] rules.**
> Once a modeling standard has been selected, the model must adhere to it.

> **Involves domain experts.**
> "You cannot build a data model without the direct and informed participation of individuals who understand the domain, have an ownership interest in the product, and are empowered to make decisions in business rules. There is no guarantee of success when business experts are involved. But there is no chance of success if they are not."

> **Can be transformed into high-quality design.**
> "The goal of building business-oriented models is not contradictory to the need to establish quality criteria ensuring a data model serves its role in driving database and system designs."

> **Is created in the context of other business architecture elements.**
> "Data models ... must be consistent with other elements of the business architecture, including but not limited to business processes, organiztional contraols and authorities, and geographic distribution of data and systems."

> **Is created in the context of the entire enterprise.**
> "We are not suggesting that every model cover all data requirements of the enterprise. We are suggesting that if you build a data model, you should do so only after thinking long and hard about how your model scope relates to other areas of the enterprise, and what the boundaries of your enterprise really are."

> **Is created in the context of overall data quality lifecycle.**
> Data modeling is a step in a much larger process (e.g. information systems development) designed to deliver to the key stakeholders of the enterprise a single primary output—high quality data.

> **Depends on support infrastructure.**
> Consistent development of high-quality models is dependent on the existence of an infrastructure to support data modeling and management.

---

[177]   Michael C. Reingruber, William W. Gregory. 1994. *The Data Modeling Handbook*. (John Wiley & Sons, Inc.).

> ➤ **Involves the right stakeholders.**
> The mix of players will vary from project to project, but in general, you need the cooperation of:

- ✓ Business experts
- ✓ Data modelers and facilitators
- ✓ Data management professional
- ✓ Information systems developers, and in particular, database administrators
- ✓ Business Managers[178]

While the industry has matured since 1994, the basic principles still stand.

Table 5: Hoberman Schemes[179]

	Relational	**Dimensional**
Conceptual	Broad scope concepts and rules	Broad scope metrics and slicing
Logical	Normalized	All metrics and levels shown
Physical	Relational, Dimensional, Column, Key-value, Document, Graph	

In 2015, **Steve Hoberman** published *Data Model Scorecard: Applying the Industry Standard on Data Model Quality.*[180] Here he describes concisely the principles that he has been using to review data models over many years. He has established ten categories for quality, along with discussions on how to evaluate each:

1. Correctness
   How well does the model capture the requirements?

2. Completeness
   - ✓ Completeness of Requirements
     All requirements requested appear on the data model, with "nothing extra".

   - ✓ Completeness of Metadata
     All of the descriptive information surrounding the model is captured.
     - Physical Model – formatting and length of each attribute
     - Logical Model – business names of each attribute
     - Conceptual Model – definitions for each key term

3. Scheme
   How well does the data model match its schema? Mr. Hoberman describes this in a two dimensional table, as shown in Table 5 two sets of categories:

4. Structure
   How structurally sound is the model?

---

[178] Ibid. pp. 13-18.

[179] *Ibid,* p. 67.

[180] Steve Hoberman: 2015. Data Model Scorecard: Applying the Industry Standard on Data Model Quality. (Technics Publication).

5. Abstraction
   How well does the model make use of generic structures?

6. Standards
   How well does the model follow naming standards?
   - ✓ Structure – Are entities singular nouns; are relationship names present tense verbs[♣]? Are attribute names built from subject area name (known also as "prime", typically the table/entity name) plus one or more modifiers plus the "class word" (such as "name", "code", or "amount")?
   - ✓ Term –The proper [sic] name is given to the attribute or entity.
   - ✓ Style – Are spaces allowed between words? If not, is it an underline (for database designs) or "camelCase" (for object-oriented designs)?

7. Readability
   How well has the model been arranged for readability?

8. Definitions
   How good are the definitions?

9. Consistency
   If it exists, how consistent is the model with the enterprise?

10. Data
    How well does[sic] the metadata [the model elements] match the data [real instances]?

While your author disagrees with Mr. Hoberman on some of the details about dealing with the Schema and standards topics, the overall list is very useful. The two lists shown above represent appropriate assertions to make about how to create quality data models. Your author, on the other hand would like to drill down on three issues, which go to the heart of Mr. Hoberman's Standards, Readability, and Definitions topics. Specifically, here are elaborated your author's best practices for

- ➤ Aesthetics
- ➤ Definitions
- ➤ Naming conventions

Best Practices for Aesthetics

The primary purpose of the three versions of *conceptual models* is to communicate the analyst's understanding of the enterprise to the enterprise representatives. These people may have had no prior experience with data modeling, and they may have little patience with highly technical diagrams. Sure, some may have studied engineering and are comfortable with wiring schematics, but you cannot assume that.[♣]

For this reason, the aesthetics of the presentation is of critical importance to the success of the modeling effort. This includes four basic design standards, that are important regardless of the notation selected:

1. Show sub-type boxes *inside* super-type boxes
2. Eschew bent lines

[♣] even if the verb is an implied "to be"

[♣] Mind you it is not a terrible thing for a database designer to understand the models as well …

3. Orient the entity type boxes so that the "crows' feet" point up and to the left
4. Create the presentation in a systematic way

Show sub-type boxes inside super-type boxes

So far, the tools that support the Barker/Ellis approach to displaying sub-types have been used when presenting the conceptual models with this approach*. If, however, you are making use of Information Engineering, IDEF1X, or UML, the tools that support these techniques only do so with difficulty. Presenting sub-types this way is recommended, even so. The argument for this is two-fold:

➤ **Too many boxes -**
There are already too many boxes on the diagram. Nesting boxes makes the appearance more tidy

➤ **Inheritance -**
More significantly, nested boxes make it clear that an instance of a sub-type *really is* an instance of its super-type.

Figure 69 shows how a model using Information Engineering might portray a sub-type structure. In addition to relationship lines between entity types, there are lines connecting sub-types to super-types. This adds to the complexity of the drawing.

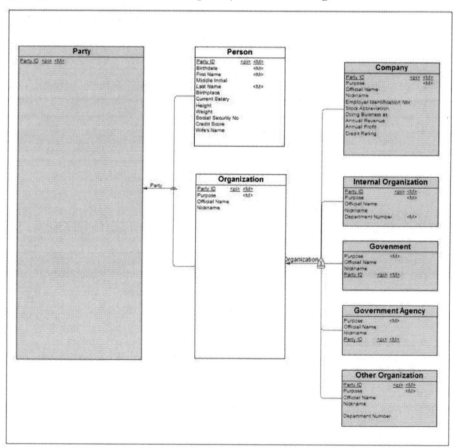

Figure 69: A Common View of Sub-types

---

* Specifically, SAP's PowerDesigner.

Figure 70 shows the much more compact Barker/Ellis approach. It is clear that **Internal Organization, Government, Government Agency,** and **Other Organization** all have "Official Name" as an attribute. Moreover, each of these (as well as **Person**) may be *the vendor of* one or more **Orders**, and may be *the customer of* one or more **Orders**.

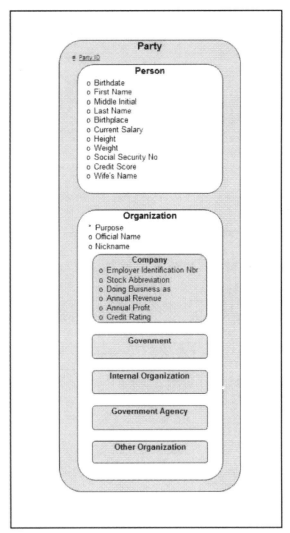

Figure 70: An Alternative View of Sub-types

In the descriptions above, we acknowledged that when the model is converted to a *Logical Model* (especially of the relational variety), the sub-types have to be separated. But during the requirements analysis phase, keeping them collapsed makes the model much more accessible to the public.

Eschew▲ Bent Lines

Figure 71 shows a model that is all too representative of what is produced in the data industry these days. What is it about? Samples? Observations? Tests? How am I to make sense of it?

The first order of business is to orient (and stretch, if necessary) boxes so that every relationship is represented by a straight line between two boxes. The line between **Direct Observation** and

---

▲   "avoid; abstain from", from *DK Illustrated Oxford Dictionary*. (Dorling Kindersley Limited & Oxford University Press). p. 274.

Laboratory Test meanders so that it is not obvious that they are connected. Is **Sample** related to **Laboratory Test, Expected Observation, Physical Observation,** or **Parameter**?

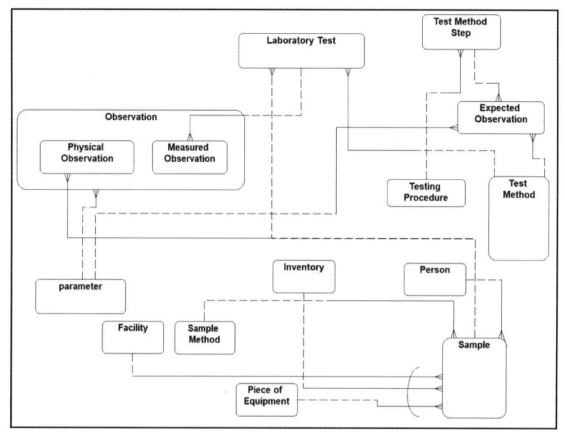

Figure 71: A Typical Data Model?

Organize the Page

A second step that will make the drawing *much more* readable, is to arrange the boxes so that crows' feet toes point to the top or the left. Think "dead crows"♦.

Figure 72 shows the transformation of Figure 71 to something more readable. Not only are all the relationship lines now straight, but the boxes are organized so that the "reference data" (**Sample, Person, Test Method,** etc.) are in the lower-right, and the "transaction data" (**Laboratory Test** and **Observation)** are in the upper-left.

Now, even if you know nothing about laboratory activities, you can understand the gist of this model. Apparently this is a manufacturing environment. Even without knowing the relationship names, it appears that **Samples** are *taken from either* an **Inventory** *or* a **Piece of Equipment,** or somewhere in a **Facility.** Each **Laboratory Test** is *an implementation of* a pre-defined **Test Method,** just as, indeed, the original **Sample** was *drawn according to* a pre-defined **Sample Method.** Each **Observation** is either of one **Sample** or a **Measured Observation** from one **Laboratory Test.**

♦   Ok, it's true: Some would contend that the crows' feet should point down and to the right. Clearly, this is heresy. But if that convention is followed consistently, it should have the same effect.

Note that Richard Barker's argument for doing it his way was that then it would <u>not</u> give you the impression of it's being a hierarchy—which, often, it is not. *It is a network.* Anyway, that's what Richard said.

The diagram as drawn here highlights the distinction between the *transaction* entity types (describing *what's done*) and the *reference* entity types (describing *who or what is doing it*).

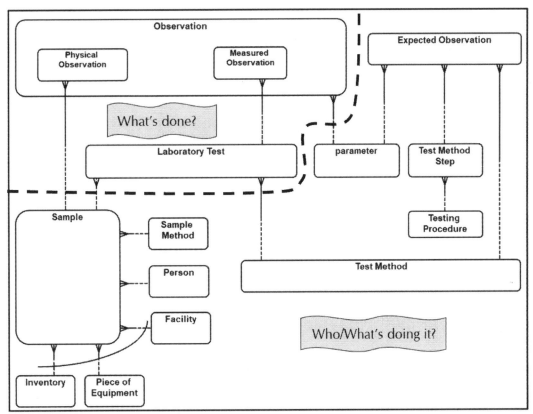

Figure 72: A Better Data Model

Prepare an Interesting Presentation

Psychologist George Miller, back in the 1950s, published a landmark paper called "The Magical Number Seven, Plus or Minus Two..."[181] In it, he revealed the results of research concluding that the human brain can hold only about seven (plus or minus two) "things" in active memory at one time. Thus, if a PowerPoint slide has dozens of lines, the viewer turns off. If there are only 2-3, it's boringly simple. About seven provides something the viewer can think about.

For those of you old enough to remember when there were few enough area codes (and no more than one or two in your neighborhood), memorizing a 7-digit phone number wasn't a problem. Now that you have to dial all ten digits (and "area code" isn't as meaningful as it once was), it's hopeless. "Speed dialing" was invented in the nick of time.

Chapter 5 describes "The Development Process" for data architecture. One step is to "Prepare and Present Models", which describes in detail how to divide up the model for a clean, coherent presentation, and then how to give the presentation. This approach constrains you by having no more than about 5 highlighted entity type boxes on any one slide, even though there may be more,

---

[181]   Miller, G. A. 1956. "The Magical Number Seven, Plus or Minus Two: Some Limits on Our Capacity for Processing Information", The Psychological Review, Vol. 63, No 2 (March, 1956), pp 81-97.

un-highlighted, left over from previous slides. This takes advantage of Mr. Miller's discovery (see pages 140-142.).

Understand, of course that those rules for presentation presume that the underlying model itself was coherent. Actually, during the modeling process, paying attention to these rules helps make models more coherent in the first place.

Best Practices for Definitions

For every entity type, a definition must be captured and recorded. While the same term may have different definitions in different contexts, at least within that context, it should be agreed upon.

In addition to entity types, other terms describing the enterprise will come up as well. Ideally the CASE tool being used will allow them to be captured as well.

Throughout history, various people and enterprise have come up specific rules for constructing a definition. They are virtually all the same.♣

The particularly articulate version presented here can be found in *Building Ontologies with Basic Formal Ontology*, by Robert Arp, Barry Smith, and Andrew D. Spear.[182] The ontologies they are describing focus on the scientific community, but nearly all their rules are relevant to defining enterprise terms as well.

1. Use Aristotelian definitions

What category (genus) is the thing in, and how is it different from all other members of that category (differentia)?[183] For example, "Enterprise" is "a collection of people with a purpose". The category is "collection of people", and the differentia is "with a purpose".

Recognize that Aristotle distinguished between something's "essential" features (those whose values defined it) and "accidental" features (those which may be of interest, but, if they are missing, the thing's existence is not compromised). For example, essential features of an automobile are that it has four or more wheels, it is motor-driven, and it has at least some section for carrying passengers. Accidental features might be its color and whether it has a manual or automatic transmission.

2. DO NOT define a word in terms of itself

…for example, "Order number is the number of an order." There is a name for this: *tautology*.♥

3. Use simpler terms than the term you are defining

The terms used in a definition should be more intelligible—for example, by being more scientifically, logically, or ontologically basic—than the term that is being defined.

♣   Unfortunately, for many of us, these rules were not covered in our English classes. Pity.

182   Arp, Robert, Barry Smith, and Andrew D. Spear. 2015. *Building Ontologies with Basic Formal Ontology*. (MIT Press).

183   Aristotle. 323 BCE. *Posterior Analytics, Book II*. From Great Books Foundation Ninth Year, Volume Two. Page 26.

♥   Even Merriema-Webster defines tautology it as "An instance of tautology". Retrieved 4/23/2018 from *https://www.merriam-webster.com/dictionary/tautology*.

4. Make the definition unpackable

That is, a definition should be **unpackable**, that is, *substitutable* for the defined term, without a change of meaning. Thus, if the definition of "contract" is "a business arrangement for the supply of goods or services at a fixed price," then we could discuss entering into "a business arrangement for the supply of goods or services at a fixed price" even as we could discuss entering into a "contract".

Best Practices for Naming Conventions

In standards for naming, at least for the three kinds of *conceptual models*, a good source is also *Building Ontologies with Basic Formal Ontology*, by Robert Arp, Barry Smith, and Andrew D. Spear.[184]

1. Strive to insure maximal consensus with the terminological usage of [subject matter experts] in the relevant discipline.

2. Identify areas of disciplinary overlap where terminological usage is not consistent. Look for and keep track of synonyms for terms already in the terminology list.

3. Don't re-invent the wheel. In term selection, stay as close as possible to the usage of actual domain experts. Note that in some cases (invariably the word that is at the heart of the nature of the business), there are too many definitions for the term to be useful. Find a different way to describe each of the concepts involved.

4. Use singular nouns.

5. Throughout this book, the convention is that specialized terms are represented in **bold face.** Entity type names are represented by **Bold Face (Calibri font)** and have initial capital letters. In your glossary, be sure you have a standard for fonts.

6. Avoid acronyms. Even if it a commonly used term, always spell it out, with the acronym in parentheses. "NATO" is acceptable ♥. So is "DNA". Pretty much every other acronym in the world is not. If it is to be used, of course, include the definition. This is in two parts: what the letters mean (that is, for example "North Atlantic Treaty Organization"), and what the acronym means (that is, "An alliance of European and North American nations originally set up to defend against the Soviet Union").

7. Ensure univocity of terms. That is, each term should have the same meaning on every occasion of its use.

8. Avoid nouns that describe masses. We are concerned with instances of things. We cannot speak of "all equipment". We need something like "each piece of equipment".

   Because of constraints in the technology being used, names in a physical database design have some additional constraints.

---

[184] Arp, et. al. *Ibid.*

♥ It is true that times have changed. The millennial generation didn't have the "North Atlantic Treaty Organization" drilled into their brains, so maybe this one should be spelled out. For current times, think "ISIS".

9. They must conform to the maximum length allowed by the DBMS, so use abbreviations where necessary. The enterprise should publish a standard list of abbreviations to be used for all systems.

10. While *conceptual* names use blank spaces as separators between words, logical and physical names suppress spaces. If the target is a relational database, underscores are used. If the target is an object-oriented system, the words are adjacent, in something called *camel case*. (the second and all subsequent words have a capitalized first letter.

   Whichever is used, do so consistently throughout the model.

BIBLIOGRAPHY

The descriptions of various data modeling methods was not meant to be comprehensive. In for each method of interest to the reader, 'e is strongly encouraged to seek out source materials which are much more comprehensive. Most of those required are described in this bibliography.

It is in two parts: the first part is a complete, alphabetical by author, listing. The second part is the same set, but organized by category and kind of model.

Complete Bibliography

Aristotle. 323 BCE. *Posterior Analytics, Book II*. From Great Books Foundation Ninth Year, Volume Two.

Armstrong Laboratory AL/HRGA. 1994. *Information Integration for Concurrent Engineering*. Knowledge Based Systems, Inc.

Arp, Robert, Barry Smith, and Andrew D. Spear. 2015. *Building Ontologies with Basic Formal Ontology*. (MIT Press.)

Bakema, Guido, J.P. Zwart, and H. van der Lek. 2002. *Fully Communication Oriented Information Modeling (FCO-IM)*. (Privately published.) (Available at *http://fco-im.nl/index.php?option=com_content&view=article&id=47:fully-communication-oriented-information-modeling-&catid=35:books&Itemid=5*.)

Barker, Richard. 1990. *CASE*Method: Entity Relationship Modeling*. (Addison Wesley).

——————————, Cliff Longman. 1992. *CASE*Method: Function and Process Modelling*. (Addison-Wesley).

Beer, Stafford. 1979. *The Heart of Enterprise*. (John Wiley).

Blaha. Michael 2014. *UML Database Modeling Workbook*. (Technics Publications).

Bracket, Michael H, 2000. *Data Resource Quality*. (Addison-Wesley.

Bruce, Thomas. 1992. *Designing Quality Databases with IDEF1X Information Models*. (Dorset House).

Bryla, Bob, Kevin Loney. 2013. *Oracle Database 12c The Complete Reference (Oracle Press) 1st Edition*. (Berkley: McGraw-Hill Education).

Burbank, Donna and Steve Hoberman. 2011. *Data Modeling Made Simple with CA ERwin Data Modeler R8*. (Technics Publications).

Carlis, John and Joseph Macguire. 2001. *Mastering Data Modeling: A User-driven Approach*. (Addison-Wesley).

Chapin, Donald. 2008. *MDA Foundational Model Applied to Both the Organization and Business Application Software*. Object Management Group (OMG) working paper March,. (Quoted in McGilvray. 2008.)

Chen, Peter. 1976. "The Entity-Relationship Model: Towards a Unified View of Data", *ACM Transactions on Database Systems*, Vol. 1, No 1, (March 1976).

Codd, Edward F. 1970. "A Relational Model of Data for Large Shared Data Banks". *Communications of the ACM*, 13, No. 6 (June).

Computer Systems Laboratory of the National Institute of Standards and Technology (NIST). 1993. *FIPS Publication 184. IDEF1X*. 21. December.

DAMA International. *DAMA-DMBOK: Data Management Body of Knowledge*. 2017. "Data Modeling and Design". (Technics Publications).

Data-Warehouse.net. 2017 "What is a Dimensional Model?". (Retrieved 10/12/2017 from *https://data-warehouses.net/glossary/dimensionalmodel.html*.)

Date, C. J. 2003. *An Introduction to Database Systems (8th Edition)*. (Pearson).

Date, C.J, Darwen, Hugh. 2000. *Foundation for Future Database System: The Third Manifesto*. (Addison-Wesley).

DeMarco, Thomas. 1978. *Structured Analysis and System Specification*. (Prentice-Hall).

Finkelstein, Clive. 1989. *An Introduction to Information Engineering: From Strategic Planning to Information Systems.* (Addison-Wesley).

Fowler, Martin. 1997. *Analysis Patterns; Reusable Object Models.* (Addison Wesley).

Gane, Chris and Trish Sarson. 1979. *Structured Systems Analysis: Tools and Techniques.* (Prentice Hall).

Halpin, Terry. 1995. *Conceptual Schema & Relational Database Design, Second Edition.* (Prentice Hall).

Halpin, Terry. 2015. *Object-role Modeling Fundamentals.* (Technics Publications).

Hay, David C. 1996. *Data Model Patterns: Conventions of Thought* (Dorset House).

_____. 2006. *Data Model Patterns: A Metadata Map.* (Morgan Kaufmann).

_____. 2011. *Enterprise Model Patterns: Describing the World.* (Technics Publications).

_____. 2003. *Requirements Analysis: From Business Views to Architecture.* (Prentice-Hall).

_____. 2011. *UML and Data Modeling: A Reconciliation.* (Technics Publications).

_____ 1998. "Making Data Models Readible". *Information Systems Management* 15(1) Winter, pp 21-33. (Available at: *http://www.essentialstrategies.com/publications/modeling/makingrd.htm.*)

Hoberman, Steve. 2015. *Data Model Scorecard: Applying the Industry Standard on Data Model Quality.* (Technics Publications).

Hoberman Steve. 2009. *Data Modeling Made Simple: A Practical Guide for Business and IT Professionals, Second Edition.* (Technics Publications).

Jardine, Donald A., Editor. 1977. *The ANSI/SPARC DBMS Model.* (The North-Holland Publishing Company).

Kimball, Ralph. 1996. *The Data Warehouse Toolkit.* (John Wiley & Sons).

Kemmerling, G. 2002. *Philosophical Dictionary.* (Encyclopaedia Britannica). Available at *http://www.philosophypages.com/dy/o.htm#onty*

Linstedt, Daniel and Michel Olschimke. 2016. *Building a Scalable Data Warehouse with Data Vault 2.0.* (Morgan Kaufmann). pp. 217-218.

Kipling, Rudyard. 1902. *Just So Stories.* "The Elephant's Child". (Digireads.com Publishing).

Liyang Yu. 2014. *A Developer's Guide to the Semantic Web, Second Edition.* (Springer).

Marco, David. 2000. *Building and Managing the Meta Data Repository.* (John Wiley & Sons).

McGilvray, Danette. 2008. *Executing Data Quality Projects: Ten Steps to Quality Data and Trusted Information.* (Morgan Kaufmann).

McMenamin, Steven and John Palmer. 1984. *Essential Systems Analysis.* (Yourdon Press).

Martin, James and J. Leben. 1989. *Strategic Information Planning Methodologies.* (Prentice Hall).

Martin, James and N. McClure. 1985. *Diagramming Techniques for Analysts and Programmers.* (Prentice Hall).

Merriam Webster Editors. 2017. *Merriam-Webster On-line Dictionary.* (Retrieved from *http://Merriam-webster.com*).

Microsoft authors. 2015 *C# Language Reference.* Retrieved, 4/10/2017 (Microsoft Press). (Available from *https://docs.microsoft.com/en-us/dotnet/csharp/language-reference/keywords/namespace*).

MongoDB, Inc. 2017. "Top 5 Considerations When Evaluating NoSQL Databases". (Available at: *https://www.mongodb.com/collateral/top-5-considerations-when-evaluating-nosql-databases.*)

Nijssen, Gerardus Maria and T Halpin. 1989. *Conceptual Schema and Relational Database Design.* Prentice-Hall.

Object Management Group. 2015. *Business Motivation Model (BMM).* (Available at http://omg.org/bmm/1.3.)

_____. 2008. *Working Paper:* "MDA Foundational Model Applied to Both the Organization and Business Application Software".

_____. 2001. *Model Driven Architecture (MDA).* (Available at: *http://www.omg.org/cgi-bin/doc?ormsc./*)

_____. 2014.*MDA Specifications.* 2014. (Available at: *http://www.omg.org/mda/specs.htm.*)

_____. 2014. *Model Driven Architecture® (MDA®) MDA Guide rev. 2.0*. 2014. (*Available at http://www.omg.org/cgi-bin/doc?ormsc/14-06-01.*)

_____. *Semantics of Business Vocabulary and Rules℠*. (2017. Available at: *http://www.omg.org/spec/SBVR/1.4*)

_____. 2015. *Unified Modeling Language™ (UML®)* Version 2.5. (Can be downloaded from *http://www.omg.org/spec/UML/2.5/PDF/*.)

Oxford Editors. 1971. *The Compact Edition of the Oxford English Dictionary*. (Oxford University Press).

Reingruer, Michael C. and William W. Gregory. 1994. *The Data Modeling Handbook*. (John Wiley & Sons.)

Schmidt, Bob, edited by David Warren, Ph.D. 1999. *Data Modeling for Information Professionals*. (Prentice Hall).

Silverston, Len, W. H. Inmon, Kent Graziano. 1997. *The Data Model Resource Book*. (John Wiley).

Silverston, Len. 2001. *The Data Model Resource Book Revised Edition: Volume 1 A Library of Universal Data Model for All Enterprises* (Wiley Computer Publishing).

_____. 2001. *The Data Model Resource Book Revised Edition: Volume 2 A Library of Universal Data Model by Industry Types*. (Wiley Computer Publishing).

_____ and Paul Agnew. 2009. *The Data Model Resource Book Revised Edition: Volume 3 Universal Patterns for Data Modeling* (Wiley Computer Publishing).

Simsion, Graeme and Graham Witt. 2005. *Data Modeling Essentials, Third Edition*. (Morgan Kaufmann).

Simsion, Graeme. 2007. *Data Modeling: Theory and Practice*. (Technics Publications).

Sowa, John and J. A. Zachman. 1992. "Extending and Formalizing the Framework for Information Systems Architecture", *IBM Systems Journal*, Vol 31, No 3. IBM Publication G321-5488.

Sullivan, Dan. 2015. *NoSQL for Mere Mortals*. (Addison-Wesley).

Tannenbaum, Adrienne. 2002. *Metadata Solutions*. Addison-Wesley.

Teamco, Inc. *Mitrol History*. 1980. (Retrieved 9/11/2017 from *http://www.mitrol.com/html/history.html#top*.)

von Halle, Barbara. 2002. *Business Rules Applied*. (John Wiley and Sons).

Walmsley, Priscilla. 2002. *Definitive XML Schema*. Prentice Hall.

Witt, Graham. 2012. *Writing Effective Business Rules: A Practical Method* (Morgan Kaufmann).

World Wide Web Consortium. 2004. *The Semantic Web*. (Described on *https://www.w3.org/standards/semanticweb/*.)

World Wide Web Consortium 2012. *OWL 2 Web Ontology Language Primer (Second Edition)*. (Retrieved 6/2017 from *https://www.w3.org/TR/owl2-primer/*)

_____. 2017. *RDF 1.1 XML Syntax: W3C Recommendation 25 February 2014*. Retrieved 6/ from https://www.w3.org/TR/2014/REC-rdf-syntax-grammar-20140225/

_____. 2014. *RDF 1.1: Terse Triple Language*. Retrieved 6/2017 from *https://www.w3.org/TR/turtle/*

_____. 2014. *RDF Schema 1.1: W3C Recommendation 25 February* Retrieved 6/2017 from *https://www.w3.org/TR/rdf-schema/*.

Zachman, John. 1987. "A Framework for Information Systems Architecture," *IBM Systems Journal*, 26:3 (IBM Publication G321-5298).

_____ and Stan Lock. 2011 *The Zachman Framework™*. Retrieved 2011 from *http://zachmaninternational.com/index.php/home-article/13#maincol*.

Zwart, Jan Pieter, Marco Engelbart, and Stijn Hoppenbrouwers. 2015. *Fact Oriented Modeling with FCO-IM*. (Technics Publications).

Sorted by Category

Across Categories

Barker, Richard, Cliff Longman. 1992. *CASE*Method: Function and Process Modelling.* (Addison-Wesley).

Bracket, Michael H, 2000. *Data Resource Quality.* (Addison-Wesley.

DeMarco, Thomas 1978. *Structured Analysis and System Specification,* (Prentice-Hall).

Finkelstein, Clive. 1989. *An Introduction to Information Engineering: From Strategic Planning to Information Systems.* (Addison-Wesley).

Gane, Chris and Trish Sarson. 1979. *Structured Systems Analysis: Tools and Techniques.* (Prentice Hall).

Hay, David C. 2003. *Requirements Analysis: From Business Views to Architecture.* (Prentice-Hall).

_____. 2011. *UML and Data Modeling: A Reconciliation.* (Technics Publications).

Jardine, Donald A., Editor. 1977. *The ANSI/SPARC DBMS Model.* (The North-Holland Publishing Company).

Kipling, Rudyard. 1902. *Just So Stories.* "The Elephant's Child". (Digireads.com Publishing).

Marco, David. 2000. *Building and Managing the Meta Data Repository.* (John Wiley & Sons).

McGilvray, Danette. 2008. *Executing Data Quality Projects: Ten Steps to Quality Data and Trusted Information.* (Morgan Kaufmann).

Object Management Group. 2015. *Business Motivation Model, Version 1.3.* (Available at *http://www.omg.org/cgi-bin/spec/BMM/1.3/pdf.*)

_____. 2014. *MDA Specifications.* 2014. (Available at: *http://www.omg.org/mda/specs.htm.*)

_____. 2014. *Model Driven Architecture® (MDA®) MDA Guide rev. 2.0.* 2014. (Available at http://www.omg.org/cgi-bin/doc?ormsc/14-06-01.)

Oxford Editors. 1971. *The Compact Edition of the Oxford English Dictionary.* (Oxford University Press).

Robinson, Ian, Jim Webber, & Emil Eifram. 2015. *Graph Databases: New Opportunities for Connected Data.* (O'Reilly Media).

Sowa, John and J. A. Zachman. 1992. "Extending and Formalizing the Framework for Information Systems Architecture", *IBM Systems Journal,* Vol 31, No 3. IBM Publication G321-5488.

Tannenbaum, Adrienne. 2002. *Metadata Solutions.* Addison-Wesley.

Zachman, John. 1987. "A Framework for Information Systems Architecture," *IBM Systems Journal,* 26:3 (IBM Publication G321-5298). 1987.

_____ and Stan Lock. 2011. *The Zachman Framework™.* Retrieved 2011 from *http://zachmaninternational.com/index.php/home-article/13#maincol.*

Overview Modeling

Object Management Group. 2015. *Business Motivation Model.* (Available at: http://www.omg.org/spec/BMM/1.3/.)

Semantic Modeling

Ontologies

Aristotle. 323 BCE. *Posterior Analytics, Book II.* (From Great Books Foundation Ninth Year, Volume Two.)

Armstrong Laboratory AL/HRGA. 1994. *Information Integration for Concurrent Engineering.* (Knowledge Based Systems, Inc.)

Arp, Robert, Barry Smith, and Andrew D. Spear. 2015. *Building Ontologies with Basic Formal Ontology.* (MIT Press).

Gruber, Tom. "What is an Ontology". (Knowledge Systems Laboratory, Stanford University). (Retrieved 2/27/2018 from *www-ksl.stanford.edu/kst/what-is-an-ontology.html*.)

Kemmerling, G. *Philosophical Dictionary*. 2002. (Encyclopaedia Britannica) (Available at *http://www.philosophypages.com/dy/o.htm#onty*.)

Merriam-Webster Editors. *Merriam-Webster On-line Dictionary*. 2017. (Available at *http://Merriam-webster.com*.)

Semantic Web

Allemang, Dean and Jim Hendler. 2011. *Semantic Web for the Working Ontologist: Effective Modeling in RDFS and OWL*. (Morgan Kaufman).

Liyang Yu. 2014. *A Developer's Guide to the Semantic Web, Second Edition*. (Springer).

World Wide Web Consortium. 2004. *The Semantic Web*. (Described on *https://www.w3.org/standards/semanticweb/*.)

World Wide Web Consortium. 2012. *OWL 2 Web Ontology Language Primer* (Second Edition). (Retrieved 6/2017 from *https://www.w3.org/TR/owl2-primer/*.)

World Wide Web Consortium. 2014. *RDF 1.1 XML Syntax: W3C Recommendation 25 February*. Retrieved 6/2017 from https://www.w3.org/TR/2014/REC-rdf-syntax-grammar-20140225/

World Wide Web Consortium. 2014. *RDF 1.1:Terse Triple Language*. Retrieved 6/2017 from *https://www.w3.org/TR/turtle/*

World Wide Web Consortium. 2014. *RDF Schema 1.1: W3C Recommendation 25* February Retrieved 6/2017 from *https://www.w3.org/TR/rdf-schema/*.

Fact-based Modeling

Bakema, Guido, J.P. Zwart, and H. van der Lek. 2002 *Fully Communication Oriented Information Modeling (FCO-IM)*. (Privately published). Available at *http://fco-im.nl/index.php?option=com_content&view=article&id=47:fully-communication-oriented-information-modeling-&catid=35:books&Itemid=5* .

Halpin, Terry. *Conceptual Schema & Relational Database Design, Second Edition*. (Prentice Hall).

Halpin, Terry. 1995. *Object-role Modeling Fundamentals*. (Technics Publications). 2015.

Nijssen, Gerardus Maria and T Halpin. 1989. *Conceptual Schema and Relational Database Design*. (Prentice-Hall).

Zwart, Jan Pieter, Marco Engelbart, and Stijn Hoppenbrouwers. 2015. *Fact Oriented Modeling with FCO-IM*. (Technics Publications).

Semantics of Business Vocabulary and Rules

Object Management Group. 2017. *Semantics of Business Vocabulary and Rules*[tm]. (Available at: *http://www.omg.org/spec/SBVR/1.4*).

von Halle, Barbara. 2002.*Business Rules Applied*. (John Wiley and Sons).

Witt, Graham. 2012. *Writing Effective Business Rules: A Practical Method* (Morgan Kaufmann).

Essential Modeling

Barker, Richard. 1990. *CASE*Method: Entity Relationship Modeling*. (Addison Wesley).

Hay, David C. 1996. *Data Model Patterns: Conventions of Thought* (Dorset House).

Hay, David C. 2006. *Data Model Patterns: A Metadata Map*. (Morgan Kaufmann).

Hay, David C. 2011. *Enterprise Model Patterns: Describing the World*. (Technics Publications).

McMenamin, Steven and John Palmer. 1984. *Essential Systems Analysis*. (Yourdon Press).

Silverston, Len, W. H. Inmon, Kent Graziano. 1997. *The Data Model Resource Book*. (John Wiley).

Data Modeling in General

Bachman, Charles W. 1969 Summer. "Data Structure Diagrams," ACM *Data Base* (1:2). pages 4 - 10.

Barker, Richard. 1990. *CASE*Method: Entity Relationship Modeling.* (Addison Wesley).

Carlis, John and Joseph Macguire. 2001. *Mastering Data Modeling: A User-driven Approach.* (Addison-Wesley).

Chapin, Donald. *MDA Foundational Model Applied to Both the Organization and Business Application Software.* Object Management Group (OMG) working paper March, 2008. (Quoted in McGilvray. 2008.)

Chen, Peter. 1976. "The Entity-Relationship Model: Towards a Unified View of Data", *ACM Transactions on Database Systems*, Vol. 1, No 1, (March 1976).

DAMA International. 2017. *DAMA-DMBOK: Data Management Body of Knowledge.* "Data Modeling and Design". (Technics Publications).

Hay, David C. 1996. *Data Model Patterns: Conventions of Thought.* (Dorset House).

_____. 2006. *Data Model Patterns: A Metadata Map.* (Morgan Kaufmann).

_____. 2011. *Enterprise Model Patterns: Describing the World.* (Technics Publications).

_____. 2003. *Requirements Analysis: From Business Views to Architecture.* (Prentice-Hall).

_____. 2011. *UML and Data Modeling: A Reconciliation.* (Technics Publications).

_____ 1998. "Making Data Models Readible". *Information Systems Management* 15(1) Winter, pp 21-33. (Available at: *http://www.essentialstrategies.com/publications/modeling/makingrd.htm*).

Hoberman Steve. 2009. *Data Modeling Made Simple: A Practical Guide for Business and IT Professionals, Second Edition.* (Technics Publications).

Hoberman, Steve. 2015. *Data Model Scorecard: Applying the Industry Standard on Data Model Quality.* (Technics Publications).

Martin, James and N. McClure. 1985. *Diagramming Techniques for Analysts and Programmers.* (Prentice Hall).

Reingruer, Michael C. and William W. Gregory. 1994. *The Data Modeling Handbook.* (John Wiley & Sons.)

Schmidt, Bob, edited by David Warren, Ph.D. 1999. *Data Modeling for Information Professionals.* (Prentice Hall).

Silverston, Len, W. H. Inmon, Kent Graziano. 1997. *The Data Model Resource Book.* (John Wiley).

_____. 2001. *The Data Model Resource Book Revised Edition: Volume 1 A Library of Universal Data Model for All Enterprises* (Wiley Computer Publishing).

_____. 2001. *The Data Model Resource Book Revised Edition: Volume 2 A Library of Universal Data Model by Industry Types.* (Wiley Computer Publishing).

_____ and Paul Agnew. 2009. *The Data Model Resource Book Revised Edition: Volume 3 Universal Patterns for Data Modeling* (Wiley Computer Publishing).

Data Flow Diagramming

Gane, Chris and Trish Sarson. 1979. *Structured Systems Analysis: Tools and Techniques.* (Prentice Hall).

DeMarco, Thomas. 1978. *Structured Analysis and System Specification*, (Prentice-Hall).

McMenamin, Steven and John Palmer. 1984. *Essential Systems Analysis.* (Yourdon Press).

Logical Modeling

Data Vault Modeling

Linstedt, Daniel and Michel Olschimke. 2016. *Building a Scalable Data Warehouse with Data Vault 2.0.* (Morgan Kaufmann). pp. 217-218.

Dimensional Modeling

Kimball, Ralph. 1996. *The Data Warehouse Toolkit*. (John Wiley & Sons).

Jaspersoft. 2017. *What is a Dimensional Model?* (Data-Warehouses.net).
(Retrieved 10/12/2017 from *https://data-warehouses.net/glossary/dimensionalmodel.html*)

NoSQL Modeling

MongoDB, Inc. 2017. "Top 5 Considerations When Evaluating NoSQL Databases". (Available at: *https://www.mongodb.com/collateral/top-5-considerations-when-evaluating-nosql-databases*).

Robinson, Ian, Jim Webber, & Emil Eifram. 2015. *Graph Databases: New Opportunities for Connected Data*. (O'Reilly Media).

Sullivan, Dan. 2015. *NoSQL for Mere Mortals*. (Addison-Wesley).

Object-oriented Modeling

Fowler, Martin. 1997. *Analysis Patterns: Reusable Object Models* (Addison Wesley).

Gama, Eric, Richard Helm, Ralph Johnson, John Vlissides. 1995. *Design Patterns*. (Addison Wesley).

Object Management Group. 2015. *Unified Modeling Language™ (UML®)* Version 2.5. (Can be downloaded from *http://www.omg.org/spec/UML/2.5/PDF/*).

Walmsley, Priscilla. 2002. *Definitive XML Schema*. (Prentice Hall).

Relational Modeling

Bachman, Charles W. 1969 Summer. "Data Structure Diagrams," ACM *Data Base* (1:2). pages 4 - 10.

Blaha. Michael 2014. *UML Database Modeling Workbook*. (Technics Publications).

Bruce, Thomas. 1992. *Designing Quality Databases with IDEF1X Information Models*. (Dorset House).

Burbank, Donna and Steve Hoberman. 2011. *Data Modeling Made Simple with CA ERwin Data Modeler R8*. (Technics Publications).

Codd, Edward F. 1970. "A Relational Model of Data for Large Shared Data Banks". *Communications of the ACM*, 13, No. 6 (June).

Computer Systems Laboratory of the National Institute of Standards and Technology (NIST). 1993. *FIPS Publication 184. IDEF1X*. 21 December.

Date, C. J. 2003. An Introduction to Database Systems (8th Edition). (Pearson)

Date, C.J, Darwen, Hugh. 2000. *Foundation for Future Database System: The Third Manifesto*. (Addison-Wesley).

Hoberman Steve. 2009. *Data Modeling Made Simple: A Practical Guide for Business and IT Professionals, Second Edition*. (Technics Publications).

Martin, James and N. McClure. 1985. *Diagramming Techniques for Analysts and Programmers*. (Prentice Hall).

Other Technologies

Teamco, Inc1980. *Mitrol History*. (Retrieved 9/11/2017 from *ttp://www.mitrol.com/html/history.html#top*).

Physical Modeling

Bryla, Bob, Kevin Loney. 2013. *Oracle Database 12c The Complete Reference (Oracle Press) 1st Edition*. (McGraw-Hill Education).

Date, C. J. 2003. An Introduction to Database Systems (8th Edition). (Pearson)

Microsoft. 2017. *C# Language Reference*. (Retrieved, 4/10/2017 from *https://docs.microsoft.com/en-us/dotnet/csharp/language-reference/keywords/namespace*).

APPENDIX A – GLOSSARY

Term	Definition	Source	Chapter	Page
<fk>	(See Foreign Key)	PowerDesigner	5	98
<pk>	(See Primary Key)	PowerDesigner	5	99
#	(See Octothorpe)			
=>	When the CASE Tool *PowerDesigner* generates a default logical model from a conceptual model, relevant "crow's feed" (>) symbols are modified to do this to indicate that the relationship is "identifying". Thus, the generated foreign key will be identifying.	PowerDesigner	5	99
0NF	(See Zeroth Normal Form	DCH	5	100
1NF	(See First Normal Form.)	DCH	5	101
2NF	(See Second Normal Form.)	DCH	5	101
3NF	(See Third Normal Form.)	DCH	5	103
4NF	(See Fourth Normal Form.)	DCH	5	105
5NF	(See Fifth Normal Form.)	DCH	5	106
ACID	**Atomicity, Consistency, Isolation**, and **Durability** – desirable characteritics of transaction in a database. Relational databases do this. NoSQL databases, not so much.	Sulivan[185]	5	128
alternative primary key	a candidate key that, although unique, was not chosen as the *primary key*. Even though a table may contain more than one candidate key, only one candidate key can serve as the primary key for a table. An alternative key can still be used to find specific table instances. Often the primary key is a surrogate key and the alternative keys are business keys.	DMBOK	5	100
app	an application. That is, a computer program, typically written for a hand-held computer (also known colloquially as a "smart phone").	DCH	6	135
architect perspective	(in the Zachman Framework), the point of view of those concerned with the "essence" of the enterprise. This is a relatively abstract point of view, reflecting the use of generic pattern to identify common structure.	JZ, DCH	2	12
Aristotelian definition	What category (genus) is the thing in, and how is it different from all other members of that category (differentia)? [186] For example, "Enterprise" is "a collection of people with a purpose". The category is "collection of people", and the differentia is "with a purpose". Recognize that Aristotle distinguished between something's "essential" features (those whose values defined it) and "accidental" features (those which may be of interest, but, if they are missing, the thing's existence is not compromised. For example, essential features of an automobile are that it has four or more wheels, it is motor-driven, and it has at least some section for carrying passengers. Accidental features might be its color and whether it has a manual or automatic transmission.	DCH	6	162

---

[185] Dan Sullivan. 2015. *NoSQL for Mere Mortals.* (Addison Wesley Professional). P.54.

[186] Arp, R., B. Smith, A. Spear. 2015. Building Ontologies with Basic Formal Ontology

Term	Definition	Source	Chapter	Page
assessment	the determination of the extent to which an *influencer* affects the operation of an enterprise.	OMG, "Motivation Model"	4	33
association	In *UML*, this is a link between two classes. The name which identifies each association end is a *role name*. Because a UML role name describes processing, the association is not a structural statement the way it is in conceptual modeling. (See your author's book on *UML and Data Modeling* for details.[187])	Object Management Group	5	114
atomic fact	(in ORM) a fact that can't be split into two or more facts involving the same object types without information loss.	ORM, Halpin	4	46
atomicity	(NoSQL) A transaction is not complete until every step is complete	Dan Sullivan[188]	5	128
attribute	a characteristic evaluated for or describing instances of an entity type	DCH	4	38
attribute unique identifiers	the use of one or more *attributes* to identify instances of an entity type.	DCH	4	79
Barker / Ellis notation	developed by Richard Barker and Harry Ellis, this is an approach to data modeling that is specifically oriented to presenting the model to non-technical business people	DCH	1	7
BCNF	(See Boyce/Codd Normal Form.)	DCH	5	103
BASE	(See *Basically Available, Soft State,* and *Eventually Consistent.*)	Dan Sullivan[189]	5	128
basically available	(NoSQL) There can be a partial failure in some part of a distributed system and the est of the system continues to function.	Dan Sullivan[190]	5	128
big data	Computers. data sets, typically consisting of billions or trillions of records, that are so vast and complex that they require new and powerful computational resources to process: Supercomputers can analyze big data to create models of global climate change.	Dictionary. com[191]	5	121
binary relationship	A relationship between exactly two entity types.	DCH	4	85
Boyce/Codd Normal Form	a constraint on data structure that resolves *overlapping composite candidate keys*. A candidate key is either a *primary* or an *alternative* key. 'Composite' means more than one (e.g. two or more columns in an entity's primary or alternate keys), and 'overlapping' means there are hidden business rules between the keys.	DCH	5	103
business function	(See function)			
business information requirement	information needed in the context of one or more business *functions* and/or *processes*.	DCH	6	139
business manager perspective	(in the Zachman Framework), the point of view of those responsible for the day-to-day operation of the enterprise—the managers and other "owners" of the enterprise's data.	JZ, DCH	2	12

---

[187] David C. Hay. 2011. *UML and Data Modeling: A Reconciliation.* (Technics Publications).

[188] Sullivan. 2015. *Op. cit.*

[189] Sullivan. 2015. *Op. cit.*

[190] Sullivan. 2015. *Op. cit.*

[191] Based on the Random House Dictionary, © Random House, Inc. 2018.

Term	Definition	Source	Chapter	Page
Business or Domain Models	in the 2014 version of MDA, these are models of the actual people, places, things, and laws of a domain. The "instances" of these models are "real things", not representations of those things in an information system. In MDA® domain, models have historically been called "CIM" for "Computation Independent Models	OMG, MDA, 2014	2	13
business policy	a non-actionable *directive* that guides the activities of the business or governs them in a general way. note that it "governs"; it does not control or shape courses of action. for example, to say that "we will not permit on-site visits" constrains the tactics available for meeting the *strategy* to "increase market share". It does not specify what those *tactics* should be.	OMG, "Motivation Model"	4	33
business rule	a *directive* that is "the set of conditions that govern a business event so that it [the event] occurs in a way that is acceptable to the business"[192]	OMG, "Motivation Model"	4	33
buzzword	"an important-sounding usually technical word or phrase often of little meaning used chiefly to impress laymen."	Merriam Webster[193]	Preface	viii
buzzword compliant	the state where you fully understand the meanings of those buzzwords that actually have real meanings in the data architecture industry.	DCH	Preface	viii
candidate primary key	any set of columns that uniquely identify a table instance. A candidate key is a minimal set of one or more columns (i.e., a simple or compound key) that identifies the table instance to which it belongs. A table may have multiple candidate keys.	DMBOK	5	99
cardinality	for an entity type, determination of whether each instance of it is associated with *one and only one* instance of a related entity type, or *more than one*.	DCH	4	40
CASE tool	(See Computer-aided System Engineering tool.)			
categorization scheme enumeration	(SBVR) defines members of at categorization scheme that are *mutually exclusive*, and *jointly exhaustive*. That is, <u>no</u> individual object can be a member of <u>more than one</u> category in the scheme, and <u>each</u> member of the class with which the scheme is associated <u>must belong to one</u> category in the scheme.	SBVR, Witt[194]	4	56
child table	the table with a *foreign key*, where a table is related to a second table via that foreign key.	DCH	5	98
CIM	(See Computation Independent Model.)	OMG, MDA, 2014	2	13
Class of Platform (technology) Independent Model	a model of the semantics of a business.	Chapin/OMG 2008	2	13
Class of Platform (technology) Specific Model	an arrangement of data to be used by a particular data management technology to accommodate technical constraints and expected usage.	Chapin/OMG 2008	2	13
closed world assumption	the conventional data analysis assumption that if it doesn't *follow the specified rules*, then <u>it must be false</u>. (As opposed to the open world assumption.)	W3C	4	64

---

[192] Barbara von Halle. 2002. *Business Rules Applied*. (John Wiley and Sons). p. 28.

[193] Merriam Webster. 1946 (first known use). "buzzword". Retrieved, 3/3/2018 from https://www.merriam-webster.com/dictionary/buzzword?utm_campaign=sd&utm_medium=serp&utm_source=jsonld

[194] Witt. 2012. ...Effective Business Rules... op. cit.

Term	Definition	Source	Chapter	Page
code set	in a database *domain*, this is a set of descriptors corresponding to a *value set* defined for the original essential model. For example, a "value set" might be "the set of Canadian Provinces", while one "code set" may name them in English, while another would name them in French.	DCH	4	42
column-oriented (NoSQL) model	a kind of NoSQL database that can work with more complex data types including unformatted text and imagery. This data can also be defined when they are entered. This is as opposed to a relational database which works with a predefined structure and simple data types, (e.g., "number" and "date").	Dan Sullivan[195]	5	96
column-oriented database	A *NoSQL* database is closest to the RDBMS. Both have a similar way of looking at data as rows and values. The difference, though, is that RDBMSs work with a predefined structure and simple data types, such as string, number and date, whereas column-oriented databases, such as Cassandra, can work with more complex data types including unformatted text and imagery. This data can also be defined on the fly.	W3C	5	122
(document) collections	a list of (NoSQL) *documents*.	Dan Sullivan	5	121
column-oriented database	similar to a relational databse, but can work with more complex data types, including unformatted text, collections, and imagry.	Dan Sullivan	5	96
compact form	(in ORM) a layout of an ORM model in which the identifying attribute of each class is displayed inside that class's symbol.	ORM, Halpin	4	47
compound primary key	a set of two or more columns that together uniquely identify a table instance. Examples are US phone number (area code + exchange + local number) and credit card number (issuer ID + account ID + check digit).	DMBOK	5	99
Computation Independent Model	(See Business or Domain Model, and *Class of Platform Independent Model*.)	OMG, MDA, 2014	2	13
computer-aided software engineering tool.	software used to create and maintain data models, data dictionaries, and other system artifacts. Also referred to as a *CASE tool*.	DCH	6	138
conceptual model	a domain-oriented model not in any way concerned with technology used to manage the information describing its things of significance	DCH	1	1
conceptual schema (ANSI)	"embodies the 'real world' view of the enterprise being modeled in the database. It represents the current 'best model' or 'way of doing business' for the enterprise." It encompasses the meanings of most or all of the external schemas	ANSI-SPARC, 1977	2	9
conformed dimension (dimensional model)	dimension tables shared across multiple data marts or fact tables the practical importance is that the row headers from any answer sets from conformed dimensions must be able to match exactly.	DMBOK	5	112
conformed fact (dimensional model)	use standardized definitions of terms across individual marts. Different business users may use the same term in different ways. Developers need to be keenly aware of things that may be named the same but actually represent different concepts across enterprises, or conversely things that are named differently but are actually the same concept across enterprises.	DMBOK	5	113
consistency	(NoSQL) A transaction does not leave a database in a state that violates the data's integrity	Dan Sullivan[196]	5	128

---

[195] Sullivan. 2015. *NoSQL. Op. cit.*

[196] Sullivan. 2015. *Op. cit.*

Term	Definition	Source	Chapter	Page
continuant	an entity that *continues* or *persist* through time, including: (1) independent objects (for example, both people (like Julia Roberts) and organizations (like Microsoft), and inanimate things (such as your computer and my smart phone); (2) dependent continuants, including qualities (such as your temperature and my height), and functions (such as the function of this switch to turn on this light); together with (3) the spatial regions these entities occupy at any given time (like Cleveland, Ohio). ("Basic Functional Ontology")	Spear, IFOMIS	4	30
convergent model	an enterprise or other large-scope entity / relationship model that has been reduced in size from larger, more complex models. This is typically done via the introductin of patterns.	DH	2	72
course of action	an approach or plan for configuring some aspect of the enterprise. This involves *the use of* things, processes, locations, people, timing, or motivation.	OMG, "Motivation Model"	4	32
CPIM	(See Class of Platform Independent Model			
CPSM	(See Class of Platform Specific Model.)			
data	(See *Datum*)	DCH	1	1
data definition language	provides for the definition or description of database objects.	Date	6	128
data format	A *domain* that constrains an attribute's layout to correspond to a pattern, such as a social security number, telephone number, etc.	DCH	4	43
data flow diagram	a model of the information flows in an enterprise or a portion of it. The model describes *processes*, *external entities*, *data stores*, and *data flows* among them.	Gane/Sarson [197]	6	139
data flow	in a *data flow diagram*, representation of the fact that data may pass from one element (*external entity*, *process*, or *data store*) to another.	Gane/Sarson [198]	6	139
data store	in a *data flow diagram*, representation of the fact that a body of data are stored at least temporarily in one place, beit in a computerized file or on a piece of paper.	Gane/Sarson [199]	6	139
data type	in a *domain* an option that constrains an attribute value to a particular kind of data, such as "integer", "string", etc.	DCH	4	43
datatype property	a property of a class that describes something about it. This is analogous to an entity type *attribute*. It consists of a *domain* (the class) and a *range* (a data type)	W3C	4	64
data vault	originally, an approach to modeling the structure of a data warehouse. Data Vault 2.0 is "a solution comprising Architecture, Methodology, Modeling and Implementation". The structure includes all of the data's history.	Daniel Lindstedt	5	115
datum	something given or admitted as a basis for reasoning or inference	MW	1	1
DDL	(See data definition language)			
deductive approach (to patterns)	make use of existing patterns to identify common characteristics with the target model	DCH	4	77
default logical (relational) model	a *logical data model* that is created by a *CASE* tool from an *essential data model*. Each entiy type becomes a table, with its attributes becoming columns. Each relationship is implemented by the creation of a *foreign key* in the "child" table that points to an instance of the "parent" table.	DCH	6	143

---

[197] Chris Gane and Trish Sarson. 1979. *Structured Systems Analysis: Tools and Techniques*. (Prentice Hall).

[198] Gane/Sarson. 1979. Op.cit.

[199] Gane/Sarson. 1979. Op.cit.

Term	Definition	Source	Chapter	Page
definitional rule	a constraint as to how we define various constraints created by the enterprise (or the industry within which it operates	OMG (SBVR)	5	54
denormalization	the deliberate transformation of normalized logical data model entities into physical tables with redundant or duplicate data structures. In other words, denormalization intentionally puts one attribute in multiple places. After a normalized default database design has been created, the following tradeoffs must be addressed in order to make the database design "fit" into a real database: 1. Convert the inheritance structure (super-types and sub-types) into relational two-dimensional tables. 2. Determine whether the specified derived columns should be evalu-ated and stored on input or derived when queried. 3. Where parameters have been defined as separate tables with "value" intersect tables, determine which of these should in fact become columns in the parent table.	DCH	5	108, 150
derived column	a column that is not stored in the 3NF tables, but rather is derived from others. This may be: - A calculation from other columns in the same table - An inference from a column in a *parent table* - A summation on a column from a *child table.*	DCH	6	145
desired result	an *end* that is a state or target that the enterprise intends to maintain.	OMG, "Motivation Model"	4	32
dimension table (dimensional model)	represents a hierarchy of object types that constitute the business. For example: - *Time*: year, quarter, month, day of month. - *Geography*: region, state, city, store - *Product Level*: product line, brand, group, stock-keeping unit. Each fact describes the intersection of two or more dimensions. Dimension tables contain mostly textual descriptions.	DMBOK	5	111
dimensional (logical data) model	a model in relational terms, but organized for efficient access, in terms of *dimensions* (structured keys) and *facts* (underlying information).	Kimball	5	95
directive	a specification that constrains *courses of action*. it does this in two ways: *first* it may simply be designed *to govern* one or more *courses of action*. for example, "a loan is not to be granted to someone whose credit rating is lower than b" governs the course of action concerned with granting loans. A *second* kind of directive may itself be a source of one or more *courses of action* whose whole purpose is to enforce that directive.	OMG, "Motivation Model"	4	33
divergent model	a very large semantic model that is based on either the entire enterprise or a large part of it. It is created from multiple interviews, with a wide variety of jargon terms.	DCH	5	35
document database	A *NoSQL* database that stores a business subject in one structure called a "document." For example, instead of storing Student, Course, and Registration information in three distinct relational structures, properties from all three will exist in a single document called Registration. Document-oriented modes are generally application focused, whereas table-oriented models are more data focused.	W3C	5	121
domain (database)	a set of validation rules, format constraints and other properties that apply to a group of attributes.	Barker	4	42
domain (generic)	a particular area of interest in an enterprise, such as a department or technical specialty.	DCH	1	1

Term	Definition	Source	Chapter	Page
domain ontology	an *ontology* that only addresses a particular subject area.	Reeves, "Simple Bio Upper Ontology	4	30
durability	(NoSQL) Once a transaction or operation is completed, the resulting data will remain, even in the event of a power loss.	Dan Sullivan[200]	5	128
domain-oriented (data model)	a picture of the underlying structure of an enterprise's information. (See Domain)	DCH	1	1
elementary fact	(in ORM) an atomic fact that applies a logical predicate to one or more objects.	ORM, Halpin	4	46
end	something that an enterprise sets out to accomplish.	OMG, "Motivation Model"	4	31
engineer's perspective	(in the Zachman Framework), the point of view of those responsible for designing both databases and programs.	JZ, DCH	2	12
enterprise data model	a conceptual model (overview, semantic, or essential) that encompasses the enterprise as a whole.	DCH	4	30
enterprise perspective	(in the Zachman Framework), the point of view of those using the finally constructed system.	JZ, DCH	2	12
entity (Barker/Ellis)	a thing of significance to the enterprise, about which it wishes to collect information. An *instance* of an **entity type**.	Barker/Ellis	4	36
entity (Bachman)	a particular object being considered.	Bachman	2	5
entity (Chen)	something real or imaginary that is of interest.	Chen, 1976	2	6
entity set	an entity grouping that associates a group of entities of one entity class with one entity of a different entity class in a subordinate relationshipm	Bachman	2	5
entity type (Barker / Ellis)	the definition of a *set of* **entities**—things of significance to the enterprise, about which it wishes to collect information. It is these sets, not instances of them (entities) that are represented in an entity/relationship diagram.	Barker/Ellis	4	36
entity type (Chen)	a category of **entities**	Chen, 1967	2	6
entity/relation-ship diagram	"in its simplest form, entity relationship modelling involves identifying the things of importance in an enterprise (known as **entity types**), the properties of those things (known as **attributes**), and how they are related to one another (known as **relationships**)."[201]	Barker/Ellis	4	35
Environment Model	a Sketch that includes primary entities.	Chapin/OMG 2008	2	14
eschew	"avoid; abstain from"	DK Illustrated Oxford Dictionary[202]	6	159
essential data flow diagram	a *data flow diagram* that represents only the contents of data stores and data flows, without regard to the technology required to either store or transmit them.	McMenamin and Palmer[203]	2	16
essential data model	(produced for the **Architect View** of the Zachman Framework), a modle of the fundamental *things of significance* to the enterprise. Its purpose is to capture the *fundamental, underlying* nature of the enterprise.	DCH	2	16
essential process	a collection of atomic processes that comprise the *complete response* to an **external event**.	McMenamin/ Palmer	2	17

[200] Sullivant. 2015. *Op. cit.*

[201] Barker. 1989. Op. cit.

[202] Various editors. Retrieved 3/9/2-18. *DK Illustrated Oxford Dictionary.* (DK, Oxford University Press).

[203] McMenamen and Palmer. 1984. Op. cit.

Term	Definition	Source	Chapter	Page
executive perspective	(in the Zachman Framework) the point of view of top management, in terms of basic concepts, used for defining the overall scope of efforts.	JZ, DCH	2	12
eventually consitent	(NoSQL) There may be many times when a network database is in an inconcistent state—as transactions are being processed through the network—but eventually they well all be updated.	Dan Sullivan[204]	5	128
existential fact	(in ORM) an atomic fact that simply asserts the existence of a single object.	ORM, Halpin	4	46
extended form	(in ORM) a layout of an ORM model in which the identifying attribute of each class is displayed as a separate, related, symbol, with the roles "has / is of".	ORM, Halpin	4	47
extensional definition	(SBVR)of a term is a complete disjoint list of the terms that are the *hyponyms* of that term.	SBVR, Witt[205]	4	180
external entity	a source or destination of data on a data flow diagram	Gane/Sarsen [206]	6	139
external event	something that is initiated by something in the environment. This is the basis for creating an *essential data flow diagram*.	McMenamen / Palmer[207]	6	140
external schema (ANSI)	"the various users of the database management system [that] operate on sub-sets of the total enterprise model which are relevant to their particular needs.".	ANSI-SPARC, 1977	2	9
fact	(in ORM) an atomic or conjunctive proposition taken to be true by the relevant business community.	ORM, Halpin	4	46
FCO-IM	(See Fully Communication Oriented Information Modeling.)			
fact-based modeling	a family of conceptual modeling languages that are based in the analysis of natural verbalization (plausible sentences) that might occur in the business domain. Fact-based languages view the world in terms of objects, the facts that relate or characterize those objects, and the role that each object plays in each fact.[208]	Nijssen and Halpin	4	45
fact table (dimensional model)	represents a particular measurement and is numeric, such as *amount*, *quantity* or *count*. Some measurements are the results of algorithms, in which cases metadata documentation is critical to proper understanding and usage. Fact tables take up the most space in the database (90% is a reasonable rule of thumb), and tend to have a large number of rows.	DMBOK	5	111
fact type	(in ORM) a collection of facts of a given kind.	ORM, Halpin	4	46
Fifth Normal Form	a constraint on data structure that resolves inter-entity dependencies into basic pairs, and all join dependencies use parts of primary keys. Note that the criteria for whether something is in fifth normal form is not internal. It has to do with whether the model describes what is actually going on. If it does, it's in fifth normal form. If not, then it is not.	DCH	5	106
First Normal Form	a constraint on data structure that each instance has no repeating groups. That is, each attribute is atomic.	DCH	5	101
Foreign Key	as a way of implementing relationships in a relational database, *foreign key* columns in one table correspond to primary key columns in the related table.	Codd	5	98
Fourth Normal Form	a constraint on data structure that resolves all many-to-many-to-many relationships (and beyond) in pairs until they cannot be broken down into any smaller pieces.	DCH	5	105

---

[204] Sullivan. 2015. *Op. cit.*

[205] Witt. 2012. …Effective Business Rules… op. cit.

[206] Gane/Sarson. 1979. *op. cit.*

[207] McMenamen and Palmer. 1984. *op. cit.*

[208] Gerardus Maria Nijssen and T Halpin. 1989. Conceptual Schema and Relational Database Design. (New York: Prentice Hall).

Term	Definition	Source	Chapter	Page
Fully Communica-tion Oriented Modeling	derived from NIAM, a *fact-based modeling* technique, it differs in that it views fact types and object types as one thing. That is, an object type is a kind of fact type.	Zwart, *et. all.* 2015	5	51
function	what a business does.	Barker/Longm an[209]	6	139
Function Column	(Zachman Framework) activities performed in the enterprise or by automated systems. (How?)	Zachman, Locke, 2008	2	11
goal	a **desired result** that is a specific statement about a state or condition of the enterprise to be brought about or sustained through appropriate **means**. a **goal** is an amplifier of a **vision**. that is, whereas a vision describes a *future state* of the enterprise in general, a goal is one of the *steps to be taken* to accomplish that vision. a **goal**, by definition is narrower than a **vision**.	OMG, "Motivation Model"	4	32
graph (NoSQL) model	a kind of NoSQL database that is for data whose relations are well represented as a set of nodes with a variable number of connections between these nodes. Examples include social relations (where nodes are people), public transport links (where nodes could be bus or train stations), or roadmaps (where nodes could be street intersections or highway exits). This may entail traversing a graph to find the shortest routes, nearest neighbors, etc.	Robinson, *et. al*[210]	5	96
graph database	A *NoSQL* database that is designed for data whose relations are well represented as a set of nodes with an undetermined number of connections between these nodes. Examples where a graph database can work best are social relations (where nodes are people), public transport links (where nodes could be bus or train stations), or roadmaps (where nodes could be street intersections or highway exits). Often requirements lead to traversing the graph to find the shortest routes, nearest neighbors, etc., all of which can be complex and time consuming to navigate with a traditional RDMBS.	W3C	5	123
hash key	A 32-character string derived from a specific algorithm to generate unique *surrogate key* from a combination of *natural keys*	Daniel Lindstedt	5	117
hash term	(See *octothorpe.*)			
hierarchical (logical data) model	an organization of a database that links elements in a hierarchical fashion, with multiple "branches" for every "root". This makes retrieval of high-level elements very fast, but retrieving in terms of low-level elements very slow.	DCH	5	18
hierarchy	A recursive relationship in which each lower level instance may only be related to one upper level instance. For example, each sub-type may have only one super-type. This is also referred to as a *taxonomy*, "the study of general principles of classification".[211] That is the dictionary definition, but in fact a "taxonomy" is a hierarchy.	DCH	4	85
horizontal denormaliz-ation	when one recognizes that an entire portion of a candidate table applies to only one geographic area, while other portions apply to other geographic areas. (Or departments or years, or whatever.) The point is that instances come from different places, so it is appropriate to put them in different tables.	DCH	5	129
hub	In a *data vault* structure, a collection of business keys that points to an underlying thing of significance to the enterprise.	Daniel Linstedt	5	115

[209]   Richard Barker, Cliff Longman. 1992. *Case*Method: Function and Process Modeling.* (Addison Wesley).

[210]   Robinson, Ian, Jim Webber, and Emil Eifrem. 2015. *Graph Databases: New Opportunities for Connected Data.* (O'Reilly).

[211]   Merriam Webster. Merriam-Webster On-line Dictionary: "taxonomy". (Retrieved 2/15/2017 from https//www.merriam0webstercom/dictionary/taxonomy)

Term	Definition	Source	Chapter	Page
hypernym	(linguistics) a word with a broad meaning constituting a category into which words with more specific meandings fall; a superordinate. For example, "color" is a hypernym of "red"'	(SBVR) Witt[212]	5	55
hyponym	(linguistics) a word of more specific meaning than a general or superordinate term applicable to it. For example, "red" is a hyponym of "color".	(SBVR) Witt[213]	5	55
IDEF1x	(See Integration DEFinition for Information Modeling.)			
IE	(see information engineering.)	Martin, 1985 Finklestein, 1989	2	6
Implementation Models	the way in which a particular system or subsystem is implemented such that it carries out its functions. Implementation models are typically tied to a particular implementation technology or platform." These are referred to as "PSM", or "Platform-specific Models".	OMG, MDA, 2014	2	14
inductive approach (to model patterns)	examine various semantic models to identify patterns.	DCH	4	74
influencer	both external and internal factors constitute ***influencers*** of the business, and the extent of that influence is determined by one or more ***assessments***.	OMG, "Motivation Model"	4	33
information engineering	an approach to developing systems developed by Clive Finkelstein and James Martin. It includes the ***waterfall approach*** to organizing a systems development effort, along with a particular approach to modeling data. The term applies to both the method and the data modeling notation	Martin, 1985 Finklestein, 1989	2	6
Information Grammar Diagram	a diagram using the Fully Communication Oriented Modeling approach.	FCO-IM	4	51
information resource	a set of data (such as a document, letter, artwork, photograph, or video) that describes something else.	DCH	4	78
Integration DEFinition for Information Modeling	a modeling notation that is specifically directed to designing relational databases. Based on **IDEF1**, and **Logical Design Database Technique (LDD)**. Used extensively by the Department of Defense in the creation of relational databases.	FIPS, 1993	2	6
intentional definition	consists of the ***hypernym*** of the term, plus characteristics that distinguish it from other members of the same set. (See also ***Aristotelian definition***.)	SBVR, Witt[214]	4	55
internal schema (ANSI)	"the 'machine view' of the data. This schema describes the stored representation of the enterprise's information."	ANSI-SPARC, 1977	2	9
intersect table	a table that replaces a *many-to-many* relationship, with two ***foreign keys***. Each refers to one of the tablesconnected in the original many-to-many relationship.	DCH	5	101
isolation	(NoSQL) The data created in isolated transactions are not visible to any other transactions, until the first transaction is complete	Dan Sullivan[215]	5	128
JAD	(See joint application development session.)	DCH	6	137
joint application development session	a *modeling session* as conducted by IBM.	DCH	6	137

---

[212] Witt. 2012. …Effective Business Rules… op. cit.

[213] Witt. 2012. …Effective Business Rules… op. cit.

[214] Witt. 2012. …Effective Business Rules… op. cit.

[215] Sullivan. 2015. *Op. cit.*

Term	Definition	Source	Chapter	Page
key-value (NoSQL) model	a kind of NoSQL database that allows an application to store its data in only two columns (*key* and *value*). More complex information may be stored within the "value" columns. (It's not limited to one value.)	Dan Sullivan[216]	5	96
key-value database	A *NoSQL* database that stores its data in only two columns ("key" and "value"), with more complex information sometimes stored within the "value" column	W3C	5	121
link	in a *data vault* structure, a collection of the attributes that describe either a *hub* or a *link*.	Daniel Linstedt	5	117
logical data model	a detailed representation of data requirements, specifically organized in terms of a particular database management architecture. While logical data models do each reflect a particular modeling approach, these are still independent of any specific implementation constraints.	DCH	5	95
logical schema (ANSI)	the organizational approach used by any particular data management technology (e.g. relational ("relnl" in the figure), XML, hierarchy, network, flat files, etc.).	ANSI-SPARC, 1977	2	9
Logical System Models	in the 2014 version of MDA, these are models of the way the components of a system interact with each other, with people and with enterprises to assist an enterprise or community in achieving its goals." [217] They are independent of particular vendors' approaches to data management, although they are specific to a particular approach—such as *relational database management*, so these are "PIM" for "Platform Independent Models".	OMG, MDA, 2014	2	14
MD5	a widely used hash function producing a 128-bit hash value. Although MD5 was initially designed to be used as a cryptographic hash function, it has been found to suffer from extensive vulnerabilities. It can still be used as a checksum to verify data integrity, but only against unintentional corruption.	DCH	5	117
MDA®	(See Model Driven Architecture.)	OMG, MDA, 2014	2	12
Metadata (Bracket)	any data about the organization's data resource.	Bracket[218]	2	20
Metadata (Marco)	all physical data and knowledge from inside and outside an organization, including information about the physical data, technical and business processes, rules and constraints of the data, and structures of the data used by a corporation.	Marco[219]	2	20
Metadata (Tannenbaum)	the detailed description of instance data; the format and characteristics of populated instance data: instances and values, dependent on the role of the metadata recipient.	Tannenbaum[220]	2	20
Metadata (Hay)	the data that describe the structure and workings of an organization's use of *information, and which describe the systems it uses to manage that information.*	Hay[221]	2	21
metadata column	a column added to a table to describe the table's circumstances, such as "creator", "creation date", "last update", etc.	DCH	6	151

[216]   Sullivan. 2015. *Op. cit.*

[217]   Object Management Group. 2014."MDA Specifications". (Retrieved 7/2017 from *http://www.omg.org/mda/specs.htm*)

[218]   Michael H. Bracket. 2000. *Data Resource Quality.* (Addison-Wesley). p. 149.

[219]   David Marco. 2000. *Building and Managing the Meta Data Repository.* (John Wiley & Sons). p. 5.

[220]   Adrienne Tannenbaum. 2002. *Metadata Solutions.* (Addison-Wesley). p. 93.

[221]   David C. Hay. 2006. *Data Model Patterns: A Metadata Map.* (Morgan Kaufman). p. 4

Term	Definition	Source	Chapter	Page
method	In *UML*, the implementation of an *operation*.[222]	Object Management Group	5	113
mission	An overall method for the ongoing operation of the enterprise. (That is, what the business is or will be doing on a day-to-day basis.)	OMG, "Motivation Model"	4	32
Model Driven Architecture®	represents and supports everything from requirements to business modeling to technology implementations. By using MDA® models, we are able to better deal with the complexity of large systems and the interaction and collaboration between enterprises, people, hardware, software."[223]	OMG, MDA, 2014	2	12
modeling session	introductory meetings with a few managers and a few more subject mater experts. If you have some patterns available, begin by sketching out elements on the whiteboard. Most significantly, solicit from the audience what else to add. Add the relationships necessary (with proper names, so that they can be read as simple—assertive—sentences.)	DCH	6	137
motivation column	in the Zachman Framework, goals, strategies, means, plus policies and rules (Why?)	Zachman,Locke, 2008	2	11
namespace	In *UML*, a part of the model in which the names ay be defined and used. Within a namespace, each name has a unique meaning.	Object Management Group	5	114
n-ary relationship	a relationship between three *or more* entity types. This is supported in the Chen, ORM, and UML notations, but not in Barker/Ellis notation.	DCH	4	89
natural key	A combination of business-oriented columns in a table that provide a *candidate primary key*. This is as opposed to a *surrogate primary key* that is unrelated to business concepts.	DCH	5	99
Natural-language Information Analysis Method	a family of conceptual modeling languages that are based in the analysis of natural verbalization (plausible sentences) that might occur in the business domain. Fact-based languages view the world in terms of objects, the facts that relate or characterize those objects, and the role that each object plays in each fact.[224] (Also NIAM)	Nijssen and Halpin	4	45
network	A recursive relationship in which any instance may be related to any number of other connected instances at any level. That is, each lower-level instance may be related to one or more instance of its immediate parent.	DCH	4	87
network column	business and technology locations and their connections (Where?)	Zachman,Locke, 2008	2	11
NIAM	(See Natural-language Information Analysis Method.)			
Normalization	the process of applying rules to organize business complexity into stable data structures.	DCH[225]	5	100
NoSQL	category of databases built on non-relational technology. NoSQL is not a good name for what it represents as it is less about how to query the database (which is where SQL comes in) and more about how the data are stored (which is where relational structures comes in).	W3C	5	121

---

[222] James Rumbaugh, Ivar Jacobson, Grady Booch. 1999. The Unified Modeling Language Reference Manual. (Reading, MA: Addison-Wesley). P. 340.

[223] Object Management Group. 2014. "Model Driven Architecture® (MDA®) MDA Guide rev. 2.0." Page 1. (Retrieved 7/2017 from *http://www.omg.org/cgi-bin/doc?ormsc/14-06-01*).

[224] Gerardus Maria Nijssen and T Halpin. 1989. *Conceptual Schema and Relational Database Design*. (Prentice Hall).

[225] David C. Hay. 2003. Requirements Analysis: From Business Views to Architecture (Prentice Hall).

Term	Definition	Source	Chapter	Page
NoSQL (logical data) model	an approach to very large databases that is "Not only SQL". Instead of taking a business subject and breaking it up into multiple relational structures, NoSQL databases frequently store the business subject in a structure called a **document**. In this case, "document" refers not to a piece of paper of business significance, but to a piece of (typically) JavaScript Object Notation (JSON) code. There are currently three versions of this: Key-value – an application stores its data in only two columns (**key** and **value**). Column-oriented – work with more complex data types including unformatted text and imagery. Graph – This is for data whose relations are well represented as a set of nodes with a variable number of connections between these nodes.	Carlo Strozzi Johan Oskarsson Morteza Javan [226]	5	96
object role modeling	a model-driven engineering approach that starts with typical examples of required information or queries presented in any external formulation familiar to users, and then verbalizes these examples at the conceptual level in terms of simple facts expressed in a controlled natural language—a restricted version of natural language that is unambiguous, so the semantics are readily grasped by humans, and is also formal, so it can be used to automatically map the structures to lower levels for implementation. [227]	ORM, Terry Halpin	4	46
objective	an attainable, time-targeted and measurable **desired result** the enterprise seeks to meet in order to achieve its **goals**.	OMG, "Motivation Model"	4	32
object-oriented (logical data) model	a model oriented towards object-oriented programming, where entity types are implemented as **object classes** and relationships become **associations**.	Object Management Group	5	96
object property	a property of a semantic web class that is its relationship to another class. It consists of a **domain** (the class itself) and a **range** (the related class).	W3C	5	68
Occam's Razor	(See Ockham's Razor.)			
occurrent	an entity that *occurs* or *happens*, variously referred to as an "event" or "process" or "happening", which we take to comprise not only (1) the processes that unfold in successive phases (for example, business processes) but also (2) the boundaries or thresholds at the beginnings or ends of such processes (e.g., "Process xy-23 start time"), as well as (3) the temporal and spatiotemporal regions in which these processes occur (such as, for financial accounting, "Third Quarter, 2017").	Spear, IFOMIS	4	30
Ockham's Razor	William of Ockham, a Franciscan friar who studied logic in the 14th century, first made this principle well known.[1] In Latin it is sometimes called lex parsimoniae, or "the law of briefness". William of Ockham supposedly (see below) wrote it in Latin as: *Entia non sunt multiplicanda praeter necessitatem.* This translates roughly as: "Entities must not be multiplied beyond necessity". [228]	DCH	4	73

---

[226]   Wikipedia. 2017. "NoSQL". (Retrieved 10/5/2017.)

[227]   from Terry Halpin. 2015. *Object-role Modeling Fundamentals.* (Technics Publications). Page 3.

[228]   Encyclopedia Britannica. Encyclopedia Britannica Online. 2010. (*Retrieved 12 June 2010*).

Term	Definition	Source	Chapter	Page
octothorpe	It's the official name for the # symbol, but what does it mean? It's actually a made-up word, invented in the same laboratories where the telephone came from. The scientists at Bell Laboratories modified the telephone keypad in the early 1960s and added the # symbol to send instructions to the telephone operating system. Since the # symbol didn't have a name, the technicians thought one up. They knew it should be called octo-something because it had eight ends around the edge An unverifiable report is much more etymologically satisfying: The Old Norse word thorpe meant "farm or field," so octothorpe literally means "eight fields." (Since 2015 and Twitter, it's been called a "Hash Term")	Dictionary. com	4	59
ontology (modern)	a catalogue of terms describing the types of things that are *assumed to exist*: 1) in a domain of interest; 2) with rules governing how those terms can be combined to make valid statements; 3) along with sanctioned inferences' that can be made.	Knowledge Based Systems. 1994	2	88
ontology (philosophy)	the branch of metaphysics concerned with identifying, in the most general terms, the kinds of things that *actually exist*.	Kemmerling, 2002	2	88
open world assumption	as the basis for semantic web analysis, the assumption that if the rules don't completely *rule it out*, the assertion may be true.	W3C	4	64
operation	In *UML*, a specification of a transformation or query that an object may be called to execute. A procedure to execute this specification is called a *method*.[229]	Object Management Group	5	113
operative rule	what must or must not happen in particular circumstances	OMG (SBVR)	5	54
optionality	For an entity type, determination of whether instances of a related entity type are *mandatory* or *optional*.	DCH	4	40
organization column	people, organizations, and their roles. (Who?)	Zachman,Lock e, 2008	2	11
ORM	(see Object Role Modeling)	DCH	1	7
ORM	(See *object role modeling*.)			
overview model	a synopsis of the enterprise's information structure. It is typically created during the strategic planning phase of a data management project. It is often sketched out on a whiteboard in response to discussions of objectives for the effort.	DCH	4	31
OWL	(See Web Ontology Language)	World Wide Web Consortium	1	7
parent table	the object of a *foreign key*, where a table is related to a second table via that foreign key.	DCH	5	98
partition	a division of a logical **database** or its constituent elements into distinct independent parts. **Database partitioning** is normally done for manageability, performance or availability reasons, or for load balancing	Wikipedia - Partition_ (database)	5	150
physical model	is typically not a graphic model at all. It describes the specific ways data are stored on a medium. In the case of relational databases, it is represented by a script in a *data definitin language*. This includes defintions of such database-specific structures as *tablespaces* and *partitions*	DCH	5	127
PIM	(See Platform Independent Model.)	OMG, MDA, 2001	2	13
Platform Independent Model	in an early version of the Object Management Group's "Model Driven Architecture", a description of the business without regard to any technology that might be involved in implementing it. (See also *Logical Systems Models)*	OMG, MDA, 2001	2	13

[229] James Rumbaugh, *et. al.* 1999. *UML Reference. Op. cit.* P. 369.

Term	Definition	Source	Chapter	Page
Platform Specific Model	In an early version of the Object Management Group's "Model Driven Architecture", a description of data in terms of a particular database management system. (See also *Implementation Models.*)	DCH; OMG, MDA, 2001	2	13
Primary Key	a set of columns that uniquely identifies each row.	Codd	5	99, 100
process	1. Unlike a *function*, this is something to be done by a system, rather than by the business. It is defined by input and output data. 2. A set of operations transforming data, logically or physically, according to some process logic.	1. Barker/ Longman [230] 2. Gane/ Sarsen [231]	6	139
process entity	(See occurrent.)	Spear, IFOMIS	4	30
PSM	(See Platform Specific Model.)	DCH; OMG, MDA, 2001	2	13
range	a *domain* that constrains an attribute to specified minimum and/or maximum values.	DCH	4	43
RDF	(See Resource Definition Framework)	World Wide Web Consortium	4	60
RDF Schema	In the *Semantic Web*, a language for describing membership of instances in classes. The word in RDFS for a semantic group is *class.* In any modeling exercise, each term that describes a class has to be designated an instance of the RDFS term "class".	World Wide Web Consortium	4	61
RDFS	(See RDF Schema)			
recursion	(See Recursion)			
recursive relationship	A relationship between two instances of the same entity type.	DCH	4	85
relational (logical data) model	the representation of entity types and attributes, with their identifiers, as *tables* and *columns* with *primary keys*. It further represents each relationship between pairs of tables as *foreign key* columns in one table corresponding to primary key columns in the related table.	Codd	5	95
relationship	the fact that instances of an *entity type* are logically related to other instances of the same or a different *entity type*. The Barker/Ellis approach to data modeling places special emphasis on naming relationships. If this is supposed to be an *Ontology*, representing *what exists* in a domain, simply listing things (or classes of things) is not sufficient. What is also needed are *assertions* about how these things are related to each other.	DCH	4	39
relationship unique identifiers	the use of one or more *relationships* to uniquely identify instances of an entity type.	DCH	4	79
requirements	(See *Business Information Requirements*.)			
reserved word	a word used as part of a programming language (in this case *Resource Definition Framework*)	W3C [232]	4	58
resource column	data structures used to build the architecture (What?)	Zachman, Locke, 2008	2	11
Resource Definition Framework	framework for representing information in the Web…RDF graphs are sets of subject-predicate-object triples, where the elements may be IRIs, blank nodes, or datatyped literals.	W3C [233]	4	58

---

[230] Barker/Longman. 1992. Op. cit. p. 161.

[231] Chris Gane & Trish Sarsen. 1979. *Structured Systems Analysis: Tools and Techniques*. (Prentice-Hall). P. 61

[232] World Wide Web Consortium. 2012. RDF 1.1 XML Syntax: W3C Recommendation 25 February 2014. (Retrieved 6/2017 from *https://www.w3.org/TR/2014/REC-rdf-syntax-grammar-20140225/*).

[233] World Wide Web Consortium. 2012. RDF 1.1 XML Syntax: W3C Recommendation 25 February 2014. (Retrieved 6/2017 from *https://www.w3.org/TR/2014/REC-rdf-syntax-grammar-20140225/*).

Term	Definition	Source	Chapter	Page
reverse engineer	the process of documenting an existing database in terms that can allow it to be rebuilt. Reverse engineering of the *physical data model* is completed first to understand the technical design of an existing system, followed by creation of some sort of *logical data model* to document the business solution that the existing system meets.	DCH	6	133
role name	In *UML*, the name which identifies each association end. It is used to navigate from an object to neighboring related objects. Each class "sees" the associations attached to it and can use them to find objects related to one of its instances. Because a role name can be used like an attribute name to extract values, a role name enters the *namespace* of the class on the far side of the association. Note that this means the associated class cannot be part of the role name, since that is different namespace.[234] The Barker/Ellis naming conventions cannot be used directly, therefore. (See your author's book on *UML and Data Modeling* for details.[235])	Object Management Group	5	114
Second Normal Form	a constraint on data structure that ensures each table has the minimal primary key and that every column depends on the *complete* primary key. That is, the value of each column must be *dependent on* the *entire primary key.*	DCH	5	101
semantic model	a model of the language used in the enterprise. Its purpose is to capture the terms (with their definitions) that concern one or more areas of interest for the enterprise.	DCH	2	14
semantics	"the study of *meaning*"	Merriam Webster[236]	5	35
semantic ring constraint	in ORM, if an instance of a recursive relationship from A is to B, then an equivalent relationship is from B to A.	OMG	5	50
semantics of business vocabulary and rules	a way to capture and define *business rules* in a coherent, natural language way	OMG	1	54
simple primary key	one column that uniquely identifies a table instance. Universal Product Codes (UPCs) and Vehicle Identification Numbers (VIN codes) are examples of simple keys.	DMBOK[237]		99
snowflake schema (dimensional model)	takes the dimensions from a *star schema* and splits them out into their more normalized component tables.	DMBOK	5	112
soft state	(NoSQL) Data will expire if not refreshed. In NoSQL, it means that they may eventually be overridden.	Dan Sullivan[238]	5	128
star schema (dimensional model)	A *star schema* is a dimensional model with simple dimensions around each *fact table*. For example, product sales could be indexed by the dimensions **Time**, **Geography**, and **Product Level**.	DMBOK	5	110
strategy	the essential *course of action* attempted to achieve an enterprise's *end*—particularly its goals. moreover, a *strategy* must be *to carry out* exactly one mission. in general, *strategies* address *goals*, while *tactics* address *objectives*.	OMG, "Motivation Model"	4	32

[234] Rumbaugh, *et al.* 1999. UML *Reference.* Op. cit. P. 353.

[235] David C. Hay. 2011. *UML and Data Modeling: A Reconciliation.* (Technics Publications).

[236] Merriam Webster. Semantics. Merriam Webster On-line Dictionary. (Retrieved 2/12/2017 from *https://www.merriam-webster.com/dictionary/semantics.*)

[237] Data Management Association. 2017. *Data Management Body of Knowledge.* (Technics Publications). Pp. 133-134.

[238] Sullivan. 2015. *Op. cit.*

Term	Definition	Source	Chapter	Page
subject area	a collection of related topics that are appropriate as a sub-section of an *enterprise data model*.	DCH	6	30
substantial entity	(See continuant.)	Spear, IFOMIS	4	30
Surrogate Primary Key	A surrogate key is a unique identifier for a table. In the case of long tables, like Product or Person, it could be a system-generated integer. If it is a short "type" table with only a handful of instances, it could be a human-assigned abbreviation. Surrogate keys serve technical functions and typically are not be visible to end users of a database.	DMBOK	5	99
syntax	"the way in which linguistic elements (as words) are put together to form *constituents* (as phrases or clauses)"	Merriam Webster[239]	5	35
tablespace	a storage location where the actual data underlying database objects can be kept. It provides a layer of abstraction between physical and logical data, and serves to allocate storage for all DBMS managed segments.	Wikipedia - Tablespace	5	127
tactic	a *course of action* that represents one or more details of a *strategy*. a *strategy* may be implemented via one or more *tactics*. in general, *strategies* address goals, while tactics address *objectives*.	OMG, "Motivation Model"	4	32
tag	an XML component that encapsulates a piece of data. Tags always appear in pairs, beginning with a name, and ending with the same name preceded by "/". It can consist of a single string or it can include a complex set of other tags.	W3C	5	119
tag attribute	a qualifier of a *tag*. For example, "effDate=2001-04-02" could be an *attribute* of the tag <product>, as in <product effdate="2001-04-02">	W3C	5	119
tautology	a definition that is in terms of itself. For example "Order number" is the number on an order.	DCH	6	162
taxonomy	(See Hierarchy.)	DCH	4	85
technician perspective	(in the Zachman Framework), the view of those looking at target systems in detail.	JZ, DCH	2	12
technological model	a picture of the way data will be managed and stored, using one or more particular kinds of technology.	DCH	1	1
ternary relationship	a relationship between three entity types. This is supported in the Chen, ORM, and UML notations, but not in Barker/Ellis notation.	DCH	4	89
the Semantic Web	a standard for registering all definitions (with their owners) on the World Wide Web, plus reporting languages for manipulating the terms in conventional language. The languages include a structure for expressing natural language sentences (*Resource Description Framework*), the ability to define classes (*RDF Schema*), and the ability to describe inferences (*Web Ontology Language*).	World Wide Web Consortium (W3C)	2	15
Third Normal Form	a constraint on data structure that ensures each entity has no hidden primary keys and that each column depends on no columns outside the primary key ("the key, the whole key and nothing but the key"[*]).	DCH	5	103
timing column	intervals, events, cycles, and schedules (When?)	Zachman, Locke, 2008	2	11
triple	a statement type in the *Resource Defition Framework*, in the form <subject><predicate><object>	W3C[240]	4	58

[239] Merriam Webster. "Syntax". Merriam Webster On-line Dictionary. Retrieved 2/12/2017 from https://www.merriam-webster.com/dictionary/syntax.

[*] ... so help me Codd." (Sorry, couldn't resist.)

[240] World Wide Web Consortium. 2012. RDF 1.1 XML Syntax: W3C Recommendation 25 February 2014. (Retrieved

Term	Definition	Source	Chapter	Page
UML	(See Uniform Modeling Language)	Object Management Group	1	113
unary relationship	a relationship between two instances of a single entity type. There are two of these: *Hierarchical (Taxonomy)* and *Network*.	DCH	4	85
Uniform Modeling Language	A combination of notations to serve object-oriented design. This includes modeling "classes" (the analogy to data models), process flows, events and responses, and other software components	Object Management Group	5	113
Universal Resource Identifier	A specialized *URL* that is used to locate the definition of a single term, in the context of that URL.	DCH	1	7
Uniform Resource Locator	A text term used in the world wide web for identifying an "IP address".	DCH	1	7
universe of discourse	the part of the real world of relevance to a data modeling exercise.	Simsion 2007, p. 40	1	1
unpackable	substitutable for the defined term, without a change of meaning.	Arp, Smith, Spear 2015	6	163
upper ontology	a model that covers the language of the world as a whole	Reeves, "Simple Bio Upper Ontology	4	30
URI	(See Universal Resource Identifier)	DCH	1	7
URL	(See Uniform Resource Locator)	DCH	1	7
value expression	a *domain* that constrains an attribute to values which are the result of mathematical functions. Most likely is a *value range*.	DCH	4	43
value set	In a conceptual model *domain* a set of things described by an attribute. This may be implemented with one or more *code sets* each of which is a set of column values that corresponded to the values in this set. For example, a "value set" might be "the set of Canadian Provinces", while one "code set" may name them in English, while another would name them in French.	DCH	4	42
Vendor Platform Independent Model	(See Class of Platform (technology) Specific Model.)			
Vendor Platform Specific Model	a model that organizes data in terms of one or more physical media.	Chapin/OMG 2008	2	13
vertical denormalization	If the Persons data (for example) is categorized as "employment information", "sales performance", etc. it may be appropriate to define different tables for each kind of Persons data. Note that, to the extent that the "columns" are in fact implemented as Person Characteristics, this division is simpler to do	DCH	5	129
vision	an *end* that is a desired future state of the enterprise, without regard to how it is to be achieved.	OMG, "Motivation Model"	4	32
VPIM	(See Vendor Platform Independent Model.)			
VPSM	(See Vendor Platform Specific Model)	Chapin/OMG 2008	2	13
waterfall approach	an approach to developing systems that begins with **strategy**, follows with **requirements analysis**, then **design** and **construction**, and finally, **implementation**.	Finklestein[241] / Martin[242]	2	6

6/2017 from *https://www.w3.org/TR/2014/REC-rdf-syntax-grammar-20140225/*).

[241] Clive Finkelstein. 1989. *An Introduction to Information Engineering.* (Addison Wesley).

[242] James Martin, Joe Leben. 1989. *Strategic Information Methodologies (Second Edition).* (Prentice Hall).

Term	Definition	Source	Chapter	Page
Web Ontology Language	an extension of RDF Schema that incorporates the ability to define properties of classes. These include *datatype properties* (known to the relational world as "attributes") and *object properties* (known to the relational world as "relationships"). In addition, software can be applied to OWL statements to make logical inferences from other statements.	DCH	4	63
XML	a language developed to support data communication.	W3C	5	119
XML schema (logical data) model	a description of a type of XML document, typically expressed in terms of constraints on the structure and content of documents of that type, above and beyond the basic syntactical constraints imposed by XML itself. It is expressed in terms of *element* (the definition of an XML term or "tag") plus *simpleType* (a class definition with simple restrictions) and *complexType* (a class definition that encompasses multiple other elements).	World Wide Web Consortium	5	96
XMLSchema	a mechanism for defining *XML tags*. This "language" consists of some specialized *XML tags*: *element, complex type, sequence, simpleType, restriction*, and others.	W3C	5	120
xsd:attribute	See tag attribute.	W3C	5	119
xsd:complextype	an *XMLSchema tag* that consists of an xsd:sequence consisting of other xsd:elements	W3C	5	120
xsd:element	an *XMLSchema Tag* that defines a particular tag of the schema.	W3C	5	120
xsd:maxinclusive	an *Muschamp tag* that constrains the <u>maximum</u> value that the parent **xsd:simpleType tag** can take.	W3C	5	120
xsd:minInclusive	an *XMLSchema tag* that constrains the <u>minimum</u> value that the parent **xsd:simpleType tag** can take.	W3C	5	120
xsd:restriction	an *XMLSchema tag* consisting of tags that constrain the values of an xsd:simpleType tag.	W3C	5	120
xsd:schema	an *XMLSchema tag* that defines the boundaries of a script.	W3C	5	120
xsd:sequence	an *XMLSchema tag* that precedes a set of elements that define tags.	W3C	5	120
xsd:simpleType	an *XMLSchema tag* that consists only of *xsd:restrictions* that control values associated with *tags*.	W3C	5	121
Zeroth Normal Form	determines that tables are, in fact, relational tables. A body of data is in zeroth normal form meets these restrictions: 1. Data shall be organized into tables, each of which is defined by a set of unduplicated. columns 2. The sequence of rows in a table is not significant. 3. The sequence of columns in a table is not significant. 4. Each row is uniquely identified by a set of columns called a *primary key*. ("Unique identifier" in the table's source entity type in its corresponding *conceptual data modes*.	DCH	5	100

APPENDIX B – SEMANTIC WEB SYNTAX

Table 6: RDF Statements

Tags for statements
<rdf:statement>
<rdf:subject>
<rdf:predicate>
<rdf:object>
<rdf:property>
<rdf:type>
<rdf:value>
Plus tags for collecting instances
<rdf:Bag>
<rdf:Seq>
<rdf:Alt>
<rdf:List>
<rdf:First>
<rdf:Rest>
<rdf:XMLLiteral>

Table 7: RDF Schema

About Resources
<rdfs:resource>
<rdfs:class>
<rdfs:subClassOf>
<rdfs:subPropertyOf>
Documentation
<rdfs:comment>
<rdfs:label>
Extent of properties
<rdfs:range>
<rdfs:domain>
Definitions
<rdfs:seeAlso>
<rdfs:isDefinedBy>
Containers
<rdfs:container>
<rdfs:>
<containerMembershipProperty>
<rdfs:member>
Miscellaneous
<rdfs:literal>
<rdfs:datatype>

Table 8: Web Ontology Language

Classes
<owl:ontology>
<owl:nothing>
<owl:thing> (complement of nothing)
<owl:class>
<owl:alldifferent>
<owl:restriction>
<owl:deprecatedclass>
<owl:deprecatedproperty>
<owl:datarange>
<owl:equivalentclass> (class 1, class 2)
<owl:disjointwith> (class 1, class 2)
<owl:sameas> (thing 1, thing 2)
<owl:differentfrom> (thing 1, thing 2)
<owl:distinctmember> (alldifferent, &rdf;list)
<owl:unionof> (class, &rdf;list)
<owl:intersectionof> (class, &rdf;list)
<owl:complementof> (class 1, class 2)
<owl:oneof> (&rdfs;class, &rdf;list)

properties (domain, range)
<owl:dataproperty>
<owl:objectproperty>
<owl:transitiveproperty>

<owl:symmetricproperty>
<owl:inversefunctionalproperty>
<owl:datatypeproperty>
<owl:deprecatedproperty>
<owl:ontologyproperty>
<owl:functionalproperty>
<owl:annotationproperty>
<owl:equivalentproperty> (property 1, property 2)
<owl:onproperty> (restriction, &rdf;property)
<owl:allvaluesfrom> (restriction, &rdfs;class)
<owl:hasvalue> (restriction)
<owl:somevaluesfrom> (restriction, &rdfs;class)
<owl:mincardinality> (restriction, &xsd;nonnegativeinteger)
<owl:maxcardinality> (restriction, &xsd;nonnegatieinteger
<owl:cardinality> (restriction, &xsd;nonnegativeinteger
<owl:inverseof> (objectproperty 1, objectproperty 2)
<owl:imports> (ontology 1, ontology 2)
<owl:versioninfo>
<owl:priorversion (ontology 1, ontology 2)
<owl:backwardcompatiblewith> (ontology 1, ontology 2)
<owl:incompatiblewith> (ontology 1, ontology 2)

APPENDIX C – TYPES OF NOTATION

This appendix compares the layouts for four modeling approaches:

- ➢ Barker/Ellis
- ➢ Information Engineering
- ➢ IDEF1X
- ➢ UML

It is organized according to the following topics:

- ➢ Standard configurations (mandatory one to optional many)
- ➢ Relationship Identifiers
- ➢ Optional one-to-many
- ➢ Optional one / required many
- ➢ Optional many-to-many
- ➢ Optional one-to-one.

Standard Configuration

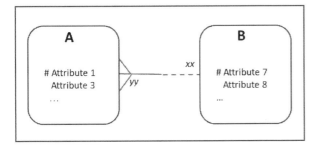

Figure C-1: Standard Notation – Barker/Ellis

Each **A** must be *xx* one and only one **B**; Each **B** may be *yy* one or more **A**.

Attributes <n> are descriptors of each entity type.

The symbol # designates Attribute 1 and Attribute 7 as *identifying* attributes, whose values uniquely identify each instance of the entity type.

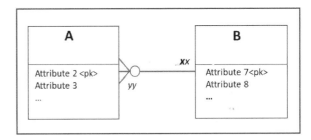

Figure C-2: Standard Configuration – Information Engineering

A *xx*s one and only one **B**; **B** *yy*s zero or more **A**s.

Attributes<n>. are descriptors of each entity type.

The symbol <pk> designates Attribute 1 and Attribute 7 as *primary key* attributes, whose values uniquely identify their respective entity types.

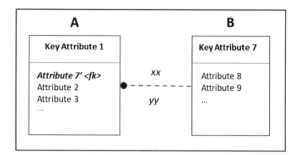

Figure C-3 Standard Configuration – IDEF1X

A *xx*s one and only one **B**; **B** *yy*s zero or more **As**.

Attributes <n> are descriptors of each entity type. **A's** Attribute 7' is a *foreign key (<fk>)* linking to Key Attribute 7 on **B**.

"Key" attributes, in **upper boxes** designate Attribute 1 and Attribute 7 as *primary keys* of **A** and **B**, respectively. Their values uniquely identify each entity type

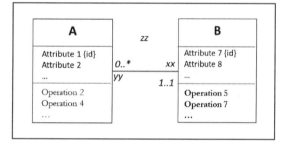

Figure C-4: Standard Notation– UML

A *zz*s one and only one **B**, where **B** plays the role of *xx;* **B** has an unnamed association with zero, one or more **As,** where **A** plays the role of *yy*.

Attributes <n>. are descriptors of each entity type (here called "class").

The symbol {id} designates Attribute 1 and Attribute 7 as *primary key* attributes, whose values uniquely identify each entity type.

Operation <n> designates an activity that may be carried out on each entity type.

Relationship Identifiers

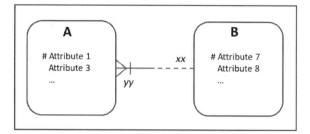

Figure C-5: Relationship Identifiers – Barker/Ellis

The vertical line (|) next to entity type **A** indicates that the relationship *xx* to **B** is part of **A's** unique identifier.

Later, in the Logical Model, this will be implemented by including in **A** a copy of **B's** unique identifier (Attribute 7),. combined with Attribute 1 to form **A's** complete unique identifier.

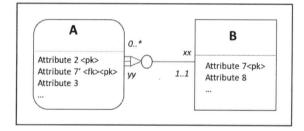

Figure C-6: Relationship Identifiers – Information Engineering

The enhanced crow's foot (⇒) next to entity type **A** indicates that the relationship **xx** to **B** is part of **A's** unique identifier. That entity type **A** is so identified makes it "dependent", and the box is now a rounded rectangle.

This will be implemented by adding a copy of **B's** unique identifier (Attribute 7) to **A** (designated with <fk>). This will combine with Attribute 2 (designated with <pk>), to form **A's** complete unique identifier.

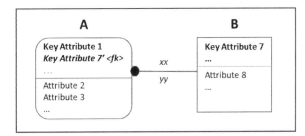

Figure C-7: Relationship Identifiers – IDEF1X

The solid line between **A** and **B** designates *xx* as an *identifying relationship.*

This is implemented by adding a copy of **B's** *primary key* (Attribute 7') to **A** (designated with <fk>). This will combine with Key Attribute 1, to form **A's** unique identifier

Also, the rounded corners on **A**, indicate that the relationship *xx* is part of the unique identifier of **A**

.

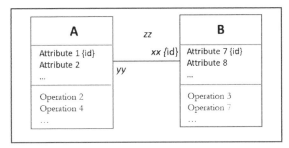

Figure C-8: Relationship Identifiers – UML

The symbol {id} shows that both Attribute 1 and **B's** playing the role *xx* together constitute the unique identifier of **A**.

Later, in the Logical Model, this will be implemented by including a copy of **Bs** unique identifier (Attribute 7'),. combined with Attribute 1 to form **A's** unique identifier.

Optional One-to-many

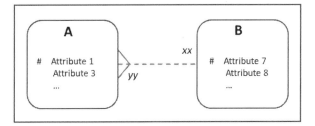

Figure C-9: Optional One-to-many – Barker/Ellis

Each **A** may be *xx* one **B**; Each **B** may be *yy* one or more **A**s

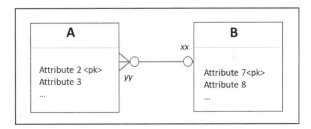

Figure C-10: Optional One-to-many – Information Engineering

Each **A** *xx*s zero or one **B**. Each **B** *yy*s zero or more **A**s.

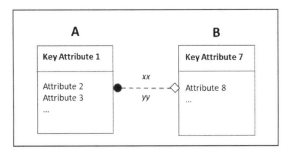

Figure C- 11: Optional One-to-many – IDEF1X

Each **A** *xx*s zero or one **B**. Each **B** *yy*s zero or more **A**s.

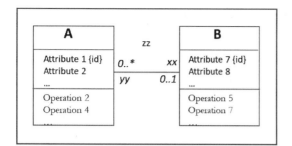

Figure C-12: Optional One-to-many – UML

A *zzs* zero or one **B**, where **B** plays the role of *xx*; B has an unnamed association with zero, one or more **A**s, where each **A** plays the role of *yy*.

Optional One / Required Many

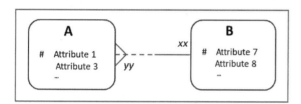

Figure C-13: Optional One / Required Many – Barker/Ellis

Each **A** may be *xx* (up to) one and only one **B**; Each **B** must be *yy* at least one but possibly more **A**s.

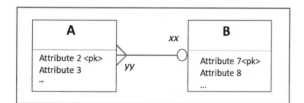

Figure C-14: Optional One / Required Many – Information Engineering

Each **A** *xxs* zero or more **B**. Each **B** *yys* at least one but possibly more **A**s.

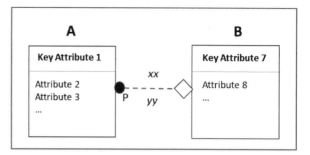

Figure C-15: Optional One / Required Many – IDEF1X

Each **A** *xxs* zero or one **B**; Each **B** *yys* at least one but possibly more **A**s.

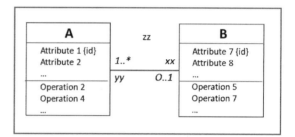

Figure C-16: Optional One / Required Many – UML

Each **A** *zzs* zero or one **B**, which in turn plays the role *xx*; each B has *an unnamed association* with at least one but possibly more **A**s, each of which in turn plays the role *yy*.

Optional Many-to-many

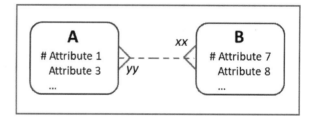

Figure C-17: Optional Many-to-many – Barker/Ellis

Each **A** may be *xxed* one or more **B**s; Each **B** may be *yyed* one or more **A**s.

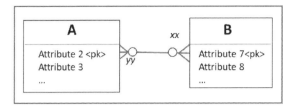

Figure C-18: Optional Many-to-many – Information Engineering

*Each **A** xxes zero, one or more **Bs**; Each **B** yys zero, one or more **As**.*

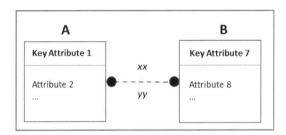

Figure C-19: Optional Many-to-many – IDEF1X

Each **A** *xxes* zero, one, or more **Bs**; Each **B** is *yys* zero, one or more **As**. (No foreign keys are involved.)

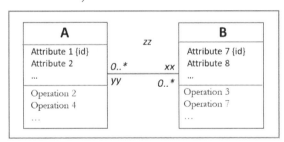

Figure C-20: Optional Many-to-many – UML

Each **A** *zzs* zero or more **Bs**, each of which in turn plays the role *xx*; Each **B** plays *an unnamed relationship* with zero or more **As**, each of which in turn plays the role *yy*.

Optional One-to-one

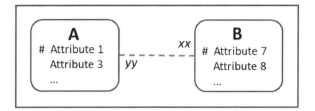

Figure C-21: Optional One-to-one – Barker/Ellis

Each **A** may be *xx* one and only one **B**; Each **B** may be *yy* one and only one **A**.

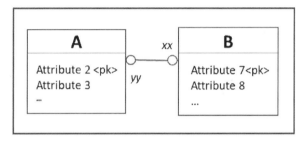

Figure C-22: Optional One-to-one – Information Engineering

Each **A** *xxs* zero or one **B**; Each **B** *yys* zero or one **A**.

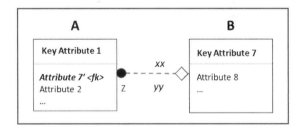

Figure C-23: Optional One-to-one – IDEF1X, Version 1

A *xxs* zero or one **B** (implemented with a foreign key); **B** *yys* zero or one **A** (no foreign key)).

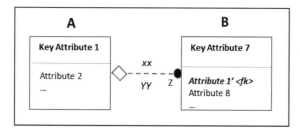

Figure C-24: Optional One-to-one –IDEF1X, Version 2

A *xxs* zero or one **B** (no foreign key); **B** *yys* zero or one **A** (implemented with a foreign key).

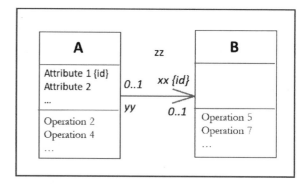

Figure C-25: Optional One-to-one – UML

Each **A** *zzs* zero or one **B**, which in turn plays the role *xx*; Each **B** plays *an unnamed relationship* with zero or more **As**, with in turn each play the role *yy*.

APPENDIX D – OBJECT ROLE MODEL SYMBOLS

The following pages contain a catalogue of the symbols used in the Object Role Modeling approach. Copyright Terry Halpin. (Used with permission.)

ORM Notation - 1

Construct	Examples	Description/Notes
Entity Type	Country or Country or Country	Named soft rectangle, named hard rectangle, or named ellipse. The soft rectangle shape is the default.
Value Type	CountryCode or CountryCode or CountryCode	Named, dashed, soft rectangle (or hard rectangle or ellipse).
Entity type with popular reference mode	Country (.code) Course (.code) Company (.name) Building (.nr)	Abbreviation for injective reference relationship to value type, e.g. Country has / is of CountryCode
Entity type with unit-based reference mode	Height (cm:) Mass (kg:) Salary (USD:) Price (EUR:) Height (cm: Length) Salary (USD: Money) Price (EUR: Money)	Abbreviation for reference type, e.g. Height has / is of cmValue Optionally, unit type may be displayed.
Entity type with general reference mode	Book (ISBN) Website (URL) WebLink (URL)	Abbreviation for reference type, e.g. Book has / is of ISBN
Independent Object Type	Country ! CountryCode !	Instances of the type may exist, without playing any elementary fact roles
External Object Type	Address^	This notation is tentative (yet to be finalized)
Predicate (unary, binary, ternary, etc.)	smokes was born in ... speaks ... very well ... played ... for ... ... in ... on ... ate ...	Ordered set of 1 or more role boxes with at least one predicate reading in mixfix notation. If shown, object placeholders are denoted by "...". If placeholders are not shown, unaries are in prefix and binaries are in infix notation.
Duplicate type or predicate shape	Person StateCode was born in	If an object type or predicate shape is displayed more than once (on the same page or different pages) it is shadowed.
Unary fact type	Person smokes	The smokes role may be played by instances of the Person object type
Binary fact type	Person was born in Country Person [employee] employs Company [employer] Car Person [manager] reports to / manages Product made drives ▲ Person	By default, predicate readings (binary or longer) are read left-to-right or top-to-bottom. An arrow-tip is used to display a different reading direction. Role names may be displayed in square brackets beside their role. Forward and inverse readings for binaries may be shown together, separated by "/".

ORM Notation - 2

Construct	Examples	Description/Notes
Ternary fact type	Sport [player] Person played ... for ... Country; Person introduced ... to ...; Food Date ... ate ... on ... Cat; Food Cat Date [Cat] ate [Food] on [Date]	Role names may be added in square brackets. Arrow-tips are used to reverse the default left-right or top-down reading order. Reading orders other than forward and reverse are shown using named placeholders.
Quaternary fact type	City Date Person ... in ... on .. ate ... Food	The above notes for the ternary case apply here also. Fact types of higher arity (number of roles) are also permitted.
Objectification (a.k.a. nesting)	"Enrolment !" Student enrolled in Course resulted in Grade	The enrolment fact type is objectified as an entity type whose instances can play roles. In this example, the objectification type is independent, so we can know about an enrolment before the grade is obtained.
Internal uniqueness constraint (UC) on unaries	Person smokes; Person smokes	These are equivalent (by default, predicates are assumed to be populated with sets, so no whole fact may be duplicated).
Internal UC on binaries	Gender is of Person was born in Country; Language speaks Person is president of Country	The examples show the 4 possible patterns: 1:n (one-to-many); n:1 (many-to-one); m:n (many-to-many); 1:1 (one-to-one0
Internal UC on ternaries. For n-aries (n > 1) each UC must span at least n-1 roles	Place Team ... got ... in ... Competition; Sport Person ... played ... for ... Country	The first example has two, 2-role UCs: the top UC forbids ties; the other UC ensures that each team gets only place per competition (a dotted line excludes its role from the UC). The second example has a spanning UC (many-to-many-to-many).
Simple mandatory role constraint	Person was born in Country; Person was born in Country	The example constraint means that each person was born in some country. The mandatory role dot may be placed at either end of the role connector.
Inclusive-or constraint (disjunctive mandatory role)	has Passport; Visitor has DriverLicence	The constraint is displayed as a circled dot connected to the constrained roles. The example constraint means that each visitor referenced in the model must have a passport or a driver licence (or both).
Preferred internal UC	Country has / is of CountryCode	A double bar on a UC indicates it underlies the preferred reference scheme.

ORM Notation - 3

Construct	Examples	Description/Notes
External UC (double-bar indicates preferred identifier)		Here, each state is primarily identified by combining its country and state code. Each combination of country and state name also applies to only one state.
Object Type Value Constraint	Gender (.code) {'M', 'F'} Rating (.nr) {1, 2, 3, 4, 5, 6, 7}	*Enumerations*
	Rating (.nr) {1..7} Grade (.code) {'A'..'F'} Age (y:) {0..} NegativeInt {..-1} PassScore (%) {50..100} PositiveScore (%) {(0..100)} NegativeTemperature (°C:) {-273.15..0)}	*Ranges* are inclusive of end values by default. Round brackets are used to exclude an end value. Square brackets may be added to explicitly declare inclusion, e.g. the constraint on PositiveScore may also be specified as {(0..100]}.
	ExtremeTemperature (°C:) {-100..-20, 40..100} SQLchar {a'..'z', 'A'..'Z', '0'..'9', '_'}	Multiple combinations are allowed.
Role value constraint	Person (.name) has Age (y:) {0..} {0..140}	As for object type value constraints, but connected to the constrained role. Here, an age of a person must be at most 140 years.
Subset constraint	is cancer prone — Person — enrolled in — Course, smokes, ... for ... obtained ... Grade	The arrow points from the subset end to the superset end (e.g. if a person smokes then that person is cancer prone). The role sequences at both ends must be compatible. A connection to the junction of 2 roles constrains that role pair.
Join subset constraint	speaks — Language (.name) — is often used in, Advisor (.nr), serves in, Country (.code)	The constrained role pair at the superset end is projected from a role path that involves a conceptual join on Language. The constraint declares that if an advisor serves in a country then that advisor must speak a language that is often used in that country.
Exclusion constraint	is married — authored — Person — Book, is widowed, reviewed	These constraints mean that no person is both married and widowed, and no person reviewed and authored the same book. Exclusion may apply between 2 or more compatible role sequences, possibly involving joins.
Exclusive-or constraint	is male — is tenured — Academic — Date, is female, is contracted till	An exclusive-or constraint is simply the conjunction of an inclusive-or constraint and an exclusion constraint. Also known as an xor constraint.

ORM Notation – 4

Construct	Examples	Description/Notes
Equality constraint	has systolic- Patient ⊜ BloodPressure has diasystolic-	This constraint means that a patient's systolic BP is recorded if and only if his/her diastolic BP is recorded. An equality constraint may apply between 2 or more compatible role sequences, possibly involving joins.
Derived fact type, and derivation rule	[languageSpoken] Person speaks Language speaks* NrLanguages *For each Person, nrLanguages = count(languageSpoken).	A fact type is either asserted, derived, or semiderived. A derived fact type is marked with an asterisk "*". A derivation rule is supplied. A double asterisk "**" indicates derived and stored (eager evaluation).
Semiderived fact type, and derivation rule	is a parent of Person is a grandparent of $^+$ $^+$Person$_1$ is a grandparent of Person$_3$ if Person$_1$ is a parent of some Person$_2$ who is a parent of Person$_3$.	A fact type is semiderived if some of its instances may be derived, and some of its instances may be simply asserted. It is marked by "$^+$" (half an asterisk). "$^{++}$"indicates semiderived and stored (eager evaluation for derived instances).
Subtyping	Person (.nr) Student (.nr) Employee (.nr) Student Employee Lecturer	All subtypes are proper subtypes. An arrow runs from subtype to supertype. A solid arrow indicates a path to the subtype's preferred identifier (e.g. here, student employees are primarily identified by their employee number). A dashed arrow indicates the supertype has a different preferred identifier.
Subtyping constraints	Animal TeamMember Person ⊗ ⊙ ⊗ Dog Cat Player Coach Male Person Female Person	A circled "X" indicates the subtypes are mutually exclusive. A circled dot indicates the supertype equals the union of the subtypes. The combination (xor constraint) indicates the subtypes partition the supertype (exclusive and exhaustive).
Subtype derivation status	Person Person is of Gender (.code) {'M', 'F'} MalePerson MalePerson* *Each MalePerson is a Person who is of Gender 'M'. is a parent of Person Grandparent$^+$ $^+$Each derived Grandparent is a Person who is a parent of some Person who is a parent of some Person.	A subtype may be <ul><li>asserted,</li><li>derived (denoted by "*"),</li><li>or semiderived (denoted by "$^+$").</li></ul>If the subtype is asserted, it has no mark appended and has no derivation rule. If the subtype derived or semiderived, a derivation rule is supplied.

ORM Notation – 5

Construct	Examples	Description/Notes
Internal frequency constraint		This constrains the number of times an occurring instance of a role or role sequence may appear in each population. Here: each jury has exactly 12 members; each panel that includes an expert includes at least 4 and at most 7 experts; each expert reviews at most 5 papers; each paper that is reviewed is reviewed by at least 2 experts; and each department and year that has staff numbers recorded in the quaternary appears there twice (once for each gender).
External frequency constraint		The example constraint has the following meaning. In this context, each combination of student and course relates to at most two enrolments (i.e. a student may enroll at most twice in the same course)
Ring constraints		A ring predicate R is locally reflexive if and only if, for all x and y, xRy implies xRx. E.g. "knows" is locally but not globally reflexive.

Reflexive, symmetric and transitive properties may also be enforced using semiderivation rather than by constraining asserted fact types.

The example constrains the subtyping relationship in ORM to be both acyclic (no cycles can be formed by a chain of subtyping connections) and strongly intransitive (no object type A can be both a direct subtype of another type B and an indirect subtype of B, where indirect subtyping means there is a chain of two or more subtyping relationships that lead from A to B).

Ring constraints may be combined only if they are compatible, and one is not implied by the other. ORM tools ensure that only legal combinations are allowed. |
| Value-comparison constraints | | The example constraint verbalizes as: For each Project, existing enddate >= startdate. |

ORM Notation – 6

Construct	Examples	Description/Notes
Object cardinality constraint	# = 1 # ≤ 100 [President] (Senator)	The example constraints ensure there is exactly one president and at most 100 senators (at any given time),
Role cardinality constraint	is the president (Politician)—□ # ≤ 1	The example constraint ensures that at most one politician plays the role of president (at any given time).
Deontic constraints	Uniqueness o— ⊖ Mandatory o ⊙ Subset, Equality, Exclusion ⊆ ≐ ⊗ Frequency °f Irreflexive Acyclic Asymmetric Asym-Intrans Intransitive Acyclic-Intrans Antisymmetric Symmetric Strongly Intransitive etc. e.g. [Person] is a parent of	Unlike alethic constraints, deontic constraint shapes are colored blue rather than violet. Most include "o" for "obligatory". Deontic ring constraints instead use dashed lines. In the parenthood example, the alethic frequency constraint ensures that each person has at most two parents, the alethic ring constraint ensures that parenthood is acyclic, and the deontic ring constraint makes it obligatory for parenthood to be strongly intransitive.
Textual constraints	{'Exec', 'NonExec'} [Rank (.code)] ◄ has [Employee (.nr)] uses² [CompanyCar (.regNr)] [1] **Each** Employee **who** has Rank 'NonExec' uses **at most one** CompanyCar. [2] **Each** Employee **who** has Rank 'Exec' uses **some** CompanyCar.	First-order constraints with no graphic notation may be expressed textually in the FORML 2 language. These examples use footnoting to capture a restricted uniqueness constraint and a restricted mandatory role constraint.
Objectification display options: link fact types, and compact display.	"Enrolment !" [Student] enrolled in [Course] ◄ was by is in ► ⊖ ⊂⊃ **Enrolment !**	Internally, link fact types connect objectified associations to their component object types. By default, display of link fact types is suppressed. If displayed, link predicate shapes use dashed lines instead of solid lines. Objectification object types may also be displayed without their defining components, using an object type shape containing a small predicate shape, as shown in this Enrolment example.

INDEX

Made in the USA
Columbia, SC
12 June 2018